READING, WRITING, AND RAGE

Reading,
Writing,
and

The terrible price paid by
victims of school failure

Dorothy Fink Ungerleider

ISBN: 1-4609-3572-1
ISBN-13: 9781460935729

To the real Petris...
for daring to trust one more time

To Muriel Davidson, in memory...
for her third ear, her spirit, her absolute
faith in the possible

To my family...
for their love, their patience

ACKNOWLEDGEMENTS

The author wishes to express deep appreciation to the dozens of teachers and professionals who submitted to interviews and allowed me access to their records, their memories, and their old files for information about "Tony Petri." To mention their names would, of course, violate confidentiality, but they must be acknowledged for their basic contribution to the credibility of this story.

Thanks must also be expressed to:

Those who called me "writer" and gave me the push that sustained over five years: Muriel Davidson, Bill Davidson, Lil Borgeson, Henry Sharp, and Joan Tobin.

My mentors: Dr. Marianne Frostig, Dr. William Morse, Dr. Phil Hansen, Dr. Ray Barsch.

My consultants on diagnostic, medical, legal, and artistic matters: Dr. Jeffrey Schaeffer, Dr. Janet Switzer, Dr. Abba Terr, Charles Silverberg, Arnold Wolf.

My editor, Suzanne Mikesell, who understood what I wanted to say.

My children, John and Peggy, who listened and made me say it better.

My husband, Tom, for his love, expertise, and impatience—without which this book might have taken even longer to complete.

"None of the teachers believed me. I was accused again and again of not doing my homework...I felt the only thing I had...was my integrity, and to have it questioned struck at my very innards."

Ann Bradford Mathias, Senator's Wife

"The more I got better known in town, the more each teacher didn't want to be the one to hold me back....They gave me better grades than I deserved....When you cut the baloney, the core was the reading problem. That set up the different problems that led to everything else."

Billy Don Jackson, former UCLA football star
convicted of manslaughter

"In dealing with learning disabled adolescents, the rescue system must deal with the whole problem and the whole organism. It cannot ignore the primary disability and it cannot succeed until it also pays more than lip service to the critical ingredients of integrity, constance, and continuity."

Albert Katzman, in *Delinquent Youth and Learning Disability*

"Powerlessness is a 'social emotion' caused by certain structures of society...that make mechanical decisions without regard to humans....A sense of powerlessness among young persons causes them to feel isolated and filled with despair."

Rollo May,
Power and Innocence: A search for sources of violence

"Many LD children...suffer serious emotional pressure and ridicule from peers, teachers, and sometimes even from their parents. These factors create...the anger and frustration that causes a child to act out. So it's not that an LD child is more prone to delinquency....In my opinion, he or she is pushed to delinquency."

Thomas P. McGee, Judge
National Council of Juvenile and Family Court Judges

FOREWORD

Dyslexia is a much misunderstood handicap, and probably no one misunderstands it more than the victim of it prior to diagnosis. When in school, I couldn't fathom why I was not capable of reading as eloquently and gracefully as others in the classroom. It was a tremendous source of discomfort and embarrassment when the teachers called upon me to read aloud. Absolutely, rage within oneself is a natural result of frustration. The mark of character, however, is the desire and ability to channel that rage into a constructive force rather than a destructive one. I gathered together all the chaos churning within me and directed it toward literally hurtling an obstacle in my life. I understand Tony's experience with learning disabilities, and I sincerely hope this book will provide insight for others who are struggling to overcome an impediment.

Bruce Jenner

PREFACE

Reading, Writing, and Rage was first published in 1985, but the requests for it continue. Colleges of special education use the book as a text supplement to help teachers-in-training understand the anguish of the helpseeking process. Therapists report its use for bibliotherapy with disturbed or incarcerated youth who were unserved at the appropriate times in their lives. Teary-eyed parents express their thanks for a story that tells what they have been through. Sadly, the message between these covers remains relevant in spite of two decades of federal legislation intended to serve handicapped, including learning disabled, individuals (PL 94-142, The Right to Education of the Handicapped Act, authorized in 1975 and renamed IDEA, Individuals with Disabilities Education Act in 1990).

In fact, little has changed--because laws do not change behavior. Laws do not assure delivery of appropriate services. Laws do not provide funds to implement themselves. Laws require a perverse kind of bureaucratic compliance that too often sacrifices human needs and substitutes paperwork instead. Laws lead to creative interpretation that obfuscates benevolent intent and substitutes fiscal circumvention. In short, laws give hope that too often leads to despair.

As this book goes to reprint, Reed Martin, scholarly advocate and attorney for the disabled, writes that the original problem creating those laws was the lack of experience of regular educators and lack of educational technology in regular settings to meet the needs of students with disabilities. Twenty-six years later, he asks, isn't that still our problem? In the 70's "regular education discovered the safety valve of special education and simply transferred students away from regular classes...The game became finding and labeling students so that more money could be obtained from Washington."[1] The money was intended to train regular educators but practically none was spent that way. Segregation of students became financially rewarding;

---

[1]Martin, Reed, *"Is This Where We Came In?"* LDA Newsbriefs.

xiii

children were labeled and stigmatized but rarely remediated. Instead of collaboration, competition grew between special and regular eduction.

The spirit and intent of these laws has been lost. IDEA has never been fully funded, fully implemented, or enforced. As IDEA faces reauthorization in 1996, powerful legislators are determined to eliminate entirely the category of "learning disabilities" from the disabilities list. In fact, the political climate of the late 90s favors release of commitment to funds for special eduction altogether. They propose to: 1) cancel all labels, leaving the domain of eligibility for services a mystery; 2) base funding on amount received the previous year, not on numbers of students needing services; 3) send monies as block grants, with dissemination determined by cash-strapped school boards; 4) serve all special ed students in regular education! (Special education was created in the first place to remove these very students); 5) trust the states (but all the federal laws were originally written precisely because we couldn't trust the states! In fact the 1990 amendments to IDEA required changes in eligibility categories and related services, all of which have been ignored by the states).

And this is why *Reading, Writing, and Rage* was first written.

The story of Tony Petri is a story of a process--the process of helpseeking for one human with learning problems. Something went terribly wrong in that process. All of those somethings are on trial here: Tony and his parents--their fears, doubts, limitations, frustrations; the schools--teachers, counselors, curriculum, bureaucracy; the helping professionals--their conflicting diagnoses, isolation from one another, and theories of deficiency.

Tony Petri was robbed of his right to literacy and became an unknowing accomplice in the crime against himself. His was no ordinary replaceable theft. It was the loss of a right that would alter his lifelong perceptions of his worth as a human being.

Tony became my obsession. Why did we lose him--the "we" being all those charged with the task of teaching, helping, fixing kids at war with the learning process? Why did the help his parents sought, over and over, fail to help? The answers I found were unexpected.

Coincidently, my work with Tony began at the time I was asked to lecture to juvenile court judges about behavioral characteristics of learning disabled youth. There was growing concern in the 1970s about the relationship between learning disabilities (LD) and juvenile delinquency (JD). Social scientists were just beginning to ask what percentage of the young people in prisons for violent crimes were also functional illiterates, for whatever reasons. Youth arrests for violent crimes had risen 254% in fifteen years coinciding in that same period with a dramatic drop in literacy skills on national achievement tests.

Over one million youth each year were entering the juvenile justice system--100,000 of whom were incarcerated for violent crimes. Varying with the researcher, anywhere from thirty to ninety percent of adjudicated delinquents were reported to be learning disabled, in contrast to ten percent in the general population. The courts could no longer ignore the question of a possible LD/JD link. In 1976, the United States Department of Justice completed a major study entitled *THE LINK BETWEEN LEARNING DISABILITIES AND JUVENILE DELINQUENCY*. Examining for the first time the learning histories of incarcerated youth, they found an overwhelming number of conflicting reports, poorly documented research, and competing definitions of the term "learning disability."

One finding in that report drew my attention: "Much of the most provocative information is nearly intractable to systematic examination. Each account is a story in itself, about a single case, and to be persuasive, it must be told in some detail."[1]

Here was my mandate. To understand the many, we have to look intensively at the few, or even at one. Stories like Tony's have to be told in detail. Tony was almost an archtype of the learning disabled child: he had perceptual and visual problems, allergies, gross, motor incoordination, and low academic performance coupled with high intelligence. Because he was fifteen when we met he represented

---

[1] Murray, Charles, *The Link Between Learning Disabilities and Juvenile Deliquency*. Washington, D.C.: U.S. Dept of Justice, April,1976. P. 30

a real challenge: prevailing opinion was that, developmentally, LD adolescents were beyond help. Fifteen also was a ripe age for proneness to delinquency.

***

We owe a debt of thanks to Tony's mother for the scope of this book. Mrs. Petri's penchant for saving every scrap of paper, report card, document, invoice, and contract allowed me great accuracy in reconstructing the chronology and details that might otherwise have been lost by fading memories.

In the sense that READING, WRITING, AND RAGE is based in the facts of the Petris' lives, with all major quotes taken from taped conversations, this book is non-fiction. But the book is also fictional. Writing it as a docudrama involved creating "Diana" as the listener and reconstructing events based on my impressions, suppositions and visualizations of actual scenes from the Petris' past. Wishing to represent their subjective experiences, the **feelings** as well as the facts, I sought to know the Petris on a more intimate level than usually is possible in the professional-client relationship.

How does one really get to "know" another human being, to get inside another's head, to imagine what it was like during a long-ago time? How does one build trust when it has been violated for so long and the imperative for secrecy has supplanted the willingness to confide? This was my challenge.

The gathering of facts took nine months and some 250 hours of searches for and interviews with those whose lives affected Tony's. I tracked down and analyzed old reports and test data, then met with the Petris individually and together as a family unit. Slowly, very slowly, I came to "know" them through their own and each other's eyes. The finished manuscript was presented to them for approval. I would not have sent this book to press without it.

They approved.

They had, indeed, allowed me to know them.

READING, WRITING, AND RAGE exposes personalities, actions, and foibles **not** to condemn but to **inform**--to allow readers to understand the Whys and, perhaps, to identify with

xvi

the wholeness, the imperfection, the vulnerability of the victims. And of the experts. We, too, feel nervous. And insecure. We sometimes wonder if we have correctly used our professional tools and sufficiently justified our diagnoses. In the silence of our private moments, we too struggle with doubt. Specialists all, we tend to hear only a specialized piece of the problem--lacking a vision of the whole, a caring for the whole. We drown in a wash of big words--the jargon of expertise, failing to listen with our "third ear" to the clients' pain behind the words.

Can a metropolitan junior high school teacher ever "know" a student when he or she is accountable for 200 of them each day? Can a school psychologist take the time to listen, to intuit emotions, when her or she has three schools and one thousand pupils to cover? Can a vision therapist guarantee that exercises alone will alter a child's academic performance? Can a pediatrician be certain an allergic child will be better off with medication for symptoms rather than shots for prevention?

No, we must not blame, but we **must** inform. We must draw attention to behaviors that leave indelible scars on young minds. As I continue to deal with secondary schools and watch the growing depersonalization of students due to increased use of computers for scheduling, as well as the growing limitations on staff time and opportunities for "knowing," I realize sadly that this story has no limitation in time.

Dorothy Fink Ungerleider

NOTE: All names and identities have been changed to protect individuals. References for professional tests, documents or reports cited in the text are provided at the end of the book.

CHAPTER 1

*Tony Petri: Extra large man
in an extra small world.*

The clock radio clicked on at exactly 4:30 a.m. Chronically fatigued, Tony lay there, his brain no longer readied for this predawn intrusion that used to be habitual. Twelve months. It had been twelve months since the last 4:30 a.m. same-every-day ritual. He felt Ginny's slim body curled up next to him, her feet still resting on his legs, where she warmed them every night before falling into her stonelike sleep. Incredible how she could fall asleep like that, in 30 seconds, and then hear nothing. Absolutely nothing. Not 'til the baby's first cry, long after Tony had left for work. When he was working.

"...and a local psychic has made a prediction today that the world will definitely come to an end on March 15th." The newscaster's voice blurred into the young man's half-consciousness until the "March 15th" registered its personal meaning. March 15th. His birthdate. Two weeks away. This one would be his twenty-first. Maybe his last, if that nut was right.

The coincidence brought him fully awake then, as he remembered why the alarm had been set for that day. Weird, that March 15th thing. Why had that announcement come today, just at the moment of his waking up? Was it a sign? He felt stupid succumbing to superstition. He hated feeling stupid. Forget the whole thing.

Tony rolled his massive body over on his left arm, cautiously uncurling his way out of bed. The twinges up and down his injured back had taught him there was only one way out of bed these days—rolling and slow. Once on his feet, he shuffled to the bathroom, flicked on the light, and, as always, was startled by his own face. There was no way of avoiding the medicine-chest mirror that faced the doorway of the miniscule bathroom.

1

Tony stared at his image, noticing the still-yellowish cast to his skin. God, he looked awful!

Should he shave? How did he want to look? Did it matter? He stared for another full minute, then plugged in the razor and shaved more carefully than usual. It did matter. He wasn't going to look like a bum. Not today. He wouldn't give that to them.

Tony hadn't thought about looks or clothes until that moment, but now he rummaged through his closet, designed so small that even a man of such tight means as to have only seven hangable shirts found the seven constantly crushed. The light from the bathroom reflected on the irridescent-green label from his gray plaid shirt. X-L, it shone. Extra-large. Extra-large Tony. For as long as he could remember, he had been extra-large Tony. Extra-large person in an extra-small world.

He grabbed the shirt from the closet and threw it on the edge of the bed. In the bathroom, he squeezed his body into the shower stall of the tract-house bathroom. Going through the motions of showering, he felt a surge of hatred for the unscrupulous builders, who must all have had extra-small bodies and minds.

The handle on the shower head nicked his ear. Same as every day. He knew it was there, but it always caught him by surprise when he was disoriented by closed eyes and shampoo.

Suddenly, surprising himself, he grabbed the tormenting handle and, with one violent wrench, snapped the entire shower head from its fitting. He stood, exposed beyond his nakedness, staring at the evidence of his rage—the stream of water falling straight down from the cracked pipe, the wounded shower head in his limp hand. He placed it in the soap dish and backed out of the stall, hating his loss of control, hating even more his regret at losing control. He had to get moving, to get out of this house.

He tried to dress quickly, fighting the weakness he felt. Extra-large didn't mean extra-strong. Not now. Not when you had hepatitis. That bitch. Why hadn't she told him she had hepatitis when she'd phoned in response to his ad for odd jobs? Why hadn't she told him when he went to her house? Don't people ever think about what they do to somebody else?

Bumping into Stephie's doll buggy in the dark hall, he stumbled and jolted the high-risk spinal muscles. A cry of pain es-

2

caped of its own will and he held his breath until the spasm passed. Luckily, this time it passed.

Disabled. Twenty years old and disabled. Crazy. Twenty years old. Almost twenty-one, if the world doesn't end. Tony Petri, husband. Tony Petri, father. Twice—with a third one growing in the sound-sleeping Ginny. What do you do well, Tony Petri? Make babies. Sorry, no job openings in that field.

Recovering from the jolt of pain, but not from the insult of his daughter's forgetfulness, the twenty-year-old with the mortgaged house, the mortgaged truck, and the mortgaged life cautiously bent down from the knees, put one extra-large hand on the handle of his firstborn's frail buggy and sent it flying. It ricocheted off the dining room table, losing a wheel and flinging its contents, an infant doll, to the floor with a dull thud. He shuddered, thinking how lifelike the little body looked.

Animal. You are an animal, Anthony Petri. Better get out of here fast. What if you wake the kids? Get out.

Passing through the kitchen, Tony paused long enough to break two eggs into a glass of milk. He gulped the mixture down like the medicine it had become. Hepatitis demanded protein, not the donut-and-coffee habit that had always sustained him before. He knew he would need as much protein energy as possible to do what he had to do today. He set the empty glass down on the plastic-tile counter, lingering for a fraction of time, studying the milk foam sitting on the bottom of the glass. Then he made his move for the garage, shutting the door firmly behind him, not looking back.

His eight-year old white Chevy pick-up, chariot of the workingman, stood waiting. The Great White Wheeler, he called it. They shared a bond, this truck and its driver. Tony was a different kind of bilingual—he spoke the language of machines. Every sound of this machine said something to him, and, at times, Tony thought the truck knew as much about him.

He kicked the troublesome left front tire testily and ran his hand over the dent in the bumper, trying not to think about that "turkey" who backed into him at the shopping center.

Enough stalling. Move, man.

Hesitantly, he walked over to the wall behind his workbench and pressed the certain spot on the fiberboard wall panel. The magnetic latch sprang open to reveal a secret niche between the wall studs. Three hooks had been affixed to the studs. On

3

each hook hung a weapon of a different caliber. Still vacillating, Tony stared at the arsenal, aware of the new purpose he was considering for his collection. Then he reached for the most devastating—the repeating rifle—and found its cartridge of ammunition in the lock-box on the floor of the compartment. He flinched at the clack of the cartridge as it snapped into place.

Carrying the now-activated weapon back to the truck, he placed it under the passenger seat, locked the passenger door, and let himself into the driver's seat. Sinking down into the familiar padded vinyl that had long ago molded to his shape, he was overcome by a sudden, crushing fatigue—the fatigue born of reluctance.

The truck, too, was reluctant. After four abortive tries, the recalcitrant engine finally yielded. It was 5:18 a.m. as man and machine headed toward the highway. The edge of the sun was just bulging over the horizon to light his way.

It was a long drive to the city. Eighty-six miles—and Tony knew them all, every hill and curve, every billboard, highway sign, and warning signal. Every gas station, way station, and eatery, especially the truck stops. Tony Petri was a trucker, had been a trucker, that is, until the accident. He hadn't wanted to think about the accident. Not today. But there was nothing to shut off his mind. His homemade, self-installed stereo had broken and silence filled the cab of the truck. Silence and the cacophony of his private thoughts.

Tony Petri, trucker, a title he'd never dreamed he could achieve. Mechanic, maybe. Or welder. He knew he could be a welder. No reading or writing needed, just patience and good hands. He knew he had good hands, and the patience could be there if he liked what he was doing. But "trucker" meant a test, a printed, written test…And he'd done it. How he'd done it was another story, but he'd done it. All that effort had finally paid off. Then came the job—with the national bottling company, to haul their soft drinks intrastate. To some it may have seemed like a menial job, but it paid dough, and to feed the kids you've got to have dough.

He grinned, remembering those first mornings when he had shared the cab of an 18-wheeler with Nick Sacco, a veteran driver. Nick told him later how impressed he was with Tony's ability to learn the rules of the road, the regs of the company, and the quirks and requirements of the gigantic rig. Tony had to be told something only once and he learned it, Nick had said. After just four months, the regional manager had become so impressed by his willingness to work, even beyond the required hours, and by his quick intelligence, that Tony earned his place at the wheel of his own semitrailer, entering that vast brotherhood of teamsters who operate the more than seventeen million trucks in the nation.

Those had been the "good" months. For some, they might not have seemed so good. Workdays started at 4:30 a.m. and often didn't end until 7:30 or 8:00 p.m. Just getting to work was a job in itself. Eighty-six miles from home to the truck barn. Tony and Ginny could not afford a home in the city, but all the jobs were there. So Tony drove his eighty-six miles, willingly, from the desert community where he and Ginny found their piece of the American dream—a home of their own, a chunk of land for the kids to run on, and, for Tony especially, a sense of being his own person.

Then, too, there was the encouragement from his buddy, Mike O'Hara. Mike, a supervisor for the bottling company, talked to the "bigwigs" and knew the ropes about moving up in the company. He had been the one who first told Tony about the job opening and kept him posted on the company's impressions of the eager young man. Mike assured Tony that the word was getting around—he was a worker, and all kinds of advancements were possible for an ambitious comer like him. Listening to Mike, Tony had already begun to plan for spending the spoils of his successive promotions.

How he worked in those early months! The dreams of his potential fed his energy. He accepted any job they offered, took on every overtime contract, and justified to Ginny the almost total devotion to work as his big chance to prove himself special, to get ahead. He lifted who-knows-how-many-thousands of cases of soft drinks, helped load and unload the giant truck daily, even on jobs where loading was not part of his responsibility. He knew the 14-hour days were long, very long for that kind of work, but he was young and strong. True, his muscles ached, but he was sure they would adapt. The opportunity was there, and he would show them that they had hired the right somebody.

As Tony maneuvered the Chevy pick-up over the familiar, wide-open highway, the mesmerizing hum of the truck wheels sent him back to the start of the nightmare days that followed those bright beginnings. First came the early backaches, the trips to the doctor, the few treatments for "strain." Then: February 26. The date was ingrained in his mind from the endless forms and insurance reports. February 26, and those fateful cases of bottles—it took only two, the first two of the day. The sudden excruciating pain, his hands unconsciously protecting, dropping the cases on top of a third that was sitting at his feet. Vague memories, sounds invading the waves of pain. Sounds of shattering bottles, tinkling glass fragments, fizzing soda pop running in bubbling streams at his feet, his body rigid, semi-paralyzed by pain, his voice barely audible, coming in short bursts. Trying to explain to his partner. No need for words. His face told his agony. Then people running, crowding around, his supervisor there, trying to sit him down, lie him down, find some relief, but no position relieved. The workingmen, all looking at his back then, saw the traumatized muscles visibly bulging like lumps of hard clay trapped under his skin.

They got him home. He couldn't remember how. Ginny was there, and the kids, looking scared. Then bed and hot packs and ointments. Rest. Rest would do it. Pain pills and rest. A few days and he'd be fine. A few days...

That was one year ago today. Happy anniversary.

Tony wished, for the first time that morning, that his stereo was working. The thoughts were becoming too painful. He hadn't wanted to replay the part with the doctors. He could hear his own words: "I got this pain, doc. Can't you do something about it? Can't you cure it?" And they'd all say the same thing, the same stay-on-your-back, use heat, relax. Relax. They had to be kidding. That union doctor...two months' rest, he said. And that jerk-doctor from the insurance company who took X-rays and said there was "nothing wrong."

Nothing wrong. Did they think he was a fake? Did they think his life's goal was to be on disability? Shit! Why did they give him pills and tell him to rest if nothing was wrong?

Dr. Morgan was his only bright memory. Tony had found Dr. Morgan on his own. He was a chiropractor. He didn't make Tony feel crazy. He took his own X-rays and showed Tony the pictures, explaining and pointing to the rotated vertebrae, showing Tony that the bones of his spine were out of alignment. Dr. Morgan started him on chiropractic manipulations, slowly,

6

cautiously, along with vitamin therapy. Dr. Morgan was big on vitamin therapy. No more pain pills unless he absolutely had to have them to sleep at night.

Tony measured the success of his therapy when, after one month, he could push a half-empty cart at the supermarket. A weird measure of hope, but he was learning to take the crumbs.

His mind strayed from the doctors and turned with even more disgust to the teamsters. His union—protector of the worker, there to help members when they're in trouble. Ha! More like, "We take your money, you fend for yourself." That was the teamsters' creed according to Petri. They'd never even returned his first three calls. He'd always thought it was a pretty shady operation; now he was sure of it. Four calls to the union office, long distance. Finally they referred him to the lawyer. More calls, long distance.

The teamsters' lawyer was always "very busy" or "in conference"—"He'll call you back, Mr. Petri." Tony waited, helpless. He couldn't afford long-distance waiting, he couldn't sit up long enough to drive the more than 90 miles to the lawyer's office in the city, and he couldn't afford the gas it would take—the Great White Wheeler really sucked up the gas—even if he *could* drive.

Then Tony thought about the passage of time—big hunks of time, it seemed to him. Time passing with no solution, only more problems. First, little Frankie got sick. Real sick. Tony couldn't believe it when the doctor said it was scarlet fever; he thought there was no more scarlet fever. Wasn't that what all those kids' shots were for? And then Stephie got a cough that went on for a month. Everybody was mean, cranky, locked in that little house together, with no place to hide, no space to be alone.

And the bills. Never-ending bills. The pediatrician had been willing to wait for payment, but there was no way the supermarket could be so personal. Food had to be cash-and-carry. Every month the insurance company was late sending the check, but the bank was never late expecting its mortgage payments. The loan company was never late expecting its truck payments. Every month, Tony tried to explain why he needed more time. They looked at him, studied him; they understood. But how he detested the pleading.

Tony's disability payments came to $616 a month. Further

7

insulting his injury, the unemployment folks had offered him a job at $3.50 an hour, minimum wage. He was outraged. He had been earning $10 an hour, and $15 per for all his overtimes, but now the bottling company wouldn't even talk to him. His supervisor friend, Mike O'Hara, couldn't do a thing but explain company policy: if you're hurt on the job and you can't come back to that same job, you're out. Out. There's no other place for you.

He'd sue them. That's what he'd thought until he'd finally got through to the lawyer. There was another bunch, those lawyers, with their world of papers—pages of papers, forms, depositions, words. Millions of words in little teeny-tiny print, words that intimidated even if you were smart enough to read them, which he wasn't. He recalled how the teamsters union lawyer, Harry Jonas, talked—negotiated, they called it—with the bottling company's lawyers, and the next thing he knew they'd ordered more doctors' tests, nerve ending tests, even arthritis tests. Did they think at 20 he had arthritis? No one ever talked to the chiropractor, Tony realized as he drove along. Dr. Morgan hadn't been part of the insurance team, and Tony hadn't said anything because he didn't know the legal "games" and he was afraid the chiropractic stuff might work against him. He was smart enough to pick up the M.D.'s basic distrust of chiropractors, but he didn't know where the lawyers stood. When in doubt, shut up, Tony. Yeah, he'd learned that pretty well.

As his foot rode the accelerator, his free-floating mental replay of events was interrupted by the sight of a billboard. The photo of a sweet-smiling woman promoting the use of the telephone had too much meaning that morning. The image swung his thoughts to the latest torture in his life. Every month, when the check was late in coming, he called the woman in charge of claims at the insurance company. It was always the same. Her indifferent, nasal voice would project annoyingly through the receiver. She offered no greeting, just a staccato "please-hold-for-a-moment." Then nothing. No one. Only the static of the instrument as the "moment" was redefined to plurals of indeterminate length. "Held" and cut off at the same time. Neat trick. The first few times, he'd voiced his outrage, hollering and swearing at the unfeeling plastic. Then only his body reacted. The adrenalin started flowing, speed-thumping his heartbeat.

Tachycardia—he'd even learned the medical word for it. The sweaty palms and feet came next, and finally the hands curling into white-knuckled fists as his helpless anger flowed into his extremities. Anger always telegraphed into his fists.

He didn't know which was worse—the waiting "on hold" or the actual conversation with that insipid clerk, who never tried to hide her annoyance with her job and his question. Her every-month-unchanging answer, "Your check is on its way, Mr. Petri," made the veins in his neck pulsate, on the brink of rupture.

One day, a call did come from the lawyers. They said something about the bottling company giving Tony a choice: to go for a cash settlement or for rehabilitation. He thought it had to be one or the other.

Tony chose rehabilitation. No one counseled him on the decision. Why would he need counsel anyway? He just needed to be an employed person, to regain his rapidly eroding pride. A job would do it, he was sure. The insurance company would arrange the rehab, he was told.

Documents came frequently to the house. Ginny read them to Tony. Her reading was good enough, but neither of them could understand the "legalese." All they could make out was that someone had decided to label his injury "permanent and stationary." No other name or medical diagnosis accompanied those words. No human being in his presence or over the phone had ever used, let alone explained the meaning of, those ominous adjectives.

Tony's decision to go for rehabilitation necessitated more phone calls to the insurance company, to the same nasal voice who continued her long distance "holding pattern." When she finally came back to the phone, she either suggested he come to the office in person or referred him to another number. He tried the new number. It was either constantly busy or, when it answered, a recording machine put him "on hold," dispensing with a living human altogether.

That did it. That was the final kicker.

These creeps had made his decision for him. Yeah, he would accept their invitation after all. Yeah, he would come to their office. In person, like they said.

He pressed the accelerator to the floor in a kind of victory stroke over his memories. The reluctance was gone.

9

CHAPTER 2

*"There's a quiet
kind of power about him."*

They scuffled and bumped out the door in couplets and triplets—popping their gum, whispering secrets, calling out 'byes, jostling and poking like pups let out of a box. Sixth-period freedom.

Inside, the littered floor, word-covered chalkboard, and cascading wastebaskets testified to the end of the school day. Hope Saltzman flopped into a desk chair and motioned for the woman who had been waiting in the back of the room to join her as she lit up her end-of-the-day smoke and took a long puff. "You've come a long way, baby," the cigarette commercial had praised. She looked around her buff-colored classroom, bursting with color-coded kits and the latest in electronic paraphernalia, and thought, "but you've still got a long way to go." Seven years in this cubicle with kids who couldn't read despite the miracles of modern technology. Some years. Some kind of endurance, lady.

Diana grinned. "My God, I forgot what it was like to work with the mob. I don't know how you do it, Hope." She slid into the chair next to the desk and propped her feet on the nearby file box.

"With a lot of help from my 'friends'," Hope said, tranquilized, gazing at her cigarette. "You're looking great, Di. How's the tennis game?"

"Oh, I've given it up. Not enough exercise when you're fighting the battle of the bulge. It's tough staying in size 10's when you're over forty," she grimaced. "I'm running now—a couple of miles a day, and working out in a gym. What about you—what are you doing for survival these days?"

"No way I can deal with that daily running routine," Hope

wrinkled her nose in disgust. "I'm still pounding the backboard under the lights, trying to get that backhand to obey me.

"But listen, Diana, I know you don't have much time and I've got to have your help." Hope shed the small talk. "I've got this kid who really has me going around in circles. He's pretty much stopped functioning in my reading class. He's supposed to be a ninth grader, but I can't even test him to find out where he's at because he's so defensive. He's like a wound-up rubber band—tight—umph! like this." She made a fist to convey the tightness and took another drag of smoke. "The counseling office says he'd had some private help in the past but they don't know much about it and—natch—there's nothing in the file. He's totally passive about the work, and he's so big that you don't want to cross him," she laughed a bit self-consciously. "With some kids, you try to kind of irritate them into working—you know what I mean. But not with Tony. It's strange, though. He never really *refuses* to do anything, but you just sort of *feel* it. There's a quiet kind of power about him and I'm never sure if he can't do the work or if he just won't."

Gentle, not a fighter, Hope described him on that day when Diana Cotter first heard about the kid named Tony Petri. He was always offering to help kids with mechanical projects, and all of his class time was spent drawing motorcycles or home-made mechanical inventions.

"In fact," Hope said, "he's actually invented this three-wheeled thing, sort of a far-out motorcycle. He designed and built the whole thing himself, and it works! Sometimes he brings it to school and the kids really make a fuss about it. That crazy cycle is his whole identity here. But as far as school-work goes, forget it!" Hope threw up her hands. "He's a complete mystery to me. I just can't get a handle on anything that'll motivate him, and I really need another point of view. I spoke to his mom a few weeks ago and told her I might be calling you in. Even got her to sign a release so you could see the records." Hope's eyes twinkled; she knew Diana would take the bait.

She was right. Hope's bafflement fed Diana's curiosity. It was out of character. Hope Saltzman, remedial reading teacher at Dalton Junior High, was unflappable, unafraid, even nourished by adolescents scarred by years of failure. Those kids were her soul food, her *raison d'être*. Hope had pioneered this

11

special program at a time when no one else thought it was necessary at the junior high level. The prevailing thinking was, "If kids can't read by age 14, forget it—it's too late." Not for all of them, Hope had proven, achieving a rare admiration from the Dalton staff.

Diana and Hope had worked together in the past, establishing a volunteer parent-tutoring program at Dalton, and had grown to respect each other as professionals. But this was the first time Hope had called Diana about a specific student. What was it about this Petri kid that had stumped such an experienced veteran?

Diana needed no time to consider. She agreed to meet with Tony the following week and have a look for herself.

All had been prearranged. The junior high expected her. She arrived eight minutes early.

Tony expected her, she thought. Wrong. Tony had never been notified of the appointment.

Tony would now be notified, she thought. Wrong. No one could find Tony. He wasn't in his scheduled class.

Diana watched the search-and-find motions that occupied the staff in the counseling office—the shuffling through file drawers in search of schedules, the scanning of manila folders and master programs, all the while handling numerous interruptions. Phones were ringing, bells dinging, and students whining, pleading for someone on the other side of the swinging door to help them.

Students crowded in rows behind the counter, dressed in a marvelous array of costumes—baggy pants, blouses, shorts, team T-shirts. The girls wobbled on their high-heeled clogs while the boys scraped through the door in their sneakers or squeaky high-topped hiking boots. One boy, up front—the next in line—waited in dreamy repose, chin on his elbow, a special thick comb stuck in his Afro, looking as if he'd been waiting so long he'd forgotten why he came in. A dapper father ushered his beautiful daughter through the door, observed the web of confusion, whispered something in her ear, and bolted the scene.

Diana glanced at her watch and asked of anyone in earshot behind the desk if there had been a meeting place assigned for her use, in case Tony showed up.

12

The blank looks and exchanged glances told her that no one had thought of that reality, either. One of the students waiting for a schedule change overheard the request and suggested the teachers' lounge, which was vacant at the time. There was no objection to the suggestion, so now Diana had the place. All she needed was the boy.

Just then, inexplicably, Tony entered the office. One of the clerks spotted his head above the shorter ones in the mob and pointed him out to Diana. How he had been found remained a mystery.

But there was no mystery to the fact that by then only five minutes remained of the hour that was to have been theirs.

No time for where-have-you-beens. Just minutes to touch base.

They walked together to the teachers' lounge, mumbling get-acquainted words. Diana watched the enormous boy, well over six feet tall, carrying more than 200 pounds on his slightly bottom-heavy, out-of-proportion frame, and made some quick mental notes. A large boy, but not muscular. Probably around 14 or 15 years old, but looking older. Dressed in the uniform of his time—blue jeans and message T-shirt. His message: "Harley-Davidson does it in the road." Straight, dark hair with a mind of its own. He'd obviously gone through puberty. All the signs were there—stubble of a beard, deep voice, raw adolescent skin problems. His walk was heavy, plodding, off-balance—ungraceful but definitely proud. Not the strut of an athlete, but the movement that told strangers he owned his space so tread carefully before entering it.

Tony's face remained a mystery. No sign of emotion. Stoical, objective, non-committal. The eyes, when he let her see them, were the kind of dark brown eyes that never reveal their pupils—solid dark brown that hide the feelings you can sometimes read in eyes. His eyes looked up, down, sideways—everywhere but at Diana. Even when he talked.

They spoke time-filling words, searching for some contact point. She confessed her frustration at the inefficiency surrounding their meeting. He nodded mutely in agreement, but not in surprise. Inefficiency was clearly not new to him.

"Miss Saltzman wanted me to work with you, Tony...to see if I could help you with your school problem."

"Yeah. She told me." Another one, eh, Tony?

"She mentioned that you invented this incredible vehicle."

"Yeah." Staring at the wall.

"Well," she went on, pulling, "what exactly is it?"

The voice came, low monotone. "Uh, sort of a cross between a motorcycle, a bike, and a wagon." Just giving the facts, ma'am.

"Did you build it all yourself here in school?"

A muffled, "No." Then an unexpected few extra words. "I did some of the heavy welding at home."

"Who helped you with the design?"

The question made a crack in the wall. First eye contact from him, and then, louder, more direct, "I designed every part myself!"

Ouch! Take note of that, Diana. No one helps Tony with designs.

"You must have had a lot of satisfaction from it," she conciliated.

Eye contact was lost now, but there was a shadow of a smile. Then silence.

Tony was in control.

They had exhausted that topic.

Three minutes gone, teacher, so you'd better get to the point and declare yourself. "Tony, I'm not here to make any promises to you. You've probably had your share of those. I could lie to you and tell you that I'll soon have you reading that ninth-grade history book you're carrying. But from what Miss Saltzman tells me, I don't understand why you're even carrying it. Doesn't your history teacher know you can't read that book?"

A sarcastic laugh was his response. No attempt to explain.

Talking fast, "I'm not here to help you pass ninth grade history, either. In fact, we probably won't even use your textbooks." She had his attention. "What I'd like to try, if you want to, is to find out once and for all just what you *know* how to do—what you've already mastered—maybe even list it all, on paper, and then look for the 'holes.' Sort of like Swiss cheese, you know what I mean? The stuff you've learned is the 'cheese,' but it's got these holes in it—the things you've missed. Can you relate to that?"

He was totally silent. Who is this nut with this cheese stuff? But Diana caught him glancing directly at her face and clung to that crumb of attention.

"We can work on filling the holes, learning the stuff you *want*

14

to know—the stuff you'll need to know for survival out there. So you can handle things yourself—not feel embarrassed. Does that make any sense to you?"

No words from him, but his posture told her he was still with her.

"What would you say is your reading level?" she went on with her monologue. No answer. Guessing, "Is it about third or fourth grade?"

Still silence. Had she offended?

Again, "Am I close? Or don't you know?"

This time, he responded. "How about first? That's what I would guess. Humph." A sarcastic snort.

"I would guess you're being pretty tough on yourself. Must be pretty discouraging," she countered, unable to hide the pain on her own face at the thought of this boy's daily humiliations.

Shifting the subject with a routine, throw-out question, "By the way, Tony, have you ever had any eye exams?"

An explosion of words followed, amazingly articulate, made all the more disarming after these minutes of muteness and monosyllables. "Are you kidding? I've been havin' eye exams every five minutes since the first grade. They wanted to do surgery. Then they gave me glasses, but they kept changing their minds. Shee-it! One thing I *don't* need is another eye exam!" He shouted to be sure his point had registered. He rested a moment, then went on, calmed a bit by the outburst. "I tried everything they said and I still lose my place when I read, whether I use a marker or my finger, or nothin'. My reading is so bad—why, you know, I can't even read all the words on this dismissal slip I'm holding."

He demonstrated.

He was right.

Pause for composure. He knew what he *didn't* know.

Diana decided to try to end their brief meeting on a more hopeful note. "Tony, what do you think you do well?" she asked.

"I make things. Fix things," he said, seeming more relaxed now. "Anything with cars and motors—mechanical stuff. I work in a gas station after school..."

A bell blared in the background, jarring their embryonic communion. Time was up.

Quickly, bootlegging an extra minute, "Look. How'd you like to give it a try? I mean—working with me—here—in the

15

school? I won't promise any miracles but I'd sure like to take a chance," Diana said. "I'll try to work around your schedule so you won't miss anything important."

"Are you kidding?" he said again. Was that a smile on his face? "You could take me out of any class in the day and I wouldn't be missing anything. Not with these creeps around here." "Creeps" was a word she would soon be hearing often.

Without ever allowing himself to say yes, Tony had implicitly accepted her offer of help.

They settled on a time for their next meeting and said the awkward goodbyes of two strangers in search of a relationship.

Diana jotted some notes and leaned back in the lounge chair.

Then it hit her. An awareness of her complete exhaustion. Only five minutes?

Walking toward the school parking lot, Diana ran through the interaction in her head. What had she learned about Tony Petri in that brief time?

Her instincts told her that he was bright, maybe very bright. And proud—a "straight shooter." But suspicious, guarded. And, yeah, passively controlling. Hope had been right about that.

She ruminated about her "plan of attack." If she leveled with this wounded boy, if she was painfully careful to do what she said she would do, he might begin to allow her some access to his insides.

All at once she stopped walking, realizing what had just happened. She had been called in only as a consultant on this case. Tony at fifteen would be a time-consuming high-risk challenge. So many years of failure would surely have compounded his problems psychologically, and his academic discrepancy was probably enormous if he wouldn't even submit to testing. She knew she had no time to get seriously involved and certainly Dalton Junior High had no money to pay her. Yet, less than an hour ago, she had made a commitment to begin working with Tony Petri.

"A quiet kind of power about him," Hope had said. The words were suddenly prophetic.

But was it just Tony's charisma? Why had she been so drawn to this case?

Inside, Diana knew why. Tony represented the end of the line in a system that had completely failed him. Her whole career had been subtly leading her to these questions about cause and effect. How, when, where had the system lost Tony? What clues had been missed? Was he "learning disabled"? What did that really mean here? What had happened, or not happened, through the years that had left this bright boy a functional illiterate at age 15? What effects did this academic failure have on his life now, and how would it affect his future?

Such questions, Diana knew, could be answered only by a detailed "autopsy" of one student's failure. Something told her Tony was that student, and it was time to begin.

She turned back to the counseling office, suddenly compelled to have a look at the records.

There was a surprising calm in the formerly chaotic office now. Classes were in session, so the staff had a respite between storms. Armed with the briefly worded release statement Hope had given her, Diana declared her intentions and was able to gain immediate access to Tony's cumulative records—the Cum, as they called it. The Cum: cream-colored manila folder—confidential bearer of numbers, commentary, statistics, and signatures condensing the entire academic career of a human being into a space easily transferable to one IBM computer card.

Diana knew that the laws regarding access to its contents were always changing, and the fear of legal repercussions from "too much in print" kept most folders spare. But not *this* spare.

Tony's Cum was an insult. Ten years in school. Ten years— with only two sets of standardized test scores? Hadn't Hope said some special help had been sought? No indication here. Just family statistics typed into proper squares, plus a few checked boxes verifying Tony's receipt of the required inoculations.

Loosely folded inside were only three kinds of information: Tony's grade cards from his two-and-a-half years at Dalton; a page of anecdotes describing contacts with the school counselor; and a page detailing incidents involving the Boys' Vice-Principal. Nothing more. Conspicuously missing was any evidence of his elementary school record. A seven-year void. She would need some better sources of information than the Dalton Cum.

Diana sat down to digest the crumbs of "significant facts" regarding Tony Petri and his junior high school career.

The Cum told so little. But it suggested so much.

It told that Tony never received higher than a D grade in

any basic academic subject, but that he also got a D in metal shop. Strange. Had the boy overestimated his mechanical aptitude to Diana or had something else been going on in metal shop?

The Cum told that when Tony entered seventh grade Mrs. Petri informed the school counselor that Tony had a problem that was "visual and non-corrective." The counselor referred the mother to some remedial centers, said the Cum. No comment on Mrs. Petri's follow-up actions. Had she followed up? Diana noted the question.

Mrs. Petri also confided, said the counselor's Cum report, that there were problems at home: that Tony didn't get along well with his father; that she tried never to leave them alone; that the Petris had "bad arguments that sometimes became physical"; and that Tony's father, who was 69 years old, "can't stand the sight of Tony, won't accept any help he needs, and won't listen." The Cum told that the family had sought counseling through the church, but that Mrs. Petri hadn't been "completely honest with the therapist then, and regrets it now." Also noted was a statement that Mrs. Petri hated to have teachers' conferences because she "breaks down."

The whole cathartic confession was recorded in the folder. The counselor's January report mentioned that she had referred Mrs. Petri to the learning centers for a second time.

Diana crossed out the question she had noted earlier. She had her answer. No follow-up had been made by the mother. Then her eyes fell on the last of the counselor's reports: "School counselor asks that Tony be put in the Opportunity Room during fourth period, his math period." No reason given for the placement, but it clearly suggested misbehavior.

Diana laughed grimly as she read the words "Opportunity Room." Some opportunity. Opportunity to join the other warriors who had chosen to act out instead of withdraw. The "holding room" for kids who misbehaved.

Diana left the page of commentary and turned her attention to Tony's "numbers"—his test results, the only two that had been recorded. On the seventh grade test in reading, Tony achieved a Stanine 1 (the lowest of the nine possible stanines, i.e., groups, into which all standard test scores were ranked). This score had placed him in Hope Saltzman's remedial reading class. The other score was from a group-administered IQ test.

Diana first saw the Stanine 2 and then was stunned by the actual recorded IQ score: 74. Borderline retarded. The score suggested Tony Petri was borderline retarded! Could this be the same Tony Petri Diana had just met, the one she sensed was so bright?

Maybe she had the wrong Cum, she joked with herself, knowing there was just one Tony Petri at Dalton. She chastised herself for her overreaction. She knew full well about the fickleness, the deception of test scores, but this one had caught her off guard. What would someone think who didn't know better?

She pushed the thought aside and turned to the document from the Boys' Vice-Principal, with its comment dated October of Tony's ninth grade. Just last month, Diana realized. The one-liner read: "With three boys in a gang, looking for revenge re Halloween incident." No description of the Halloween incident, nor of the form of the "revenge." The Vice-Principal further noted that, from seventh through ninth grades, seven encounters had brought Tony to his office, mostly for "horseplay, pushing, hitting others, or encouraging others to fight."

That was it.

What could Diana conclude from the Cum? Not much from what it told. But the suggestions were another story—strong suggestions that this was a deeply troubled family, that Tony and his father didn't get along, that perhaps there were some physical beatings going on. The Cum suggested that Mrs. Petri only *spoke* of seeking help, but apparently did nothing. It suggested that Tony was borderline retarded, maybe prone to violence and revenge-type gang behavior—this boy Hope Saltzman had described as the gentle giant who never got into fights.

As Diana pondered all the implied horrors of the Cum, she couldn't help but wonder what they were really like, these three human beings who comprised the Petri family. Was the mother indifferent, irresponsible? And the father? Could he really "not stand the sight of Tony"? Was he physically abusive? What about Tony? How could he design and build a unique vehicle from the ground up and score as borderline retarded on an IQ test—or get a D in metal shop? And what *was* his potential for violence?

As she thumbed the documents and pried into the inconsistencies, Diana rediscovered something she hadn't thought about

19

for years—that different beholders perceive the same people and the same behaviors in markedly different ways. Just a passing thought. She couldn't know then that this basic truth would reveal itself over and over during a search that was to consume the next three years of her life.

How many Tonys were out there, Diana pondered as she closed the slim folder, with how many Cums filled with inconsistencies that no one was questioning?

Yeah, Hope Saltzman, Diana took the bait.

There was no turning back.

CHAPTER 3

Ann Petri:
"I remember it all, every detail...."

Maneuvering through the big-city hospital, the teacher-therapist mastered the maze of corridors, double doors, and elevators and finally found the sub-basement location of the cafeteria.

This was dumb, unprofessional, she told herself as she was being led to the cafeteria kitchen by a helpful busboy. You should have called first, Diana. Should have made an appointment. Too late now; she found herself at her destination.

Inside the cavernous tile and stainless steel room, five women in identical light-blue uniforms were occupied with the slicing, stirring, and steaming of food and the assembling of serving trays for the next wave of hungry customers. In a hospital, there was never any set mealtime—just flows and overflows as shifts changed and hunger struck round the clock. The women had systematized their routine so that no movements were without purpose.

Diana gave the busboy the name of the person she was seeking and was soon introduced to one of the light blue figures, who appeared considerably older than Diana had anticipated. The woman was more than thin, with a pale, delicate, porcelain complexion. Even her wrinkles seemed delicate. Her whole bearing expressed fragile strength and utter efficiency. The starched uniform, mandated short hairdo, and scrubbed pink hands confirmed that she had totally sanitized herself for the job. Only the intricate cross of Jesus, which hung prominently at her neck, and the badge, titled MANAGER, personalized the hospital dress code.

21

The woman's face was kind, alert, preoccupied—and puzzled. Her knit brows gave away the confusion hiding behind the politely smiling mouth. She was clearly apprehensive about this unscheduled visit.

"My name is Diana Cotter, Mrs. Petri, and I'm an educational therapist in private practice. I think Hope Saltzman may have spoken to you about me—about my consultation with her regarding your son, Tony?"

The mention of her son drew her immediate interest. "Oh...yes? Oh, yes..." She vaguely recalled signing something for Miss Saltzman about that.

"Hope mentioned that you worked here and I was eager to talk to you," Diana stated, filling Ann Petri's expectant pause with the explanation she was awaiting. "I met with Tony briefly yesterday and he showed some interest in working with me."

Mrs. Petri's eyebrows raised in astonishment; she seemed suddenly withdrawn, almost embarrassed. "We cannot afford to pay, you know," her words declared herself instantly. "We have simply done all we can. We are not looking for more help for Tony," she said softly, then looked away.

Diana understood. "Of course. Please forgive me, Mrs. Petri, for charging in here on you like this, without even a phone call. It was just that I got so carried away. I met Tony yesterday morning and I couldn't get him out of my mind. He seemed so bright, so capable of learning, and I just kept wondering where we'd lost him. There was something about him that made me feel the two of us could work together—that maybe it wasn't too late for him to still get some help.

"There'll be no financial obligation for you, Mrs. Petri," Diana assured her quickly. "It's not your money I'll be needing—it's your memory. I'd like to learn from Tony—from his case and from your experiences so that I can have a better understanding of why kids like Tony fail. You mentioned a minute ago that you weren't looking for more help. I guess that means you've done your share of helpseeking?" Diana half-stated and half-questioned.

"Ohhh, yes," the mother told it all in the "Oh," relaxing her guard somewhat. "Oh, my, yes," she repeated, still rationing her words. Diana sensed that her ability to trust was as fragile as her appearance.

"I know Tony's had lots of years of failure, Mrs. Petri, and I sure can't promise any miracles," Diana said. "But I've been working with kids like Tony for 22 years and I'll give it my best."

"You said you were some kind of a therapist?" Mrs. Petri asked, still confused about exactly who and what this lady was about, this lady who had dropped in off the street from nowhere.

"I'm an *educational* therapist, Mrs. Petri. My major concern is for people who are failing to learn. Kids fail for lots of different reasons. Sometimes they really can't learn, and sometimes they just won't. Part of my job is to find out if they're really unable, no matter how hard they try, or if they're just unwilling—just turned off for some other reason. I look behind the learning problem for the reasons, and that involves listening to what's really going on, inside and out for these kids.

"It's such a common thing, Mrs. Petri. So many times, people look at little pieces of the problem and they miss the whole kid. If I work with Tony, I'll need to know what kinds of things he does well, because his successes will give me important clues. He's so much more than his parts, if you know what I mean...Oh, of course you know that." Now it was Diana's turn to feel embarrassed, knowing no one is more of an expert on that subject than a mother. "That's why your support is so crucial to me, Mrs. Petri. I'll need to know where you've been and what's been tried with Tony. It's late for him but I think I can do something. I just know I can't do it alone."

Just as her son had done the morning before, Ann Petri studied Diana's face, piercingly now, for long, silent seconds. Then, with her son's same conservation of words, she served up the awaited permission.

"All right," she stated simply, firmly, then repeated, "It's all right. Go ahead and try. " She would take one more chance.

Freed by her decision, she offered to help in any way she could. The two women arranged a meeting for the following week, to include Tony's father, so that Diana could begin gathering the information that only the parents possessed.

Then, glancing sideways to hide the eyes that were rapidly filling with moisture, Ann Petri said in a hushed church-voice, "Mrs. Cotter, God bless you. If you can help my Tony, you will truly be earning your place in Heaven. I'll tell you whatever you need to know." Still looking away, she announced poignantly, more to herself than to Diana, "I remember it all. Every detail."

23

With those words, the mother regained her composure, excused herself, and resumed her role as manager of the hospital kitchen. Her life offered little time for tears.

They sat across from each other at a spotless formica table in the far corner of the hospital cafeteria, where no one would intrude on their confidential exchange.

Diana had been unprepared for Mr. Petri's appearance. Hardly your typical junior high parent, she thought. He looked weary, infirm, and about twenty years older than his mate. His shoulders were rounded as if the weight of his head were a burden that forced his eyes to look downward. His facial contours, hairline and opaque, black-brown eyes suggested that he owned the genetic blueprint for his son. A mellowed-with-age version of Tony's, his heavy-set, cumbersome body spoke of many years of sitting in chairs.

Spread out on the table was a yellowing collection of documents—bills, cancelled checks, birth records, photos, health charts, test results, contracts, and assorted correspondence. These tangibles were Mrs. Petri's proof to the world that she had indeed done everything that could be expected of a mother seeking help for her child. It was too early for Diana to realize the immeasurable value of the voluminous collection.

Mrs. Petri began her recital of explanations as she held up each document or paper scrap. She was no longer the woman of few words. On this day, she had much to say.

"Now, this lady, she was the educational consultant at the Catholic school..."

"And this man was the psychologist at our health clinic..."

"This Sister—I had lots of conferences with her, but she's not with the church any more..."

"And this gentleman—this is his contract—I got his name out of the newspaper..." She handed Diana the papers.

"It's fantastic that you saved all this," Diana mumbled, unable to hide her amazement at the quantity of documents.

Mrs. Petri went on, uninterrupted, totally engrossed in clarifying the evidence.

"...and this is the contract we signed. There was another half-year contract but I can't seem to find it," she said, rummaging nervously through the pile. "This man is still there. I know he is because..."

Mr. Petri interjected hurriedly, almost inaudibly, "Yes, because he advertises."

Tony's mother continued, again unhearing, "I called him once and asked him to send a report to another clinic, but he refused to give out anything. He wrote a letter instead, saying that if I was willing to bring Tony back he would be willing to help him, but he would not send out any reports about him. I was *most* upset with him. I wish you could get it from him."

"Well, I'll sure pick at him a little bit," Diana offered, copying down the name that was printed there.

Surprisingly, Mrs. Petri added, with great sincerity, "He was a most charming man." Puzzling comment, Diana thought.

Moving on, "Now this is where I took Tony one summer." She showed the letterhead.

"And these letters are all from this learning center over near the school. They ran the remedial reading program at the Catholic school. Now—not that I care about the money, but I paid each month for the school and I paid an additional $25 a month for this remedial reading teacher.

"Then I took Tony the following year, privately, to that same center. These are the four letters he gave me. I know he gave me a report every month, but I'm sorry, I just can't seem to find all of those. It was so many years ago, you know." She paused, glancing at her husband, who was staring straight ahead at nothing in particular.

She explained, "Tony wasn't happy at that center. The girl who was taking care of him pulled his ear because he wasn't paying attention, and I don't think that's good either! I mean, here's a kid who's desperately trying to learn a *word*. So then, I just quit there...but later I went back to them again."

Another enigma. Why did she return?

Mrs. Petri felt no need to explain this last puzzler, but continued, commenting as she picked up each paper—the anecdotal reports from the sixth grade teachers, in place of report cards—the cancelled checks from one reading specialist—the height-and-weight chart that recorded every visit to the doctor.

Diana whistled, marvelling at the completeness of the files. One question generated by the Cum had been answered already. This mother had been deeply involved.

Mrs. Petri laughed at herself. "I bet you never saw anything like this before." Indeed Diana hadn't.

Finishing with the papers, Proud Mama began on the photos of Tony as a young child.

"Here's the date," she pointed to the numerals on the photograph, "and he was 5 years 9 months and 65 pounds."

Mr. Petri and Diana winked at each other, both chuckling now at her penchant for details.

"I wrote that on every picture," she said, adding sheepishly, "Well, you know, when you only have the one child..."

"I know," Diana said. "I have two children and my second one really feels cheated out of all the records and pictures."

Trying to direct the conversation back to Tony's early schooling, Diana began asking about one of the teachers at the Catholic school.

But Mrs. Petri didn't hear her. She was smiling, sentimentally lost in a photo of Tony, retelling the circumstances. "My older brother said to Tony—he was busy riding his bike and they wanted to get his picture—so my brother said, 'Tony, you don't like your mama, do ya?' and Tony said, 'Yes I do,' and my brother said, 'I don't think you do. You never hug her,' and Tony ran over to me and that's when they took this picture." Her reverie took her back to the scene of the snapshot.

Drawn back to the present by the patient silence of her audience, she explained two more photos, seeming driven to finish what she had begun. One snap bore the note, "Two years and three weeks old."

"Wow. Down to the exact moment," Diana reacted.

"Yeah. Everything was that way." The husband/father was speaking, resigned, tired. He shifted his weight, trying to find a comfort zone, and wiped a troublesome left eye with his handkerchief.

With the last fragments of the past explained, Ann Petri breathed deeply and relaxed her posture into the chair. She seemed sad that the litany had drawn to a close.

"This has been so helpful to me, Mrs. Petri," Diana said, sensing the mother's need for some support at this moment. "Would you mind if I borrow these? I'll be careful to return them just as soon as I've pieced together the order of everything."

"Oh, of course," she answered. "We're just so grateful that something might be done to help Tony, and maybe his story will help some other children so they don't have to suffer the way he did. The way we all did." So polite. So controlled.

Diana began to gather together the various papers, presuming their meeting had just about ended except for the farewell proprieties, when suddenly Mrs. Petri reached for her arm, seeking her full attention.

In a voice transformed, she said, "You know, Mrs. Cotter, it's been so hurtful! My anxiety...I mean, it has been so hurtful that Tony hasn't been able to learn all these years. I've felt so helpless. There's nothing I wouldn't do for him, if only he could learn to read!

"The hours we've spent! It wasn't just him alone, you understand." Her pitch was high now—almost a wail. "We'd sit at the kitchen table. 'Spell "wand,"' I'd say...'W-A-N-D'...Then he'd say 'W-A-N-D'...'Now put your hand over it...Now close your eyes ...NOW spell it...Now OPEN your eyes...Now spell it AGAIN.' Over and over. 'Try! You're not trying.' 'I am!' he'd say. And the next day, he wouldn't remember even one of the handful of words we'd worked on...I tell you..."

The eyes closed. The hand released Diana's arm. "That *little* child. We'd be working nights. Oh, how I wanted him to pass just one lousy little spelling test. Just one!" Her out-of-character profanity went uncensored. The passion was that intense.

"And the wondering, 'Why isn't he learning? Why can't he read?' He was so bright," her voice cracked, "such a bright little baby, all those years before he went to school. You know, Mrs. Cotter, it's a terrible frustration for a mother." She was silent for some seconds and then, slightly embarrassed, added, "Or a father."

Mr. Petri remained mute, but nodded. Had he been involved? How?

The mother's pain hung in the air. Remembering more, she went on. "And to have people say to you, 'Oh, what a nice boy you have!' Yes. A nice boy. But to know deep down inside that that 'nice boy' can't read or write, that's a heartache!"

Her husband suddenly broke the silence he had maintained throughout this unexpected release, and moved to console her. "Oh, that's not so bad," he offered, gently reaching a hand toward her shoulder.

But the hand could not soothe the pain kept private for so long. Inconsolable, Mrs. Petri continued the confession.

"None of my family knows about Tony. Oh, they suspect it

27

because they know I drag him all over. But they don't completely know. I've never told them, and they don't ask. And if they do, I give them an answer so they don't ask me any more."

Then without any change of composure, she added, "My brother lives right next door to me."

Stunning news. "They live next door and they don't know?" Diana blurted, losing her professional cool at the unexpected disclosure.

"They don't know the whole...that he can't read and write." Mrs. Petri responded casually, as if the circumstances were perfectly natural.

Mr. Petri, animated for the first time, added emotionally, "They just know that he is capable of doing almost anything. They know that! He can do what they can't do!"

Anticipating the question before Diana expressed it, Mrs. Petri explained, "We've kept the secret for Tony's sake," then quickly amended, "but he doesn't know that they don't know."

Incredible. The *secret* was even a secret—fromTony. Diana felt she had to ask, "Does Tony see these people often? Do they have children?"

"Oh yes! My family, we're *close*," Mrs. Petri responded instantly, automatically. "They have two children a couple of years older than Tony. He's on pretty good terms with his cousins, but I don't think he's that close to them that he could discuss it."

Mr. Petri became involved once again, shaking his head and wagging a finger in emphasis, "Because *they* are not of the same opinions or same qualities as Tony. He's interested in doing things mechanically. The rest of them are not. In fact, his cousin's been calling for the last three nights, trying to get Tony to fix something for him. But Tony's too busy. They go their own way—unless they need something. Then we hear from them. Oh, yes, oh yes," he nodded over and over.

"That's his cousin who's an 'A' student at St. John's. He's going to get a scholarship. He graduates this year," Mrs. Petri added, momentarily leaving her son's woes to share pride in her nephew's accomplishments. "And *he* calls *Tony* all the time for help with his car," she added with a tone of irony. She wore her hurt near the surface.

"And has Tony ever called on them for any help?" Diana asked of both of them.

"He don't need their help," Mr. Petri burst out, proud, indignant, hardly sounding like a man who "couldn't stand the sight of" his son. "Why, he can take something we wouldn't even be able to do ourselves, and all we have to do is read directions to him once, and he can do anything. He'll say, 'I got it, I got it,' and then he doesn't want you to say another word. No, he don't need their help."

"Everybody in my family asks me, 'Why do you make such an effort to go to Mass every morning, Ann?' God, if they only knew!" Mrs. Petri said.

Stopping, looking into space, she continued, "And the family would say, 'Well, if Ann didn't spoil him so much, he'd be all right.' They said it behind my back."

Wistfully now, "It's more important to me than anything in the world that people say good things about Tony...and his friends all do."

Leaning back, she ended with a painful admission, perhaps voicing it aloud for the first time. "I pushed and pushed all his younger days," she sighed deeply. "I can't push any more."

CHAPTER 4

"I don't know what I really know
and what I'm supposed to know...I just know
I feel pretty stupid most of the time."

D uring the beginning twice-a-week pieces of scheduled time, Tony Petri and Diana Cotter began the real getting acquainted, the loosening up, the poking around in the boy's splintered memories, searching for some laughter. But there wasn't much laughter to be found in Tony's memory bank. At least not in the memories connected to school.

"There was always trouble," Tony frequently repeated, wearing his old-man face. "Yeah, right from the beginning. Trouble...it's hard to remember all the stuff, especially anything good happening. I remember all those tests...for sure, they were always testing me. And...that guy, there was one guy with the eye exercises...all that weird stuff for me to do...it was just weird and it didn't do much good, far as I could tell."

The fragments of thoughts, events, people were bouncing off each other, running together as he talked: Some "other guy, a real con man," who sold them a bunch of records and books...lots of gadgets, "the fixers," Tony called them...Mom, always looking for something new, something magic, something that would finally work. Hatred flashed through his voice about some teacher and her colored slips...Teachers! All creeps, freaks...oh, one exception though. Yeah, one nice guy in fifth grade, who understood and tried but "there wasn't much he could do by then, I was so far gone." Tony forgave the man his limitations.

They were just skirting the past in those early sessions. Tony's dreams for the future were what interested Diana now; it had to be his dreams for the future, not his dread of the past, that provided a direction for their work together.

"What do you hope to do when you get out of school, Tony?"

"Well," he contemplated, "right now, I think I want to be a motorcycle mechanic." Then he did find a moment of laughter as he admitted he was trying to con his mom into buying him a motorcycle. "She's pretty much of a pushover most times, if you know what I mean. I get my way a lot with stuff—but I help her a lot too," he hastened to add. "My dad's another story, though. I just sort of handle him, kinda humor him, y'know what I mean. So he doesn't holler."

He left the subject of his parents as quickly as he'd come to it—too soon to get personal?—and headed back to her question. "Yeah, I think I'd be good working with choppers or mechanical stuff. As far as school goes, I guess I just want to be able to read well enough to get out of this rat hole and get the kind of job I want. Oh, and spelling."

"Spelling?" She couldn't disguise her surprise.

"Yeah, I guess I need some spelling. I hate spelling—never cared about it, but, much as I hate to admit it, for the first time I think I may need it. You know, though," he said, pulling a folded piece of paper out of his jeans, a folded reason that spelling was on his mind that particular Monday, "somethin's screwed up with me and spelling. I just can't get it! Look at this." He unfolded the looseleaf sheet, smoothed it flat, trying to hide its wrinkled abuse, and disclosed a page of writing. A full page of repetitions of the same word. The word was supposed to be Nicholas.

"There's one of those 'holes' in my 'cheese' you were talkin' about," he said, acknowledging he had given some thought to the analogy shared at their first encounter. "I must have spent two hours on three lousy words for this crummy history class last night!" He pointed to the history book that lay on top of his notebook. "And I still can't do 'em the same every time. Especially this one." He jabbed at "Nicholas."

Astonishing effort—probably the first he'd made for the history class all semester.

His Nicholas had gone through several evolutions on the page. The closest he'd come was a surprisingly acceptable "Nicolas" minus the h, but then he'd lost it. His effort, and the sharing of it, was his way of asking why, even when he tried to his maximum, he failed at a task that seemed so simple for others. Another clue about his brightness. Bright kids care about the Whys of their disabilities.

"Huh, all those teachers used to tell me to 'Write each word three times.' Bullshit," Tony barked, abandoning curiosity for another moment of self-protection. "What's so magic about three times? I can write it 50 times and it's still wrong! Screw it, it's all crap!" He impulsively swiped a powerful arm across the desk, flinging his pencil to the floor as he yelled, "Who cares anyway how you spell 'Nicholas'?"

Diana gave no answers—just asked him to write his name three times and then a fourth. Naturally, all the examples were identical, perfect.

"Why do you think you can do that so perfectly, Tony?"

"Because it's my NAME. Because I've written it maybe ten thousand times!" he answered, annoyed and confused by the comparison.

"Yes." Waiting for the point to sink in. "It's yours, it's important to you, and you've practiced it over and over. Now try mixing up the letters so it doesn't say 'Tony.'"

He hesitated, not sure whether to risk it, almost afraid if he mixed up the letters he'd never get them right again.

Then he took a pencil and wrote OTNY, and YNOT, and NOTY.

"Do any of them look like 'Tony' to you?" she asked.

He shook his head, surprised how clearly he saw that none of these combinations of letters even resembled "Tony."

"Why do you think they don't?"

"Well, it just doesn't *look* right. I don't know why! 'Cause I know how 'Tony' is supposed to look and that's not it." Still gruff. "It's out of order, that's why." He finally put it into words.

"Ah. Out of order," she said, matter of factly. "You got it. You have to learn the tricks about remembering the order. Crazy, eh? Just the order of the letters can change the whole word. But the point is, you *can* learn it. If you *couldn't* do it, you wouldn't be able to do it at all—ever! Not even for your name. The real question is why you can't do it more often. That's a biggy, and I don't think we'll find that out in one or two days. For some reason, you never learned *how* to look at words, Tony. Your brain played some tricks on your eyes. Some kids need to be taught how to look in special ways. It never came naturally for you."

"For me, nothing comes naturally," Tony interrupted.

"Sure it does. Look what you do with motors. I would need

to be taught how to look at motors and mechanical blueprints, but for you *that* comes naturally. For learning words, the kicker is that you need to know how to look, and then you need to be willing to practice. Sounds simple, but it's a big order, especially now, after all the years of feeling so foolish. I understand that, Tony. When you were little and couldn't do what others did, you must have been humiliated. You must have found ways to protect those hurt feelings."

He said nothing, perhaps afraid to trust his voice.

"Let me show you something. Take a look at these two words and tell me what you notice," Diana said, shifting the focus back to word analysis, a safer topic than humiliation at that moment.

Tony studied the two nearly identical words of "car" and "can," which she had written extra-small to emphasize how similar they were. These were two words he knew how to read, two words he'd seen many times, but had never really *seen,* never really looked at as she was asking him to do now, to look for their differences. He had never consciously realized that only a two-millimeter vertical line converting the "r" to an "n" made those into two distinct words with different sounds and totally different meanings.

The fifteen-year-old brow furrowed in thoughtful discovery. He saw. Fifteen, and for the first time he was understanding a never-contemplated principle about the structure of words, a principle most kids automatically compute neurologically by about age eight.

Curiosity, and the great satisfaction of understanding, took hold. With a broad grin, Tony said, "Hey, I think I get it. What else?"

What else. Diana howled at the understatement of the decade. They had just looked at the first rise of the first hill in a whole mountain range. But maybe, just maybe, Tony was ready to venture up the incline.

"Before we look at the 'what else's,' Tony," she laughed, "a few minutes ago you said you think you may need to learn to spell. Why? Why do you need it? Lots of times, I see kids your age who have trouble spelling but they just chuck the whole idea. You know, they sort of figure they can get by in the world just by using their 'smarts' and skip the whole reading-and-writing trip."

She was deliberately playing devil's advocate. There had to be some evidence from Tony that he had found a real need, in the non-school world, for the literacy skills that had evaded him. Diana knew too well that without his perception of need their therapy didn't have a chance.

He didn't disappoint her; there was no dearth of evidence in his young life. At fifteen, his first job had been in the bicycle shop. From his telling, Diana gathered that his bike repairs had been impressive for one so young. The boss, to demonstrate his pleasure with Tony's quick, precise work, decided to give him the added responsibility of greeting new customers, analyzing their bike problems—and writing up the repair tickets.

Writing up the repair tickets.

He tried.

He could write the customers' names just fine, if they spelled them slowly. Then he had to write a description of their repair needs on the work orders. How could a 15-year-old ninth grader ask the customers to spell the words they had just used to describe their problems?

He faked it as well as he could.

For one day.

By five o'clock that evening, chaos hit the bike shop. No one could read the repair tickets, and since he'd forgotten to take down phone numbers there was no way to reach the customers until they returned for their bikes.

Tony lost the job.

At 15, he'd learned from life what no teacher or parent had ever been able to get through to him: that spelling was a practical, *essential* skill.

The story reminded him of other times of feeling foolish, helpless, inadequate. He talked about his habit of eating at the local McDonald's after work, every night ordering the identical quartet—Big Mac, Regular Mac, fries, and large Coke. He began to notice that even though he would always order the same items his bills varied. Tony chuckled as he described his silent research study. During ten consecutive visits to the same McDonald's he placed identical orders and marked down what he was charged. He found that four totals were different from the other six and that none of the four were the same.

He said nothing. But secretly Tony savored his private awareness of the employees' stupidity. He couldn't risk exposure of his own "stupidity" by going public. Public protest would involve reading over the menu, listing the prices, and computing the total—in front of others. From start to finish of his "research project," Tony remained silent.

Apparently Tony often remained silent, whether he felt powerful disdain for others' stupidity or deep humiliation about his own. He described the time his parents gave a family party and ran out of ice cream. They sent him to buy some. He'd handled the task efficiently, he thought, until he heard the giggling from the kitchen as his cousins unloaded the grocery bag. He had bought ice *milk* instead of ice *cream*. Hey, Tony, cantcharead? they had chided. Of course. He could read the words "cream" and "milk." They didn't even look alike. He'd just been in a hurry, was just looking for flavors, for the best price. Anybody could have made the mistake. But anybody didn't. Tony did. The ridicule cut deep. These were his cousins, the "family scholars" who lived next door and from whom the extent of his problem had been kept secret.

Little things, everyday things, were constant reminders of his inadequacy. Whenever he had to make deliveries for the gas station, there were the street signs, and the maps with names in impossible tiny print, all running together. And those headlines with enormous print, screaming something he should know from the little glass-covered vending machines on every corner. And the special sale flyers on motorcycles and parts, the order forms and instruction manuals for all of his tools. Instantaneous messages flashed across the TV screen saying other things he should know. There were traffic tickets for riding his neighbor's cycle illegally in the hills. The drivers' manual—the Bible of every fifteen-year-old. All demanding to be read.

The evidence was more than sufficient for Diana. Tony knew he needed literacy.

Time to get on with business.

"Well, Mr. Tony Petri, what do you want to find out about yourself?" Diana asked lightly. "If you want me to test you, you're going to be in on the scoring. No more secrets. You're old enough to be a partner in this process now. Whatever I find out, you're going to find out—right away—no waiting either. What do you say?"

Tony exposed his now familiar half-smile. He liked the

partnership idea. "I don't know what I *really* know and what I'm supposed to know," he answered candidly. "I just know I feel pretty stupid most of the time." He began to tap his pencil in a drum-rhythm on the paddlearm of the desk, thinking. Then, the decision. "Go ahead and test me. I don't care."

Permission granted. Probably for the first time in his life, he had a piece of the power—the power to submit to something he hated, because it might lead to something he wanted. A big step.

They plunged into his educational inventory like a shop-keeper after the Christmas rush. They disposed of isolated phonics sounds, once and for all, as a topic worthy of attention. Isolated sounds were simply too slow, inefficient, and too emotionally tied to past years of failure. Within minutes, it was clear that Tony was master of all but a few vowel digraphs which, at his age, were not worthy of milliseconds of effort. There must have been a lot of phonics in his past, and most of it had sneaked into his brain in spite of his efforts not to let anybody know.

Next they hit the list of Common Syllables. Tony had never known there was such a list, or that anything was common about syllables. Even more astonishing to both Diana and Tony, he read thirty-two of the forty-five instantly—cautiously, slowly, but instantly—unaware of the power he already possessed.

Syllables, made up of blends of phonic sounds, are the structural units of English words. Like building blocks whose rearrangement allows infinite constructions, those thirty-two syllables Tony had mastered gave him the capacity to decode and assemble great numbers of words. Sadly, Tony had never learned to use that capacity or to understand the strategy behind it.

Once again, Diana used his name to illustrate her point. Borrowing the "ny" from "Tony," she listed words with that "nee" sound—fun-ny, pen-ny, bota-ny, and even such exotics as ebo-ny. Then she divided the word "interesting" into its four separate parts, writing each syllable in a different color. From the checklist, Diana had learned that Tony could read all four of those syllables, but he had been unable to read the word "interesting." As he read each of the colored syllables in sequence, by the time he finished "in-ter-est..." he smiled and

The copper ford O,D not
Become great until That ang#s
macke

coming ridenes
Bell

all am

op CITY camper
er
are operate RTioN
ook et ets ent
ell eD un iD

said, "Oh. 'Interesting.' I get it. Hey. Gimme another one."

Diana felt the joy that always came with teaching adolescents who were ignorant of these basic principles. By the teen years, brain and thought development are mature enough that the concepts, clarified at last, become absorbed in a flash of instant discovery.

Tony tried out his new method on the words "speed-om-e-ter," "ig-ni-tion," "gen-er-a-tor," and, of course, "mo-tor-cy-cle." The "cy" gave him trouble, but he guessed. Guessing was not only allowed, it was encouraged, recommended. Risk was going to

37

be OK now. There would be no more wrongs—only correctables.

As they explored syllables and words, Tony wrote in a tedious print, soon confessing his insecurity about, and reluctance to try, cursive handwriting. Diana demonstrated how the cursive alphabet had been invented. He watched, intrigued, as she added the connecting curves, in a different color, to the alphabet he had so ably printed in manuscript form, thereby allowing him to see the printed symbol hiding inside each cursive version of it. So simple, so obvious. One demonstration was all it took. Diana knew from experience that he would ask to try it and would form every letter perfectly by following the method. She also guessed that he had probably received many writing demonstrations from other teachers. But a concept *taught* is not a concept *learned* unless the learner has paid attention.

The evidence was mounting toward one conclusion for Diana: if you could gain Tony's attention, Tony could learn. Rapidly.

As they were talking, Tony suddenly spotted the WRAT in the pile of materials Diana had brought to the session. The WRAT—his old enemy. Wide Range Achievement Test. Really wide range—designed to test humans from 5 to 65, said the manual. The three parts, reading, spelling, and arithmetic, take twenty minutes to administer, five minutes to score. It is a valuable tool, a fine clue-provider in trained hands, especially for quick assessment at schools, prisons, hospitals, and residential institutions where time is limited.

Alas, the WRAT is also a dangerous tool as well—a potential breeder of nearsightedness. Too often, quick assessors see only the numbers, or compare the present numbers with those from other tests. Too often, quick assessors fail to notice a subject's conditioned response, a shrinking withdrawal at the mere sight of the test form that will, once again, verify failure. How could quick assessors read the mind or feel the rumbling in the bowel, the itching in the scalp, the sweaty palms, or just the silent refusal of the subject's brain to attend?

Tony confessed to being such a subject. He had already done five rounds with the WRAT. Diana had no intention of using it again and was putting it away when Tony stopped her and asked her to give it to him once more. This time, he could be a partner in the scoring. He was about to take the whisper out of all those little numbers that others had always known *about* him but had never shared *with* him.

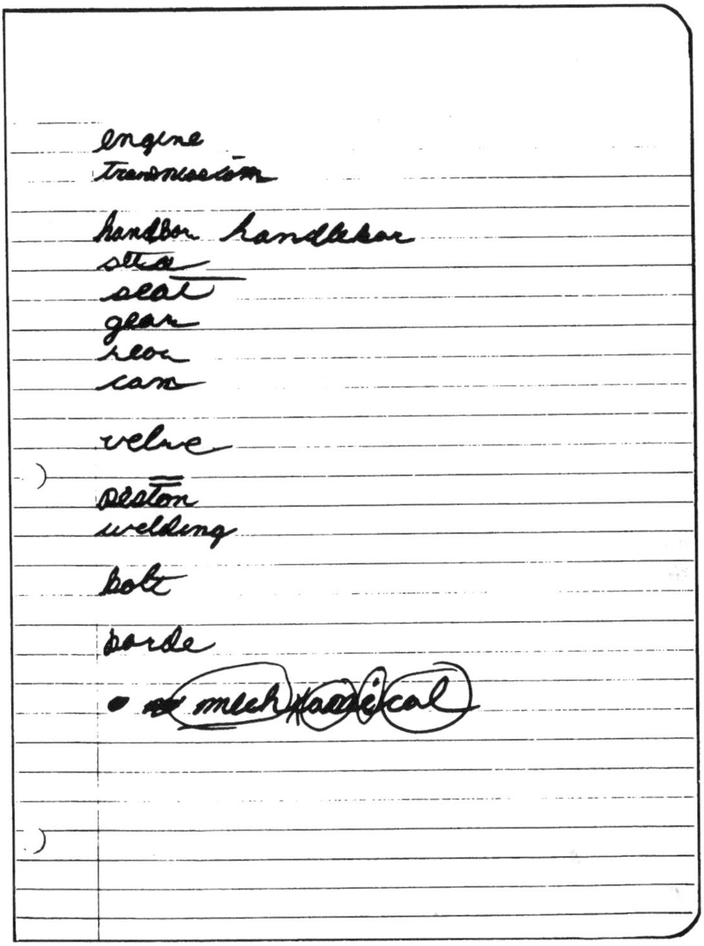

(handwritten notebook list)

engine
Transmission

handbar handlebar
stra
seat
gear
rear
cam

velve

piston
welding

bolt

parde

mech[anical]

Intrigued by his reasoning, by the unique maturity of this enigmatic youth, Diana agreed.

As a partner, Tony made an effort he'd never shown on his previous tests. He attempted to spell twenty-two words, confessing to Diana that the most he'd ever tried before had been the first seven.

He used his ears well, heard the sounds in their correct sequence. His errors were all "good errors"—phonetically readable by others. Diana's explanation of his good errors "blew him away." Never before had the word "good" been connected with Tony and spelling. Fortunately, in his excitement at the completion of twenty-two phonetically readable words, he forgot to ask his score: mid-second grade, WRAT-style. Unfortunately, the officially correct spelling of English demanded more than ears for mastery.

Diana flipped to the reading section, hoping to capitalize on his optimistic mood.

The reading portion of the WRAT has no sentences or paragraphs, only isolated words. Even though Tony had asked to take the test, the sight of the black print with its rows of unrelated morphemes still brought the chronic reflex. He backed away momentarily, turning his head abruptly. Then, remembering he had volunteered, he gave it a try. "Letter" became "Little," "deep" became "jeep," "spell" became "special" and then, with more effort, "speel." Tony was still functioning at the primitive, guess-at-clues level of a neophyte second grader.

He asked for his score, wanting a number on this one.

Diana showed him: 2.7, high second grade. Tony guarded his face. He would not show the devastation of that reality—a second-grade reading score after almost eleven years in schools. Now they both knew the numbers, both ached with the shared facts.

Diana diverted him to the math portion of the test. She was prepared for a refusal now, but Tony seemed relieved to do anything to get away from the reading. Besides, he knew math was a strength, at least in comparison to his language skills. He was right. He could compute like an average sixth grader. So said the WRAT. But the WRAT had no word problems, which meant it offered no chance to evaluate the most essential math skill of all—the ability to know which mathematical processes to use in different life situations. Diana decided to read word problems to him from his ninth-grade practical math book.

Tony proved to be a star in this essential skill. He understood process. He knew exactly what numbers to use and how to use them, and sometimes, even on problems with two or three stages, he computed the correct answers completely in his head. With such skills, it didn't matter if his division or three-place multiplication suffered from an acute case of rust. A machine could always do those higher computations for him. What did matter was that he knew what numbers and operations to put *into* a calculator. Diana made no secret of her excitement over this newly-revealed proficiency.

Tony couldn't understand why she was so excited. He'd been doing "this kinda stuff" for a couple of years. Nobody had ever asked about it and, of course, he'd never mentioned it. No big deal. Just do it and don't call attention to it—another Petri Rule of Thumb. He figured everybody could do that kind of thing. He also figured that, like his reading, he probably did it worse than other people.

Diana was beginning to know Tony and was formulating her working plan for him. She knew he would be turning sixteen four months after they began to work together and he coveted a driver's license more than life. He craved the freedom and expanded job options the cherished document would offer. The driver's manual, adapted to his needs, became an obvious choice for his textbook.

The choice was not so obvious to Tony. He balked at the suggestion that something he *wanted* to read would qualify as legitimate material for "book learning." Like so many others who had endured years of failure, he was suspicious that anything less boring and ponderous than his school textbooks would be fraudulent, deceitful. To read something enjoyable or personally meaningful was to keep him in the dark about the real secrets of reading.

"Look, Tony. Reading is reading. All those books are filled with words. Just words. And all the words follow the same rules, go by the same code," Diana explained. "Once you learn the code, you can use it anywhere—on history or science or motorcycle magazines. Learning the code with words that have interest or meaning for you just helps you get started. Give it a try. Then, whenever you feel you want to switch to the history book, let me know."

Tony began thumbing through the driver's manual Diana had brought, his skepticism giving way to enticement. Diana had read him well. The pamphlet was a perfect lure. Seeing his interest, she used the moment to give him his first homework assignment—to go through the manual, searching out and copying down any words he already knew how to read. She made it clear that he was not to attempt to read the manual as a book at all. Not yet. First they would use it as a resource to find out his "sight vocabulary"—the words he already recognized instantly, words that were not included on the WRAT or other test lists.

Tony listened curiously, nodded that he understood the task, but said nothing. Then he slowly unfolded his six-foot-plus body from around the writing arm of the chair-desk and gathered up his unused ninth-grade history book, his rarely used practical math book, his unused-but-tatooed notebook, and his new "textbook." Glancing at the cover of the manual as he headed for the door, Tony Petri, second grade reader, turned and asked, "What does 'revised' mean?"

He had indeed learned more of the "code" than any WRAT would ever reveal.

CHAPTER 5

"It's such a tough group,
the policy is to spread them around so that
no one teacher has too much burden."

Following her sessions with Tony at the junior high, Diana had begun to make a habit of dropping in on some of Tony's current and former teachers, catching them informally at lunch or on their break times. Their collective memories began to fill in the holes in her understanding of Tony's public face at Dalton.

From Peggy Boyd, the youthful, pleasingly plump Doris Day look-alike who taught a ten-week course in suspense novels, came a description of a boy who seemed more mysterious than any of the characters in the mysteries he wasn't reading.

"Withdrawn. Very withdrawn," had been her chief characterization of the Tony Petri she saw in the class. Just sitting there, kind of filling up a seat, never smiling, never opening his mouth in discussions. Only one boy he would talk to, Ms. Boyd recalled—a hoodlum-type who got expelled for throwing firecrackers. Matter of fact, that was the only type of kid he ever talked to. Pleasant, though—he was pleasant. Never hostile. But he didn't respond. She *tried* to talk to him, but he just wouldn't respond. Did he turn in work? Well, a couple of times, but the papers were "illiterate," she recalled. Strange boy...she just couldn't figure him out.

Ms. Boyd's descriptions reminded Diana of Hope Saltzman's first words about Tony—that he "never really refuses to do anything, you just sort of *feel* it." Peggy Boyd obviously got the same message.

When Diana interviewed Jim Morgan, a social studies teacher, she discovered that the new mini-course concept was popular at Dalton. Jim Morgan, fresh from the university, ded-

43

icated, optimistic, immaculate in his tweed sport coat, white-white shirt and "preppy" tie, had unexpectedly found himself teaching a *five*-week mini-course on geography. Five weeks—hardly time to learn the kids' names. Mr. Morgan had only "known" Tony for this first of their five weeks together. His comments were brief but his frustrations were abundant. He believed in giving his students unlimited extra-credit options—"Whatever they want to do with their best talents." He provided lots of films and filmstrips so they could have more than texts or lectures as sources of information. But he clearly worried whether his option plan, designed to motivate, could work within such a telescoped time span.

Mr. Morgan dug around in his memory for an image of Tony Petri. "Big guy, isn't that the one?" He nodded in agreement with himself. "Big, affable guy who doesn't say anything—absolutely no verbal interchange, as I recall. Yes. Tony. That's the one." Then, gazing into nowhere, he added, "He sits off to the right."

Diana smiled to herself. There it was again—that mind's eye game that secondary school teachers used to attach a student's name to a face. With caseloads of 150 to 200 students rotating through their doors daily and with classes changing sometimes as often as every five weeks, teachers relied on visualization-by location as an essential identification technique.

Eager to be more helpful, Jim Morgan checked his logbook and verified that Tony had turned in no homework or assignments and that his one test score on a map quiz was a dismal 4 out of a possible 25. Reality had a way of puncturing idealism. Mr. Morgan looked woeful as he shared the facts with Diana, but he urged her to remind Tony that, if he exercised his extra-credit options, he could pull up the score.

Big "if," Diana mused. If Tony was motivated enough to try. If Tony could think of an extra-credit project using his "best talents" that could in any way relate to the subject of geography. If he cared enough to begin, persevere, and complete the project within the next four weeks. Big if, Mr. Morgan.

Jim Morgan had no knowledge of Tony's reading disability; he had never been notified. Dalton Junior High had over two thousand students. Mini-courses, Diana learned, covered 5-, 8- and 10-week spans. Regular courses lasted for the semester. Students were constantly changing their schedules and programs. Who in the school hierarchy could be charged with notifying the teacher of a 5-week mini-course that one (or maybe many?) of his students couldn't read?

Of course Jim Morgan hadn't been notified. And, Diana thought, what if he had?

The week after her meeting with Jim Morgan, Diana sought out Jean Abercrombie, Tony's current English teacher, who was less bewildered by Tony because her class was populated with kids battling reading. The fiftyish Jean exuded an unruffled maturity that came from two decades of cajoling adolescents intimidated by the study of their own language.

"Yes, I know your Tony Petri," Jean responded to Diana's first inquiry in the school cafeteria that Tuesday. "Tony was the one who started late and I told him to sit and watch—just get used to things. He'd missed the first few weeks because of a schedule change." The teacher stated the reality with dispassion.

Diana flinched. How could the tragedy of weeks lost be stated so matter-of-factly, especially for a boy who couldn't afford to lose minutes? Then a second thought: had Tony cared?

Jean Abercrombie continued talking, describing the unusual ambiance of her room. Students were allowed to sit all over the room, on the floor or under the tables if they chose, because "all those kids in that group have reading and concentration problems." She was committed to the necessity of their learning to read at any cost—for their own survival. When they read, they read aloud as a group, or silently. And they could choose not to read aloud at all.

Then she spoke about Tony. "Tony's a nice boy. Quiet. He chose to sit in the back. You know, the class accepted him immediately, Mrs. Cotter. They all knew him and were glad to see him when he arrived. In the beginning, everybody read aloud," Jean went on as Diana tried to forget that Tony had missed the beginning, "and I tried to make them feel comfortable. I wanted them to see that they were all in the same boat and they didn't have to feel embarrassed, but that was the only way I could help them. They seemed to respond."

Diana studied Jean Abercrombie's soft eyes and easy smile. One of the "permissive" ones. How well Diana knew that planned permissiveness in experienced hands could move

45

turned-off kids in ways that no authoritarian stand ever could.

Jean was more than wisely permissive. She solicited suggestions, eager to know more about Tony, more about methods she might try with him. Diana shared a few, but had no expectations, knowing the multiple demands already being made upon the English teacher.

Two weeks later, Jean surprised Diana with a telephone call. She reported that Tony had been absent for another week, but when he returned she had set up an experiment utilizing one of Diana's suggestions for guided reading. The other students had thought it was stupid, but they went along with it. When Tony's turn came, he was willing to try because she had read the paragraph first. He made a few errors but she told him instantly what the words were; she then asked him to repeat the whole reading a second time. He knew every word perfectly. They were both pretty amazed. But only one of them expressed it.

"I was so pleased," Jean's voice bubbled into the receiver. "I was sure it was a tiny bit of satisfaction for him. But his behavior confused me, Mrs. Cotter. It didn't fit. I had a chance to see so clearly then how he always holds back. He says one thing, but keeps his face blank. He acts so nice, so passive, never expresses anger. But there's never any joy either," the perceptive lady added, "even when he had that success."

"I know, Mrs. Abercrombie. He can't trust success, even his own. After all those years of failure, maybe he's too suspicious that it's a trick, or not real somehow," Diana responded, and then thanked the teacher for "being out there." She expressed her appreciation that Tony had been fortunate enough to have been assigned to Jean's class for the semester. Perhaps, Diana dreamed aloud, he might be able to stay with her for the year?"

The dream died quickly.

"Oh, I would like to help," Jean responded, "but you need to know—this group will be with me for only eight weeks."

Was English a mini-course too?

"I probably won't have them longer because it's such a tough group and the policy is to spread them around so no one teacher has too much burden."

The call ended with Diana's thought stuck on the last phrase and its meaning to her. Too much burden. Were teachers being

46

reduced to "serving time"? Perhaps one of them would have some magic with the "tough ones." No matter. The risk of burnout, the strain of numbers, were too great. Eight-weeks-and rotate, team. Survival rules.

Suddenly those first few weeks lost because of Tony's schedule change were stripped of all consequence to Diana.

Bill Thorne was not the type you "drop in" on. Diana made an appointment. She crossed the threshold of the conference room to face an athletically-built man with the sharp features and stoic facial control of an ex-Marine.

He was so friendly, so interested, so complimentary about Tony. At first. His words were all the right ones, the ones she expected about a boy with Tony's struggles and about a class full of kids with similar struggles.

But his manner gave another message. He was too cooperative, almost unctuous. Diana knew the signs. Her radar told her that to this man she was an intruder, a "specialist outsider" who couldn't possibly know what it felt like to be in the shoes of a faculty insider. Her cushy, one-to-one world didn't qualify her to understand.

Guardedly, they searched for some rules for relating to each other. Since she had requested the meeting, Diana began, asking what Mr. Thorne saw as Tony's particular strengths and weaknesses in class.

He responded literally. "Tony's strengths are a very sincere effort to do the best he can on what he's asked. He pays close attention...when he's there," he quipped, but then conceded, "He has a more mature attitude than most ninth graders. His weaknesses are that his work is barely legible and his frustration level is low in doing math. He doesn't complete assignments—gets angry at himself about the problems and then he doesn't finish. He's in my D-level practical math class."

The capsule assessment seemed accurate to Diana.

Leaving Tony then, the teacher began to generalize about the D-level group. "These kids have difficulty with everything—fundamentals and basic operations. They have near nonexistent work habits, but mostly they just don't bother to *do* the work. They're lazy, apathetic...and they don't want to discuss anything academic. They're only concerned with social discussions and going to the beach."

47

Probably true, Diana thought. Often D-level math classes demonstrated apathy, the disastrous work habits, the social distractions. But Mr. Thorne's judgments seemed to go deeper.

"We review the basic operations—numbers, fractions, decimals, measurement," he droned on. "This is a very affluent community, as you know. I have them measure their swimming pools. Some assignments turn them on," he noted, his scorn oozing through.

So. It was the affluence. Wouldn't Tony have guffawed at being clumped with the Affluent Crowd! Dalton Junior High was in a community that boasted a one-to-two swimming-pool-per-home ratio. The Petri home was one of the modest originals of the vicinity—of pre-posh development vintage. Diana couldn't help but wonder how Tony had handled the assignment about "measuring his swimming pool." Her guess was that he would have missed class that day. She didn't ask.

Diana smiled and nodded, trying to show her understanding of the "D-level Phenomenon"—still hoping for Tony's sake to develop some professional rapport, no matter how tenuous.

"Tony hasn't got even 30% right on any test this year," Mr. Thorne noted. "Maybe he'd do better if he came to class more often. He doesn't grasp word problems at all. On his last test, two-thirds of the problems had very few words but he still didn't do well."

Doesn't grasp word problems at all, the man said. Diana recalled her own math evaluation of Tony.

"You know, Mr. Thorne, Tony's reading problem is pretty severe," Diana interrupted.

"Well, I had sort of guessed that, but..."

Another teacher who hadn't been notified.

"Have you ever tried reading the word problems to him?" Diana asked, trying to sound as if she'd just thought of the idea that moment.

His "No" was followed by her cautiously worded, rapidly delivered dare. "I bet, if you tried it, Tony would know what process to use and how to set up the problem, because when I work with him one-to-one, I find he's very bright."

Mr. Thorne's response this time was immediate. "Never. He could never do it," he said, rising then, his posture signalling it was time to end their dialogue.

One last try. "I just have the feeling he could, although I

realize how tough it is to do that sort of thing when you're working with a group and all, Mr. Thorne. I've always been sort of a coward that way—I just take one at a time. I really admire those of you who are brave enough to take on the whole pack."

Diana's confession was more true than he would ever know. She saw teaching as an act of heroism in these times. Taking his lead, she rose to leave. She threw out as a parting comment, "If you ever get a chance to try him at it, would you do me a favor and let me know what you find out?"

There were forty math sessions remaining for that semester. In forty sessions, Mr. Thorne never accepted the dare.

On that same day, Diana's meeting with the Boys' Vice Principal, Dominic Vitti, helped remove the Thorne from her side. Within moments she knew that the ruddy-cheeked, barrel-chested Dom Vitti was a man who liked kids, even fourteen- and fifteen-year-old kids—not always the world's most endearing population. The tone of his voice revealed his fondness for Tony, in spite of the nature of their encounters. Dom Vitti supervised disciplinary matters. It takes only one encounter for a junior high youth to know whether his school's peace-keeper really cares about his wellbeing.

Mr. Vitti expressed pleasure that Diana would be working with Tony and seemed informed about Tony's learning difficulties. Then he provided his own special testimonial. "Tony is an extremely responsible lad—sort of a leader for the good, a champion-of-the-underdog type, if you know what I mean. He's very old-fashioned in that way, a good influence on his 'bad' friends. You'll always see Tony either alone or with the 'hard guys.' And whenever you talk to him about trouble, he accepts advice, which is more than I can say for a lot of the kids around here," he chuckled. "His manners are unique, too, Mrs. Cotter. He always comes to me to ask permission to bring his three-wheeled invention to school or to leave early for work. He never seems to take anything for granted—always checks it out first."

Then Mr. Vitti went over to his files, drew out the folder marked PETRI, ANTHONY, and thumbed the pages. "Hmm. I see here that, in the past two years, I've only had to intervene with Tony seven times, and those were mostly minor problems—horseplay, pushing, hitting others, or encouraging others to fight," he read the words from the page.

Familiar words. The words from the Cum. They sang back to Diana from the recent past, those words that had suggested Tony might be prone to violence. How different was the meaning of those identical words now, in the person-to-person interpretation of them by the man who had written them.

Only seven encounters, Dom Vitti had said. He saw no cause for alarm about what he clearly regarded as minor mischiefs.

More important, Dominic Vitti saw what was right with Tony Petri. But he hadn't written the Rights on the Cum.

That is not the custom.

CHAPTER 6

*"Something is wrong with
your boy, Mrs. Petri."*

Closed semi-sheer curtains cast a dim light in the Petri livingroom, belying the reality of midafternoon on a sunlit day. Ever-drawn curtains, pulled to preserve the privacy of the inhabitants, Diana had thought when she noticed them on each of her visits. The scarce light dulled the already bland colors of the furnishings, the gray-on-gray sculpture of the patterned carpet. The statues and paintings of Jesus and the Holy Mother—permanent invited guests, mute guardians in the modest, immaculate room—created a mood of sanctuary, of haven. As Diana's knowledge of the Petris expanded, their need for home as haven became increasingly clear.

Ann Petri was weary, justifiably weary. And defensive.

"The Pushover." That was what her son and her mate both called her. There were few thanks expressed to the provider, decision-maker, and answer-seeker of this threesome.

She pondered her actions over the years, defending her role as "soft touch." "Do you realize what that little boy went through? How many times I dressed him and dragged him here, there, and everywhere? Oh, I bribed him, I must tell you. I bought him a lot of things. Yes, that's right, I did. My husband would say, 'Good God, Annie, you're not going to buy that kid...' and I'd say, 'Well, Johnny, I got a reason!' I had to! I didn't want him to go and be all upset if he was going to be tested again. He must have been tested a hundred times," she exaggerated, reflecting her own exasperation with the process.

As Tony had shown a growing trust for Diana, his mother had begun to do the same, sharing with her more and more pieces of Tony's past. Her own life, however, was not something

51

Ann Jordan Petri chose to talk about with strangers, and Diana sensed not to ask. Instead, she learned the sparse facts about the mother's early years from comments made by Tony during their sessions.

Ann Jordan had been born of a large rural family, the next-to-youngest of seven children. No doubt those children had different personalities and capabilities, but they shared one reality: they were expected to help support the family as soon as they were employable.

Ann met the expectations early. Employable at age 14, she became a "liberated woman" long before the words were fashionable—liberated to work all the weeks of her lifetime, with only childbirth or illness offering brief periods of respite.

But she didn't want to talk about her work or her unique brand of liberation now. She wanted to talk about Tony.

Diana had felt surprised and pleased when Mrs. Petri had first invited her to the home, weeks earlier, to see the books. Scores of books, children's books, piled up in foot-high stacks covering the entire three-by-five-foot dinette table. No question about it; Mrs. Petri had done her share of readiness training. Diana recalled the mother's sentiments: pride because she had read all those books to Tony, and anger at the failures once Tony had started school. "He knew every one!" she'd said. "Every one. And then he starts school and they tell me he can't read."

She'd been afraid to admit the hidden fear that something was wrong even when she read the picture books. She would always try to get Tony to repeat what she read to him as she pointed to the words. He would repeat it perfectly, but always from memory, not as "reading." The mother didn't know what was "normal" at that age, but she had a deep-seated mother's fear that there was some little quirk, something wrong.

On this day, Diana and Ann Petri were searching for signs...Signs of Wrongness. They examined the myriad clues from Tony's history for the causes of his failures.

Mrs. Petri sat on the sofa, facing Diana but not seeing her. She saw instead, through closed eyes, the scene that few mothers ever forget—the arrival of the first-born child.

The mother began to share her recollections. "I was so small, the doctor didn't even think I was pregnant. He thought it was a tumor—can you imagine! But I was sure! I felt perfect...the pregnancy was perfect. Then—it was Tuesday night—I lost my water. I remember, it was Lent and I went to all four stations of the cross at Mass. Maybe that's what made me deliver three weeks early. The pains came and the doctors said the head was showing. I felt ready, but there was no sign of birth...so they sent me home again and I waited...'til Thursday.

"Stayed home 'til Thursday morning—it seemed like forever—and finally, on Thursday afternoon, I delivered. But I didn't get my regular doctor then," she said, opening her eyes, watching Diana to see if she would understand what she was about to say. "I got some old man. I hated him! I've always believed he used undue force. He had those awful forceps—why, that boy still has the marks on his head from them. He kept yelling at me, 'Grunt! Grunt, Goddamn it! Grunt!' I can't bear to hear the Lord's name taken in vain and it really upset me."

Thus Tony was born, the only child ever conceived by Ann and John Petri. John, aged fifty-five, and Ann, ending her thirty-seventh year without prior conception, had given up the notion of parenting an offspring when Tony happened, an unexpected "gift from God" for these devout Catholics. Those first months of awe at the development of their boy-child gave them little warning of what was to follow. Oh, yes, there were some troubles with formula, bloody diarrhea, even mild asthma at six months. But those would be resolved by their beloved pediatrician, Dr. Fortunati. They felt confident of that.

The times had been hard then for Ann and John, but even John's severe bleeding ulcer, which forced the new mother back to work prematurely during Tony's first year, was a trial both felt they could bear. After all, life can't always go smoothly, and this baby was their joy. Look at him, so bright, responsive. Why, he was even walking at a year.

"His crawling was a little strange, though. Actually, he never really crawled," Mrs. Petri admitted. "He just sort of got up on one knee and pulled the other leg behind him. I didn't think anything of that. I mean, that wasn't a sign of anything, do you think?" she asked, and continued without waiting for a response.

"Lately, I've been seeing articles about kids who don't crawl, and how they teach them all over again—when they're older—how to crawl...but Tony...he seemed fine...I mean, he didn't *need* to crawl because he just went straight into walking," she said, debating with herself again, hoping to defeat another of the gnawing doubts that were continuously fed by everything she read.

Diana just listened, nodding in noncommittal absorption of the data.

Mrs. Petri went on, perking up at the more positive thought that came then. "Tony was always so busy with things he could put together or take apart, and he loved toys that could turn. Mechanical things. Why, his first words were "Turn it,'" she laughed, then pondered a moment. "Busy—that's how I'd describe him…but he wasn't hyperactive," the self-trained diagnostician emphasized defensively, "just busy."

She'd done her homework, this searching lady, and she wanted an ally to support her conclusions about what her son *wasn't.*

"You can't believe the kinds of things that child did at Christmastime. He just loved the tree," she chuckled, as she conjured up the image of Tony taking all the ornaments off one side of the tree and moving them, one at a time, to the other side. Then he'd stand on a chair to remove the highest ones he could reach and switch them to the lowest branches. He would hang any leftovers on the doorknobs and from all the hooks he could find in his bedroom.

"Of course, I let him do it because it kept him busy and happy. He was so careful. Never broke anything that I can recall. He was always such a confident little boy," she said, "until he started school."

"Were there any physical signs, any illnesses in those preschool years?" Diana asked, changing the direction of their exploration.

Mrs. Petri recalled the German measles at 15 months. He hadn't been very sick, and had had no apparent adverse side effects. At least, the doctor hadn't mentioned any.

"Tony was pretty healthy, except for all those respiratory problems and croup," she said. "He always had to stay home when it was windy, you know, because if he ran in the wind he got asthma. The wheezing made his heart pound and he'd get tired in about a minute. The medicine made him so sleepy, but it helped the wheezing," she sighed, shrugging. The dilemmas of allergies. Tony's asthma first surfaced at six months of age and he never outgrew it. His distressed breathing was

54

relieved only by a medication that altered his very functioning as a child.

More signs recalled. The night-time sweating. Such heavy sweating that his bedclothes would be soaked and he would drink huge quantities of water, "I mean, *gallons* of water," in the middle of the night. Troublesome behavior for a mother to understand. Someone said to have a Sweat Test done. Never knowing its purpose was for diagnosis of cystic fibrosis or emphysema, Mrs. Petri requested such a test and was relieved when it came back normal. The test may have been normal, but no one had explained the behavior.

Mrs. Petri turned her attention to Tony's infancy, when she'd been forced to return to work, leaving him in her sick husband's care. Had something happened then, the mother wondered now? Was it something so awful that Johnny Petri had been afraid to tell her about it? The child never appeared harmed or mistreated when she came home from work, but she still had been uneasy leaving the pair together. Something inside compelled her to return to child care duties as soon as possible. Once John Petri's health was even minimally improved, she urged him back to work, temporarily resuming her cherished role of mothering.

"I don't know if you'll understand this, Mrs. Cotter, but my husband always disapproved—he always thought I spoiled the boy. He never understood Tony—never made Tony feel good about himself, never praised him. You see, they have nothing in common—they have such totally different interests, those two. It may sound silly to you, but I think he felt jealous of Tony. He's not at all mechanical like Tony. He used to have a fine job, he was a fine musician. But he's been sick a lot, and now he's so ornery and grumpy. I tried to change him, but now I know I can't. He'll never change. He's just a stubborn 'wop'— that's what we used to say, me and my family. Just a stubborn 'wop.'"

She glanced around the room, then, gesturing, "We moved to this house when Tony was five and my mother came to live with us. In fact, she stayed with us about three years, until she died. Tony got along fine with her. He used to wake her up to play cards or read to him. But my mother always warned me, 'Ann, promise me, I beg you. Don't ever let John take care of Tony alone!' She always disapproved of the way Johnny cared for him."

Mrs. Petri explained that her husband was in and out of the hospital a lot in those years, but when he was home he was up and around, not bedridden. "But Tony avoided him as much as he could so he wouldn't get yelled at. My mother was always the buffer between them, and between Johnny and me, too, now that I think of it. She was a kind, sweet, gentle little lady. She always tried to keep the peace."

More questions answered for Diana. Ann Petri had found it necessary to serve as a constant backup provider for her ailing husband, forced frequently to return to work, leaving her child in the care of her sick, impatient husband and concerned but bedridden mother. She had no way of knowing what transpired in that house while she was away.

Still unresolved was the question of physical abuse that had been raised by the Cum. Diana decided to ask.

Mrs. Petri seemed surprised and thought for a minute before answering. She realized that Diana had misunderstood her. "My husband has no patience, no understanding of Tony, Mrs. Cotter, but he is capable of warmth and kindness. I always worried when I was away because Johnny was old and sick. I didn't know how careful he was about Tony's safety, and you have to remember that I'd never been a parent before, either. I know my husband loves Tony, but it's sort of like a friend or relative would—not like a father, if you know what I mean. There's so much difference in their ages. He's too permissive about rules and responsibilities with Tony, and then he gets so mad—yells and hollers and threatens to beat him. But he never has. And he never will. He would never intentionally have hurt that baby." She pursed her lips with the certainty of the fact.

Diana was relieved. The bark had indeed been much worse than the bite. How easily words can be misinterpreted. With that vital bit of information secured, the two women turned their attention toward other possible sources of Tony's Wrongness.

Diana was trying to isolate the beginnings—the first time the Petris had been told things were not as they should be for their son.

The first seeds of Wrongness had been sown with a phone

call requesting a school conference. Mrs. Petri had felt sure Tony was doing well in school. The caller was the young kindergarten teacher, a long-term substitute for the twenty-year veteran teacher who was on an extended leave because of illness. This had been the substitute's first full year of total responsibility for a classroom.

"Something is wrong with your boy, Mrs. Petri," the fledgling teacher said. A brief declarative sentence. A judgment rendered, undefined, over the telephone.

A conference was scheduled, and mother and teacher came together. "Something is wrong with your boy, Mrs. Petri."

Clarification now. "He writes backwards. You see?" With that, she presented the evidence: Tony's kindergarten papers, all in mirror writing. Legible, well-formed letters, but all written backwards.

The proof of the charge startled the mother. The meaning of the symptom, however, remained unexplained. The young teacher had no explanations. Only questions about Tony's development. When did he walk and talk? How did he get along at home? More questions, loosely recalled, and then the recommendation for a complete physical.

The conference ended on that note, leaving the mother to decide on the next move, and the teacher hoping the mother would know the next move.

Frightened and bewildered, Ann Petri promptly turned to the medical profession to find out about this mysterious Wrongness. After all, hadn't the teacher recommended a physical? Perhaps there was something in the brain, something that could be corrected. Or not corrected.

Mrs. Petri pushed this last thought aside and arranged for the physical. Her adored pediatrician, Dr. Fortunati, had died suddenly, and through Mrs. Petri's union insurance program the family had joined a health clinic two years before Tony entered kindergarten. The clinic pediatricians were often changing, but her current one, Dr. Lifton, had been there for awhile and had seen Tony several times for asthma.

Dr. Lifton responded to the troubled mother and did his job, checking out the basics that might have been a source of the trouble. First he checked the reflexes, which he pronounced "all perfect"—apparently no sign of any major neurological problem. Then the eyes: "Optic discs normal," wrote the doctor in his report. Hearing seemed fine, too, according to the gross kind of measurement done in pediatric offices. The doctor also recorded Mrs. Petri's comment that Tony's wheezing had declined since the family's move to their new home.

"There is absolutely nothing wrong with him—he's just fine!" Dr. Lifton had proclaimed cheerfully, adding, "but he's going to be a very big boy!" Feeling confident that he had allayed all fears, he'd added the bonus of optimistic prophecy.

And so a cycle began. A neophyte teacher had identified a differentness in her student and labelled it a Wrongness. The Wrongness had been understood by the mother to be physical—a problem in the medical domain. A doctor had been called to check out the ill-defined Wrongness and had declared everything "normal." He'd had no contact with the referring teacher to determine what she'd had in mind when she'd made her diagnosis. No doubt she couldn't have told him anyway. She just knew there was something different about Tony.

Mother had done all she knew how to do, but was left in a quandary: the doctor found nothing wrong, but Tony remained "unfixed." Nothing had been changed to help improve his classroom performance. What was the Wrongness? the mother wondered. Was it in Tony? Was it in her parenting?

Ann Petri then began digging into every possibility, appointing herself amateur diagnostician. She shared her search with Diana.

"When the teacher said, 'Something is wrong with your boy,' the first thing I thought about was that strange yelling he did when he was 18 months old. It did seem strange to me, even then. He'd go to sleep and in the middle of the night, he'd wake up and start this yelling, not crying, for no reason that I could see. He didn't seem unhappy and he didn't care if you came in the room or not. But nothing would make him stop it. That went on maybe six months. Not every night, but most. He outgrew it but I never knew the cause. At first it alarmed me terribly. I talked to Dr. Fortunati about it and he said, 'Oh, don't worry, there's nothing wrong.' He was such a beautiful doctor, and that made me feel better. I never thought about it again until that kindergarten teacher began to say all those things.

"Then, when he was about two," she continued, "he'd get out of his bed and come lie in the hall on the rug. I'd get up early and there he'd be, sound asleep on the rug, close to our room, as close as he could get. I thought that was kind of a strange little thing he did." She glanced at Diana to see if she agreed.

As Mrs. Petri spoke, Diana remembered her own mother-fears when her child would fall asleep after crying hard and then make unusual gasping noises in her sleep all night. Secretly, for years, Diana wondered why, subconsciously remembering those sounds with each new crisis of her child's growing.

Mrs. Petri went on, timidly confessing other possible peculiarities in her son. Suddenly, every commonplace quirk and childhood idiosyncrasy had become suspect as a sign of Wrongness. She talked of Tony's imaginary friends, a big sister and a baby, when he was just three or four years old. After all, there *were* no other children in the house or in the neighborhood then. Didn't lots of children have imaginary friends? Yes, of course.

"Then there was the cooperative nursery school over near our first house. Why did he go into such a frenzy when I left him there?" Mrs. Petri wondered aloud. "The other mothers said he wouldn't join in." She felt embarrassed by their disapproval and took him out after only four sessions. What if she had left him there longer? Was he different from the other children, or did he just miss his mother?

Mrs. Petri was not the only one who was searching for signs of evidence from Tony's past. During these months, Diana had expanded her own investigation. Through persistent efforts to gain the Board of Education's release, she had managed to exhume the duplicate elementary school records from the vaults downtown. No one could explain the absence of the originals.

Though incomplete, the duplicate Cum files yielded all kinds of new clues and inconsistencies about Tony Petri. For starters, he had scored 116, borderline *superior* range, on the Detroit beginning group intelligence test. Administered in kindergarten, the test involved no reading and was supposed to be a reliable predictor of school success. Diana had been told by a school principal that 90% of kids who do well on this test usually turn out to be good readers. Tony's score indicated he'd be one of the stars.

Diana was surprised to find no mention, not one word, about the mirror-writing in the kindergarten teacher's Cum comments. The symptom that had triggered the mother's intense search for signs of defectiveness was not reported in the summation of "data" forwarded to the upcoming teacher. Tony was described only as a lad who "participates in all activities, favors block-building and outdoor physical activities." With those ten words, the kindergarten teacher promoted Tony Petri to first grade.

Ann Petri told how she took it upon herself to arrange a conference early in the semester with the first grade teacher to personally inform the teacher about the Wrongness. But the first grade teacher wasn't concerned with Tony's mirror-writing. Her concerns were more global.

"Tony is just not trying, Mrs. Petri. He just doesn't seem to care."

A second teacher, in a second conference, was identifying a new kind of Wrongness. Tony, not quite six, with borderline superior intelligence, now didn't seem to care.

Mrs. Petri deferred once again to the "expert." She accepted the accusation as fact. She tried to explain to Diana, in retrospect, why she believed Tony wasn't trying. "I imagine he felt discourged right from the start. When you don't do what you're supposed to do, I'm sure you get punished for it. I asked the teacher why *she* thought Tony wasn't trying, but she just asked me the same thing. As if I had an answer! I tried to tell her how he was at home, but I doubt that she believed me."

Mrs. Petri felt increasingly uncomfortable with this second teacher's suggestions that something was wrong with Tony. She decided that perhaps the problem was with his eyes; she had been noticing that he rubbed them and blinked a lot.

She took Tony to an ophthalmologist for a complete examination. Although she could never find any official records of the exam, Mrs. Petri claimed a vivid memory for the findings of that professional.

"He said there were some irregularities there, but he didn't see how they would affect Tony's learning. The doctor said the problem could have been corrected with minor surgery when Tony was little, but now it was too late. I never knew exactly what the problem was called, but the doctor just fluffed it off. He was a *specialist*," she asserted proudly. "I didn't understand what he meant by 'too late,' but he didn't give me anything to do so I just tried to forget about it."

Tried, but never forgot.

For understandable reasons, Mrs. Petri tried to forget the problem during that particular period. Her husband's health had so deteriorated that he was forced to retire, and Mrs. Petri's employment became more essential to family survival than ever. She had no further conferences with the first grade teacher, who, like the kindergarten teacher before her, condensed the remainder of Tony's semester performance on those 3-millimeter-wide lines provided on the Cum for that purpose.

She wrote: "Tony is especially interested in social studies, seems slow to grasp abstractions in arithmetic, has difficulty learning new words. Is uncoordinated. Lacks initiative." She closed on an unexpected, positive note: "Tony is friendly and cooperative."

Friendly, cooperative schoolboy Tony was lacking initiative and not trying. Homeboy Tony, in contrast, was continually initiating new projects, driving his already impatient father crazy with requests for aquariums, shelves, easels, and materials for motorized inventions. Under pressure from Mother, Father would capitulate. If the project took too long, however, or was too complicated, Tony often moved on to something new, leaving his father abandoned and angry, with investments he could ill afford and half-completed creations he never wanted. Tony may have lacked persistence, but certainly not initiative.

Diana was getting a better feel for Tony's contribution to his father's grumpiness.

The search for causes of Tony's vaguely defined Wrongness seemed to be creating more questions than answers for Diana.

Had Tony been damaged in any significant way by the delivery process, or was Ann Petri's description of "undue force" partly the result of her dislike of a sacreligious doctor?

Had Tony's German measles left him with undetected visual defects, a not uncommon side-effect of that common disease?

Was the mirror-writing in kindergarten symptomatic of a neurologically-based problem or of delayed development?

The Petris were older than the average child-bearing couple when they conceived Tony. Ann Petri was in the age group termed "high risk" for a first pregnancy. Could Tony's problems have had a congenital basis?

The strange yelling, the profuse night sweating, the respiratory infections and allergies compounded by medicines that caused drowsiness—were these critical signs, worthy of suspicion as causes of Wrongness?

Was Tony "uncoordinated"? This same child who had moved every ornament around and around a Christmas tree without breaking a single one—could he be uncoordinated?

The Petri family had to deal with some harsh realities related to health and economic survival. Ann Petri, like thousands of other mothers of young children, was forced to work because of those realities. What part of Tony's problem was caused by the absence of his mother? Did her guilt at leaving make her overindulgent? What kind of caretaking did Tony receive while his mother was at work? Did he suffer neglect or, on the contrary, did he enjoy too much attention?

Can teachers possibly be expected to have the time and the training to find out *why* a child, at age 6, is "not caring" or "not trying"?

Most important, how did those oracular words, "Something is wrong with your child," words that never left Ann Petri's subconscious, influence this family's ensuing behavior?

A substitute kindergarten teacher—a newcomer to this business of understanding children's development and learning patterns—had begun, innocently, unwittingly, a process of doubt that would alter a lifetime.

CHAPTER 7

John Petri: "I've been through
troubles like that myself."

Diana could hear the sounds of a recorded piano concerto as she came up the walk toward the modest, frame-and-stucco house. The tiny front lawn was dust-brown from the dry spell. She climbed the shallow steps of the porch with one stride, pushed the doorbell, and waited, resisting the urge to pick at the pale green paint curling off the wooden door frame.

This would be her first solo interview with the now 71-year-old John Petri, this man whose child-care behaviors had been suspect and whose patience and temper had been under questionable control. Diana had seen Mr. Petri only twice, both times in the company of his wife. Had he stifled himself in front of his mate, or had he said all he had to say? Diana's investigation demanded a better understanding of this man Tony called "Grumps," an understanding of his view of the family circumstances.

She could feel the vibration of slow, heavy steps responding to the doorbell. Mumbling a staccato "come-in-come-in-come-in" as he opened the door, John Petri ushered her into the house and went to turn down the music. He had expected her visit. This time, she had called first.

The dimly-lit room with the drawn curtains was familiar to her now. Settling into the couch in response to Mr. Petri's sit-down gesture, Diana remarked, "Mrs. Petri told me you had a career as a musician at one time, Mr. Petri. I guess you still love to listen to music."

"Oh, yes," he replied. "But I don't dare mention it when they're around. They have no patience for it." He painfully lowered his body into the worn brocade wingback chair to her right, assuming that she knew who "they" were. She did.

"Are you a music lover?" he inquired, hoping.

"I enjoy music, but I don't know much about it. I wish I knew more," Diana said sincerely, wondering if her interest would encourage him to talk. The flow of words that followed told Diana that John Petri, unlike his son, would need no prodding.

"Well, I tried to do a little teaching to Tony, but he don't pay me no mind," the father said; his head shook in resignation, but only for a moment. He had an audience now. "Back in the twenties, Miz Cotter, we had an Italian band. Why, everyone in the vicinity was in that band, don't ya know! Of course, I played the piano...every chance I got, I would play. Well, one fella heard me one day, he says, 'Where did you learn that?' he says. It was just somethin' I was feeling." A humble smile punctuated the disclosure.

This man, who had been so silent during previous meetings, had been waiting months for *his* turn to talk. His history poured out of him like oil from a newly-drilled gusher as he verbally transported both of them to another time and place. Diana learned of the attic studio where he took his first piano lessons from a real professional. Then came the first concert, at age 21, followed by vaudeville tours from Illinois to California to Utah and back through the midwest to the east. The narration flowed freely, only occasionally marred by the inconsistencies of a 71-year-old memory. When he recalled a certain performance that demanded a more graphic depiction, he brought out several old scrapbooks filled with playbills, critical reviews, and photographs of the darkly handsome Johnny Petri.

Diana was surprised, impressed. Tony's father, too, had been a saver of evidence—evidence of his budding notoriety. Looking at him now, his pains softened by the delight of sharing those fulfilling years, Diana could picture him as he must have been in his prime.

"It must have been a wonderful time for you," she said.

"It was. A very wonderful, happy time...." He rested a moment, the rasp of his asthmatic breathing filling the silence. "Then the Depression came."

He shook his head once more, gazing at the portrait of Jesus that stared back at him from the wall. "Things were bad...bad...'33, '34, '35...those were bad years. Theatres weren't using acts anymore. Television wasn't on...radio wasn't even on...uh...no," he said, adjusting his memory, "I guess maybe radio was, but...uh...I don't recall to what extent..."

Then, full recall came. "Oh, yes!" His face brightened, excited now. "There *was* radio, because I recorded at a radio studio and I remember the *Radio News* came out and said, 'Nothing worthwhile listening to this week except for a young pianist' and then they mentioned my name! Why...hold on a minute, I can even show you."

With that, he awkwardly thumbed through one scrapbook with a patience that only old age seems to bring. It was then that Diana noticed his crippled fingers. He found the withered newspaper clipping with precisely the words he had quoted. His satisfaction was clear.

"This is really something, Mr. Petri. Did you ever play with a symphony orchestra?" Diana asked, curious about the extent of his success.

"Ah. That's where the problem comes in. I came back to the midwest to perform on the circuit again, and had this first attack of arthritis in my hands. They got stiff and swollen," he said, displaying the painful rigid knobs as if she hadn't noticed, "and I just couldn't play to my standards. Then, to top it off, I got this tooth infection that affected my sinuses and my whole face swelled up. They had to go through my nose with a reamer. Good Lord, what a mess! From then on, one day I'd be good and the next day I couldn't do anything. You know, nowadays when you have an infection they have penicillin and things, but in those days they had nothing...nothing...from then on, I had nothing but troubles, troubles, troubles. Kept goin' from bad to worse." He rested again, long this time, rocking his head back and forth in a soothing rhythm.

"It sounds like fate wasn't on your side." Diana broke the silence inanely, not wanting to disturb the fading train of thought.

"I don't know if it was fate or if it was my fault, but I just decided I had to give it up. Give up the music..." A pause again, for the breathing. Or was it a pause for the interment of a dream?

When Mr. Petri resumed talking, it was faster, almost gruff. "So I went to this restaurant—it was Italian-owned—and they gave me a job. I played a little at the piano bar, but I had lost

65

my touch and I didn't want to do it unless it was right. You know what I mean? If I couldn't do it right, I'd rather not do it at all. Stupid, isn't it?"

"You just have high standards. That's not stupid," Diana consoled, realizing then that Tony had inherited his strong sense of pride from both parents.

He went on. "Those who knew me in those days...they knew, but...here in this town, I don't have any acquaintances in the line of music...Well, after I gave up that piano bar, I worked as a *maitre d'* at the restaurant, and that's where I met Annie— Mrs. Petri. She worked for me in the restaurant and one thing led to another. She was a good Catholic girl. You see, I was married before and my wife had recently died of cancer."

Diana nodded. "How long were you married before Tony was born, Mr. Petri?"

"Oh, a couple of years."

"Were you surprised when Mrs. Petri became pregnant?"

Laughing, "I wasn't, but *she* was! I never gave a thought, at our ages and all, about having a child. But I know Annie was real pleased. She gave him a lot of time." Then, with a mutter of regret, he added, "That she did."

"I know Mrs. Petri has spent a lot of time with Tony," Diana said, acknowledging the difficulty of sharing a mate with a demanding new being, "but how does he relate to you? Does he come to you and ask for help?"

"Good heavens, no! To him, why, I don't think he thinks I'm a father. He's a big, overgrown kid. I think he thinks I'm a kid like he is. Why, he'll slap me around and grab me on the back— sort of wrassles me around, y'know. That kind of stuff. Very seldom does he say 'dad' or anything like that. Unless he needs something! Now *that's* a different story. Oh, yes." A note of annoyance here. Mr. Petri had alluded, at several earlier meetings, to all the money Tony cost him.

"How did you feel about all those troubles Tony began having at school?" Diana asked, curious to hear what he would say in private.

Mr. Petri surprised her with his direct reply. "To tell the truth, I didn't pay any attention to Tony's troubles in school. Just went along with Ann all the time. It's hard for me to say if he really had a problem, because the help he was getting

66

didn't seem to do a doggoned thing. He seemed bright enough, but I saw some kind of bottleneck. I've been through troubles like that myself. Never did like to read. But them Catholic schools were stricter than all get-out in my day. My own father came to the last classroom I was ever in and, for what reason I will never know, he hauled off and smacked me. Knocked me down on the floor! This was back in Missouri, in a Catholic school. I don't remember if I had trouble reading, but I was never told why I was slapped in the face. I made up my mind then and there that I was never going back to school, no sir. We moved to a new state anyway, and in those days nobody cared whether you went to school or not.

"You see, Miz Cotter, my mother died when I was three. My brother and I, we were raised in a German orphanage. We were in short times those days and my dad couldn't raise me. He got the travelling bug and went to Peoria and horsed around and got in with some woman. Then he sent for us—my brother and myself. Well, his new wife, she beat the living hell out of us every time she could. With a black rawhide. She was a terrible woman. Finally, we said, 'Dad, we can't stay here anymore. We'd rather be in a Home.' I was six or seven then. We went to another orphanage for two more years and they pulled a lot of funny stunts there, so Dad shipped us back to Missouri to our aunts and uncles and grandparents. Then Dad got married to a nicer lady, so we moved back with them...but I never went back to school after the fifth grade."

So ended the simple understated narration of a childhood without tenderness. Diana could only imagine what "funny stunts" he'd endured.

"Where is your brother now, Mr. Petri?" she asked.

"My brother? Oh, he's dead. Joined the army and was killed at 17. My uncle was the instigator who got him into that! Huh. You know, as I think of it now, Tony is a replica of my brother. They could have been brothers. Always in a hurry, not interested in anything except mechanical things. He had his own clique of friends, apart from me. It's hard to remember him. Such a long time ago."

He rested then, closing his eyes and mind to that past time. When he reopened them, he said, "Now I'm here and I'm the maid. Huh. I do the cooking and washing dishes and whatnot.

67

Just cleaning up. I have so much trouble with breathing. I had asthma and diabetes, but they disappeared pretty much. I still have the arthritis, but there's not much that helps."

He didn't even mention the bleeding ulcer that put him out of work during Tony's first year of life. It didn't matter. Pain and problems, generally, were the message.

"Sometimes I help Annie at her job. She's the ambitious one these days. Always go-go-go, always looking for some top position, something new to do." He worked at sounding grumbly, trying to mask his pride at her drive. "She took that job in food services so she could have better hours—you know, to be home when the boy got home from school and all. Did she tell you she was thinking of going for supervisor? She even took some courses for it. I can't remember what happened, but she's an ambitious one, that's for sure."

Diana knew what had happened. It was one of the few personal events in her life that Ann had been willing to discuss. The man who taught the course had talked down to the students, talked down to them so continually, so demeaningly that Mrs. Petri had dropped out of the course. "Why, if I starved, I couldn't work under that man!" she swore to Diana. Just dropped out, she'd said, trying to sound matter-of-fact. What she hadn't said was that she had taken a qualifying exam, passed it, and then waited six months just for an opening to the *waiting list* for the course.

How much like the branch was the tree. For mother as for father and son, the negative judgments of others were so undigestible that all three preferred to redirect their very goals in life rather than surrender their pride. Diana wondered if Ann Petri had ever told her husband the whole story.

"Mr. Petri?" Diana asked softly, noticing that the septuagenarian had closed his eyes and not wanting to disturb him if he had fallen into a sleep. He opened his eyes briefly and went on as if no time had elapsed.

"Yes? Oh, yes...well, sometimes I help Annie at her job, but my car's not going now so I'm stuck here at home being the maid," he repeated. "Probably if I get it fixed the boy'll take it anyway. I don't even walk in that garage anymore! He's out there welding all the time. That garage hasn't had a car in it for years. Now he wants a truck, so he can haul his motorsickles where he wants to go —so he can kill himself. I guess that's what he's aiming at...he and his friend, they go racing up in the hills. Last race they had, one boy got hacked up pretty bad. There was so many places they were putting him together, and the guy screaming bloody murder, and I thought, 'Well, maybe that'll make him give it up'...but it didn't....Well, that's the way it goes..." Resignation, resentment, emasculation all came through his tone. And exhaustion.

The eyes closed and silence came again.

Diana watched the reposed face and pondered the disclosure to which she'd just been privy. Johnny Petri, silent, lonely, aging man, dreamer of better days, dreamer of what might have been—suddenly no longer reticent. He had exposed himself as an *interesting* man, an owner of fascinating experiences from another era. The mere presence of a willing listener jolted a wealth of information from a fading memory. He'd grown up during the times when children were to be seen and not heard, when education took a back seat to survival, when beatings came first and explanations later, or not at all.

No one in John Petri's childhood had worried about the effects upon a growing child of constant shifting from one orphanage or relative to another. No wonder John hadn't been too concerned about his son's "troubles in school." When compared to those of his own abused childhood, Tony's problems paled. Nevertheless, Diana sensed the father's perverse admiration for the way his son manipulated him. His Tony was no pushover.

Diana waited a few minutes more but she could see that John Petri had done all the talking he had in him that day. She left him undisturbed.

Three days later, Diana mentioned to Tony that she had met with his father. Until that time, Tony spoke of his father sparingly and always as "Grumps" or "The Old Man." Occasionally, though, Tony hinted he had tried but failed to open a few doors toward relating.

When Diana mentioned that she thought Tony's father, like Tony, had a rich fantasy life, Tony agreed. "Oh, yeah, he's tripped out all the time. He's freaked out on KRFT, the classical music station. You can't even break through to him. I used to try to get him to tell me about it. I told him I didn't understand any part of that classical stuff, but I didn't put it down like he puts down *my* music—all the time! And you know what he says? He says to me, 'You never try.' I tell him I used to ask about it and he'd say, 'You'll never understand it!' You know, I've listened to millions of his concerts—why, I've even recorded herds of 'em for him off the radio, like he asked me to. But he's never once listened to any of mine." A two-generation gap in music, too.

"When you were little, when your mom went back to work, did your dad ever take care of you?"

"Ha! My dad *never* took care of me, except to yell at me. He was always home and always yelling at me and I never knew why."

I never knew why. The words had a familiar ring. They were the very words John had used about his own father's attack on him in school that day.

Tony went on with a self-assuredness he reserved for the right times.

"How could he help me? He couldn't help me with my reading!" Tony exclaimed. "He can't read himself! They didn't have schools in his day. Every time I try to read with him he stops to ask me if I know what every word means. Or he'll go off and talk about something from his music days. It's impossible! No, he didn't take care of me. Nobody took care of me. *I* took care of me. If you don't know any different, you just accept that that's the way it is."

That was the way it was. She believed him.

"Did your dad ever tell you about his childhood?" Diana was curious.

"No, he won't tell me anything. I know he had a brother, but I don't even know his name. I think it's Louis, but I don't even know for sure. My father's own brother! Can you believe it?"

A father and son, who had lived together for almost sixteen years—how was it possible they could know so little about each other? How was it possible this father had hardly mentioned the name of a deceased brother who was so like Tony, or never shared the suffering he'd endured in his own childhood?

The seclusive John Petri had allowed a total stranger, but not his own son, to see his tender side, feel his pains, and share his longings for lost dreams. He also permitted the stranger access to a secret: he loved this boy, believed in this boy, and respected his strengths.

And the boy didn't know it.

The room at the junior high where Tony and Diana usually met was not available one day, so the Vice-Principal offered them the use of the conference room behind his office.

Tony, delighted with his new self-importance, spread out his books and papers on the broad conference table, put his feet up on the edge of it, and tilted his chair back, enjoying the moments of imaginary power. He and Diana chatted idly as she prepared his lesson.

Then, without warning, the sneezing began. First it was just one loud blast, and they sniggered at the volume of it. Two more followed, without recovery time between them. Diana blurted out some automatic gesundheits, still preoccupied with her lesson plans, paying no attention to Tony. But Tony was no longer sniggering. The sneezes were coming in continuous spasms, too fast for Diana's blessings to separate them. When she glanced over at him, she saw the formerly calm teenager now in distress. He had lost control of his body. His eyes, newly reddened, were running with fluid, his face and bearing totally altered in just moments. She recognized the symptoms—allergic ones, at their most extreme—but the cause was a mystery.

The onset was so sudden—it must have been something in the room. As Tony fumbled through water-blurred eyes for his handkerchief, trying unsuccessfully to control his body-bursts, Diana spotted a large cardboard box on a chair directly behind him. The box had been overstuffed and left unsealed so that through the opening she could see its contents—coils of hemp rope and assorted balls of twine. On a hunch that these might be the culprits, she grabbed up the carton and placed it outside the door.

It was too late for that. Tony had become nonfunctional. The sneezing, the running of his eyes were out of his control. They left the room immediately, with Diana guiding the now-helpless youth outdoors into the courtyard. Tony tried to catch his breath, to hold his breath, to find some breath—anything that would relieve his symptoms.

In the fresh air, away from the problem environment, the spasms gradually subsided. The recovery took about twenty minutes, but the entire episode had left its victim wasted. His handkerchief sat on the school step, saturated and worthless, next to a mound of Kleenex and paper towels that had ultimately been enlisted for the battle. Tony, as limp now as his

71

tissue supply, was silent at last. The fatigue was total. He and Diana rested together for a few minutes, both breathing deeply to restore their equilibrium. Then Diana left him momentarily to collect her materials from the conference room.

Curiosity drew her to the open box that sat innocently near the doorway. She put her nose next to the opening and inhaled deeply, feeling, at that close range, the tiny bits of hemp dust irritating her nostrils, forcing her own protective sneeze. But only one. She was not allergic to hemp.

Unsure about Tony's need for recovery time, she brought out the drivers' manual and notebook, feeling obligated to attempt a lesson if he was able.

Neither of them knew if he was able. He was willing to try. He tried to concentrate on the readings but couldn't remember what had been read. He tried writing but reverted, interestingly, to much earlier reversal patterns and letter confusions— ones he had begun to master. He simply could not focus his attention on the tasks. The fatigue was his master.

Teacher and student mutually agreed to terminate the session.

Diana had been the learner that day—had observed, for the first time, the drama of a severe allergic reaction. For years she had read, quite skeptically, about its effects on a child's ability to pay attention, to think, and to learn. Now she understood. But the understanding led to new questions. What had been the role of chronic allergy in Tony's failure to acquire skills?

Until that day, Tony and Diana had been working quite productively for three months. They had been reading the drivers' manual and the off-highway-vehicle code for motorcycles, using a method of guided reading called Neurological Impress Method, NIM for short. Diana varied it to meet Tony's particular needs, wondering if he would be one of those who could stay with it for three months and raise his reading level three years, as the researchers claimed.

Diana's adaptation of the NIM consisted of her first reading aloud from the driver's manual, with Tony following the words as she pointed to them with a marker. He would hear in advance what the words said and how they flowed together into sentences and paragraphs. He would hear rhythm/punctuation/decoding/meaning—all in one process. Then he would read back exactly what had been modelled for him, and any words that still gave him trouble would be told to him instantly. In this way, the two read as many pages as they could cover in a fifteen- or twenty-minute period, the time being determined by Tony's patience level each day. The lengths of the passages varied according to the difficulty of the text. Diana knew the passages had to be short enough that Tony could have success, but long enough that he would be forced to pay attention to the words and not just use his fine ears to memorize the material. It was those fine ears, however, that made him such a superb candidate for the method.

The NIM wasn't for everybody, but when it worked, it worked miracles. The technique does more than model the correct reading and phrasing of thousands of words. It removes anxiety. And shame. Diana had seen it make kids like Tony *want* to read, often for the first time, because it permits them to read anything—anything they choose. No more fear of the unknown words, each one bringing memories of teachers and tutors parroting, "Sound it out," memories of trying and failing, over and over. Sound-it-out means slowing down, losing meaning. After a while, the trying stops—the fear of failure is too great.

The NIM ended that torturous pattern for Tony.

It worked so successfully with him that he became suspicious, refusing to believe that he was really reading. He thought it was a trick and that he was just memorizing the words. How could he be reading from the drivers' manual when he still couldn't fluently read a third-grade text?

The only way Diana could prove to him that he was actually learning to read was to copy a whole list of words from the pages they'd read together, present them in isolation, and show him he could still read them out of context. He could. He could even read them a week later. He astonished himself. He became a believer.

The NIM presented one problem: daily practice was essential. Diana consulted with Tony about his choice of another adult he might use as a guide on the days the two of them didn't meet.

She knew she was asking for a commitment. A commitment to homework—something Tony had artfully skirted since the kitchen-table spelling years.

He pondered her request in silence. Bright Tony knew that the rate of his progress was all up to him. Diana could help him with the whats and hows, but the doing had to come from him. He had to be a willing partner, not just in the testing but in the learning process, too—unless, of course, he had some reason to remain illiterate.

Diana used the word "illiterate" frequently and deliberately at that crossroad in Tony's therapy. He needed to know that he was, for whatever reason, illiterate, but that he no longer had to be, that he had a choice in his destiny. She was gambling that his pride would work for him.

No glowing promises burst forth from the suspicious youth. A good sign. He wasn't going to lie to her. He sheepishly agreed to try the reading with his mother, since "Grumps" would never qualify, and there was no one else he felt comfortable enough to ask. They both knew that working with mother was loaded with risk—he was conditioned for failure by years of struggle at that kitchen table. By talking openly with Tony about the risk, Diana hoped that mother and son might have a better chance for success this time.

No matter how low-key the approach, Tony was feeling pressure. Diana knew it when he immediately shifted his talk to the world of "grease." During all of their hours together, she had allowed him some time to be *her* professor, her tutor on the topic in which he was so expert. Tony relished the reversal of roles and lectured with a flair about motocross, dirt tracks, brands and models of motorcycles. Diana became familiar with "hogs," "choppers," and the dynamic principles of two-cycle engines. Once, he had even brought an 8x10 glossy of a cycle he coveted, confiding that it was being held at the cycle shop for the day when he had "the bread for it."

His conversations were rich with the vocabulary of his world, and Diana began to record in writing the lectures he was dictating. In this way, she led Tony into a form of guided writing that could also be used as a follow-up of his NIM reading. After they read together the rules from the off-highway vehicle code, they would discuss them. Then Tony would paraphrase the rules as he understood them, watching as Diana recorded his words, pronouncing them for him syllable by syllable as she wrote each one. She would do the same for his motorcycle dictations. By watching and hearing her say the syllables, he was learning to connect the spoken with the written symbols—

learning the code of literacy. Afterward, he'd read back his own transcribed dictations.

Thus—together—they developed an entire curriculum of NIM readings, dictations, and copying tasks so that Tony had specific follow-up work to do while he was in his remedial reading class, or even in other classes where he had become alienated from the assignments. For the first time, Hope Saltzman reported that Tony worked for entire hours in her class, copying over his dictated notes about the rules of the road, and creating a study guide for the drivers' test he would soon be attempting. Incidental to the copying tasks were his growing proficiency and speed at handwriting and even at his old enemy, spelling.

Slowly, very slowly, Diana was exorcizing "the demons"— those fears and doubts about literacy to which Tony had clung for nine years. She tried to make the most of this honeymoon period; the amount of time this boy would give, could give, was always in question. The more she learned of Tony's history, the more she knew the honeymoon couldn't last.

CHAPTER 8

*"All I did was
just suck it in..."*

D iana sat amid the piles of notes, time lines, and tapes,
trying to give a chronology to all the facts she'd been
assembling. She wanted to synthesize Tony's reminis-
cences with the reports and memories of others to recreate the
childhood of this boy whose school failure had become her obsession.

The semester system had confused her until she realized that
Tony had spent only one semester in kindergarten and had
entered the first grade term, paradoxically labeled B1, in January. The "B" semesters came before the "A's."

She tried to envision Tony at six-and-a-half years, frightened,
confused, entering a new school: St. Jude's, the parochial school
affiliated with the Petri's church. The kindergarten teacher's
Wrongness and the first grade teacher's Not Trying had forced
the mother's decision. He'd be better off at St. Jude's, Ann Petri
had told herself. Smaller classes, and those nice Sisters who
ran the school. Why, they'd even given Tony some sort of a
reading readiness test and he got an 86%. She'd felt so proud
when they said, "He seems to have fine potential, Mrs. Petri."
Another test had verified his fine potential. She'd known it all
the time. She hadn't objected when St. Jude's insisted Tony
repeat the B1 semester he'd just completed. After all, it was a
new school and it couldn't hurt him to have a fresh start. Ah,
the promise of a fresh start.

So the larger-than-average, brighter-than-average Tony
Petri entered the new school, watching, observing everything.
An outsider, looking in. He watched his peers effortlessly per-
form their reading, their cutting and pasting, their sports. For
Tony there was no such ease of performance. He would peek
at the papers of others, never sure if he was doing things right,

never sure which way the letters and numbers turned or which side of the paper was the correct side to begin writing on. All those squiggly lines of print confused him. He could copy them pretty well, but he couldn't remember what they should say. And the teachers were always changing what he was supposed to be doing. He'd just get the hang of that printing stuff and the teacher would tell him to stop, to put-away-the-red-book-and-take-out-the-green-book. Then he'd look over at Charles, next to him, and Charles would give him a shove and cover up his paper. Do it yourself, Tony.

By November he couldn't keep up. They were just going too fast. The kids would whisper. He was sure they were whispering about him. New school. New kids. New teachers. And now all the new ones knew that something was wrong with him.

He became increasingly quiet. "Just kind of there," one of the Sisters said about him. Just kind of there. The teachers never described him as an acting-out boy, but as a boy who tried to become invisible, to go unnoticed.

On the playground, Tony avoided the teams and group games. He ran slowly, tripped a lot, and dropped the ball when they threw it to him. He hated their laughter when he missed, and early on withdrew from athletics completely rather than risk the ridicule. Secretly, he would practice throwing and catching at home in the backyard with his dad on those few occasions when Grumps felt well enough. Even at home, though, he could never seem to be where the ball was. He became so self-critical, he gave up practicing altogether.

Tony found other activities on the playground. Using a special lure, he became the leader of his own little gang of three or four. He'd bring his own toys from home so that he could be in control, picking those few friends he'd allow to share his precious possessions. Such quiet manipulations gave him what he wanted—a speck of social control—without offending, without causing trouble. "Just quietly doing his own thing," was the way the young Sister remembered it.

Quite soon after they became aware of Tony's academic struggles in their first grade, the Sisters informed the Petris of their belief that Tony suffered from "perceptual and learning problems." They recommended that Tony be enrolled in remedial reading with some specialists who came to the school and worked with small groups of children.

After only three months in the new school, the Wrongness had surfaced again. Mrs. Petri felt upset, unsure. She returned to the health clinic, imploring Dr. Lifton, the pediatrician, to search another time. She hungered for some answers. This time, she delivered to the doctor the teacher's term, "perceptual problem," which she understood to mean "something having to do with the eyes."

Respecting Mrs. Petri's request, Dr. Lifton checked Tony's eyes once more, again for distance vision only, and again found them perfectly normal. No one had called from the school to discuss what they meant by "perceptual problem." The doctor's report made no mention at all of such a problem.

Whatever his reason, Dr. Lifton made no referral to any other professional regarding this possible disability.

Instead, he focused his attention on another problem: Tony's rapidly increasing weight. Tony Petri, aged six, now stood breast-high to his mother and weighed 76 pounds. The doctor's prediction about his becoming a "very big boy" was too rapidly becoming a reality. Dr. Lifton placed the boy on nonfat milk for his mild obesity.

Tony felt fat, awkward. Nothing seemed to be right with him. But he craved food. He had so few other satisfactions then. Maybe if he tried not to call attention to himself no one would notice the fat, the clumsiness, the "dumb" numbers and letters that went the wrong way, the trouble reading the words that his friends seemed to remember so well.

After school was different. He would spend hours in his backyard, on the homemade "jungle gym" he had customized with boards and wood strips and blankets, adapted in various ways to his fantasy of the day. Sometimes he was on a boat, the captain, and when the boat was sinking he would dive off and save the people who were drowning. Once he "saved" a nun, one of the Sisters from the school, in his heroic illusion. Some days the creative construction became his motorcycle, and he was The Cop—important, powerful, admirable. He was Somebody there on that jungle gym in the backyard. But first-grade Tony was always alone when he was Somebody.

His mother, having nowhere else to turn, followed the school's advice and enrolled Tony in the special tutorial services. Unarmed with any new diagnostic insights, the Petris felt compelled to carry on: Tony went to school, Tony failed to learn,

Tony went to tutoring, and the Petris somehow managed to pay. But payment brought no guarantees.

The Petris paid a monthly fee to the tutorial service, and an additional fee to the school, besides tuition, because of the extra help. Money was scarce, the times hard, but the mother wanted her son to have the extra help right from the start. Yet after the first year all Ann Petri could recall the tutor ever saying to her was, "He simply won't try." Ann didn't know what to believe.

Diana located the former director of the tutorial center, who used a familiar adjective to describe Tony. "Nice. Tony was always nice to work with." No recall from this man, either, of Tony being a terror during those four-days-a-week, half-hour sessions in which he'd been placed with two other children who were at about the same reading level.

"I don't recall a severe perceptual problem," the director said. "I felt—in fact, we all felt, the nurse and the psychologist and my staff, too—that it was all emotional for that boy. Tony was oversized, you know, and not particularly capable intellectually. He had trouble reading, of course, but there were lots of emotional problems. The parents were getting along badly. I never met the father, actually," he added hastily, "but the mother certainly was concerned and anxious. It was a helpless situation. The parents couldn't get anything going for Tony consistently."

The mother was concerned and anxious. Understandably so, Diana thought. No one had yet explained her son's Wrongness.

This special tutorial service had been newly formed. In fact, the whole profession of special education for children with learning disabilities was in its infancy. The inexperienced staff was just learning the process of evaluation and remediation. The role of emotions in learning problems was as yet ill-defined and hotly debated among the differing schools of thought. Even the director, so sure Tony's problems were all emotional, later confided to Diana, "We were not very knowledgeable about the psychological aspects of learning disabilities at that time in our careers."

Diagnosing learning behaviors that defied change as "emotional problems" was tempting. Too often, the words became strangely comforting to professionals who felt helpless when they had no answers, especially when answers were so desperately sought by concerned parents.

Diana had blanched at the director's characterization of Tony as "not particularly capable intellectually." The statement made her realize, however, that Tony had been as successful at hiding his Self during those half-hour group tutoring sessions as he was during regular classes. He hid all of his Self, including his capabilities. He was young, defensive. Like a wounded animal, self-protecting.

Those tutoring sessions had required that he be removed from his class four times a week, taken out of the large group where he'd just about succeeded in becoming invisible. He was placed with a newly-trained specialist in a group of three youngsters where there was no place to hide.

He had to read then. Out loud. For everyone to hear. They'd hear that he knew only about thirteen words of the thirty on the page he was expected to read. "An emotional block toward reading," the special tutor, Miss Eisen, had called it. But could the six-year-old have an emotional block toward something he was learning for the first time? Maybe his "block" was toward the particular method being used. Or the making public of a problem that needed to be worked out in private.

One day, in desperation, Tony tried a new plan. When it was his turn to read, he made up his own story from the pictures. He guessed at the words he didn't know, saying what he thought they should say to make them fit the story. That was what he had always done at home with his mom and grandma when they'd read all those books together, with Tony "reading" the pictures.

Miss Eisen wasn't amused. Out of desperation, she became determined to force his attention on the words, to abort his tendencies to guess. She thought of a plan to type up the stories separately, without pictures, so he would have to concentrate on the words themselves. Then they would have word drill together, over and over, constant repetition.

By the end of the school year, the force, drill, and constant repetition paid off. Tony had mastered twenty-eight words. The tedious, painful, joyless struggle had gained him twenty-eight words. What Miss Eisen didn't know was that the cost of those words had been too high. The printed word had become his enemy. He'd done what he was told; he'd stifled his natural tendency to guess—so essential for early readers—because guessing meant he might make an error, and errors were Wrongs. The bright, strong-willed only child couldn't—wouldn't—learn through phonics and drill. Instead, he learned to avoid risk.

Years later, an interview with Miss Eisen confirmed Diana's hypothesis: the tutor had never had the chance to discover Tony's uniqueness, had never found any means of motivating the boy. If only she had been allowed to see him alone right from the start, for just enough sessions to break through his public mask, how different the year might have been. But individual tutoring for Tony had not been a financial option. After all those years, the specialist still recalled her frustration.

Tony was promoted to the second half of first grade and continued in the tutorial service without significant progress. In March of that year, just before his seventh birthday, two incidents upset the equilibrium in the Petri household.

Tony learned about death. His grandmother died, at age 77, in her sleep. Except for some mild protest when his parents tried to give away her rocking chair, Tony showed no outward emotion. Neither parents nor child felt comfortable discussing death. It was considered a reality. A life had ended.

Shortly after the death, Mrs. Petri lost her job. Now both parents were unemployed. With Mrs. Petri at home for the next six months and Mr. Petri still unable to return to work, there was severe strain in the Petri home—uncertainty as to who or what would become the source of financial support for the family. Tension was high and grandma, the buffer for family tension, was gone.

His teachers, unaware of the changes in the Petri home, began to notice new behaviors in Tony. He became more and more lethargic, and what little conversation he offered concerned food. He often boasted about the malts and candy his father bought when he picked him up.

Miss Eisen, also unaware of the realities at home, became increasingly convinced that something was blocking the learning process. She wanted more testing done, and, admitting that their tutorial service was poorly equipped for testing, suggested to the classroom teacher many times during the semester that a thorough "psychoeducational evaluation" be arranged. It was a useful suggestion, perhaps forgotten by a well-meaning but too-busy teacher. Time passed without the testing.

Tony produced less and less work and Miss Eisen became more and more suspicious that the "block in the learning process" was the parent-child relationship. Unfortunately, the inexperienced tutor never saw Mrs. Petri and saw Mr. Petri only from a distance as he picked Tony up. She maintained, nevertheless, an opinion that things were "not as they should be at home."

Why, Diana wondered, had the special tutor never seen the Petris, never talked to them? The Petris, unemployed, had nothing but time.

"She never called us in, that's why," was Ann Petri's recollection. Was the professional waiting for the parent to call? Were the parents waiting to be summoned? Such a simple explanation for non-communication: propriety. Who makes the first move? Often, no one.

The school year was drawing to a close. Then, by some stroke of ironic logic, just before the closing Tony was scheduled for a total psychological and educational evaluation by Emma Dern, the school psychologist. The "psychoeducational test battery" that had been repeatedly requested was finally to be done.

Just in time for summer vacation.

It was early evening, a Wednesday. Tony settled his body into the mohair sofa in Diana's office at the back of the house. He glanced around at the wall, covered floor to ceiling with books, and said, "You're really into those things, aren't you?" Then he laughed sarcastically and said, "I bet we've got as many books as you do, and they're all mine. Yeah, they're all mine...and I've...I've read maybe one or two Dr. Seuss. That's about it." The painful admission made him sorry he'd brought up the subject. Diana thought of the small mountain of books Mrs. Petri had so proudly displayed for her that day in her home. Now she knew they had a different meaning for Tony. That mountain of books, only one or two word-read by him, represented his failure, not his preschool precocity as the mother had intended.

Tony had come that night just to talk. At fifteen, he was willing to talk, sparingly but passionately—to comment on the data about his life that Diana had begun to assemble. The names and places she began to recite stirred him, triggering thoughts of those early years. One of those places was the parochial school, St. Jude's.

"Yeah, when my mom took me out of public school and put me in St. Jude's, that would do it, she thought. That would save me. Ha! She figured if it wasn't for the church school, I'd end up being corrupted. So she blew money on me. She really 'saved' me, let me tell you!" He looked disgusted.

"I remember the first grade teacher. I liked her OK, but one day I had to go to the 'head' and she wouldn't let me out. So I broke out. I just went flying through the door, running out, and she came chasing me all the way to the boys' head." Tony broke into a rare, loud guffaw, remembering the chase, the nun, with robes flying, in pursuit of the minor offender.

"Hey, look. You gotta go, you gotta go, and she wouldn't let me out so I let myself out. Huh! I got detention for that."

Detention. One of the ridiculous words. Incomprehensible to a six-year-old. Diana felt her old outrage at the use by schools of mystifying, jailhouse terminology like "detention" and "citation" that instilled fear.

"In the first grade, detention?" she asked. "Sounds a little steep."

"Yeah. In the first grade. I got in more trouble in those two years at St. Jude's than in *all* the years in public school. The rules—they were stupid, man! First of all, I don't believe in anything in the Catholic church. Even in the first grade, I had my doubts, watching this goon with a cape on going around with that incense stuff. I used to laugh, so I'd get detention and have to sit in a corner and read a comic book. On Donut Day. Ha! What a laugh! I couldn't read, not even a comic book, and Donut Day was a joke. You'd have to buy a donut in the morning. Who'd want to buy a donut, man! Three ounces of total nothingness."

Who'd want to buy a donut, says fifteen-year-old Tony. Six-year-old Tony would want to buy one, that's who. Sorry, Tony. Sit in the corner.

"You sound like you were a pretty unusual first grader," Diana commented, intrigued by the types of events his mind was summoning, intrigued by this image of himself as a law-breaker, and curious to know how much was fact and how much fantasy.

"Yeah. They didn't know what to do with me. My hair had to be just so long and I didn't like to wear that stupid uniform, and I always tore it out because my legs were so big. I was an oaf, and the knees were always torn out. I was always causing trouble, and I was fat, even in the first grade. I was a little pudnick."

When Diana asked about his academic progress during those early years, Tony simply said, "I tried. I know I tried. But somehow everything always came out wrong."

Tony's portrait of himself as six-year-old holy terror lacked credibility for Diana. His self-perceptions were too different from the teachers' descriptions of him as "just kind of there" and "nice." Could this first-grader have had the maturity to be that skeptical of the rituals of the church or did the skepticism bloom later? As for his appearance, Mrs. Petri had insisted that Tony's clothes always be clean, his shoes shined, his pants pressed, without holes in the knees, when he went to the church school. Yet, in Tony's memory, everything he was, everything he did, was wrong. He was fat. Oaf. Pudnick. He was rebel and troublemaker in the first grade.

Diana sensed that Tony's rebellion was inside, his disobedience a secret wish, an unexpressed fantasy, made real in the privacy of his dreams. Nevertheless, the truth didn't matter. The child's appraisal of himself was what mattered to Diana's investigation. And his way of "reading" his world.

Some things were certain about the way Tony Petri read his world. He observed. He evaluated what he observed. He disagreed with a lot of what he observed. Secretly.

And he never forgot the negatives.

That last fact became more and more evident as Diana prodded his memory by mentioning the names of teachers from his early school years. She was unprepared for the response evoked by the name "Hinkle."

"Miss Hinkle." Tony barely breathed out the name as his usually guarded, expressionless face distorted into a snarl. "Yeah...She probably wouldn't even remember my name. But I'll never forget hers. Hinkle. How I hated her. Miserable, nasty lady. She was a real freak! She was crazy. Always pulling my ear. She was one of those real old-fashioned types—you know, the kind that, if you don't do what you're supposed to, she grabs you by the hair or smacks you on the hand with a ruler. Real cute stuff like that."

Tony's eyes narrowed, his jaw angled forward, and he shouted, "I'd like to go back and handcuff her to the car...and...and run over her face!"

Jarred by the outburst, he fell silent for a moment, lowered his voice and explained, "You know, I don't usually carry vengeance, and I only wish everybody would have a happy life and when they die, die quick, with no pain. But I really don't care what happens to Miss Hinkle. I really hope she kicks the bucket. And suffers...suffers the whole time."

This was a ninth-grader talking about his second grade teacher, a woman he had not seen in over eight years! Tony's vehement reaction to the news of Miss Hinkle's brain tumor and recent paralysis surprised Diana. She and Tony had been working together for several months. His gentleness, willingness to cooperate, and ready sense of humor dominated their hours together. Although he'd alluded to his temper several times, this was the first evidence of it

Tony sensed her surprise. "Yeah. There's lots about me you don't know. Like my friends. My friends are not the norm, if you know what I mean," he said. "They're all the bad guys around here—the delinquents. They do the things I always wanted to do but never did. I guess that's why I like to hang around 'em. I watch 'em blast out and they never seem to worry about it. Me, I'll break *things,* not people. I'll break things," he picked up a pencil from Diana's desk, "and pretend they're people!"

He snapped the pencil in half, illustrating his point, then stared at the jagged wood and softly apologized. He'd done it again. Sensing that Diana understood, he continued talking. "One time I really lost my cool. There was this bully on my block and he was always bugging me. One day I just couldn't take it any more and I hauled off and let him have it. I swung at him—just once—and knocked out his front teeth! I was so surprised. I mean, sheeez, I didn't mean to do that...but it happened."

The voice had become controlled. Tony seemed uncomfortable admitting to this fear of his true strength, of the loss of control, of his capacity to destroy if he ever really let go.

Diana listened, nodding in silent understanding.

The vengeful curses Tony had willed upon Loreen Hinkle must have shamed him then, for he began to speak with a near-tenderness Diana also hadn't heard from him before. He was not devoid of compassion. He wanted her to know that.

"You know, I had a cousin, Laura. She died...very slow. She had cancer....I miss her. I loved her a lot. She died when she was twenty-two....I felt terrible because I was closer to her than anybody....Her and Tom—that was her husband. He was like the brother I never had." Reminiscing, "He was such a little guy. But you know," he smiled, "it's not the size of the dog, it's the size of the fight in the dog that counts. He was just a neat guy. They had these two little girls. I miss them a lot. They moved away." The words were controlled, but the quavering in his voice gave him away. He mourned for Laura, anguished for her orphans.

"But...I...really...don't care...what happens...to that creep teacher," Tony repeated deliberately, making sure that Diana understood, "and I really do hope she suffers."

Tony thought a moment. Then he barely whispered these words: "I never...gave her...any trouble...but I wish...I wish I had...I didn't say anything...but I wanted to...I wanted to. All I did was...just suck it in....Yeah...just sucked it in."

Just sucked it in.

Deep scars. Indelible marks on the mind of an adolescent. A seven-year-old child had been made to feel humiliated in front of his peers. He'd never shared the feeling—not at seven. Now, almost sixteen, he had not yet forgiven the one who caused such pain.

Looking down, silent now, Tony began ripping loose tufts of mohair out of the sofa cushion, alternately pulling at them and rolling them into a ball.

CHAPTER 9

"My mom knows the secret
why I do so bad in school,
so stop asking me!"

Diana tore open the envelope with the excitement she
felt each time she was able to locate someone from
Tony's past. She had found Emma Dern, the school
psychologist, and Emma had remembered "lonely Tony" from
her end-of-the-year tests on him at St. Jude's nine years earlier!
She'd cared enough to do a record search, find a copy of Tony's
intelligence test, and write a personal letter.

Diana read it with fascination.

"Dear Mrs. Cotter,

Finally, here is Tony's record from the end of first grade. I
remember him as a confused boy who just wasn't sure of any-
thing but put up a front to hide his feelings. You'll note the
confusion as to left and right on the picture arrangement test.
He told all the stories correctly, but he put them down in reverse
order on the table. I saw no evidence of any severe perceptual
problems, just some developmental immaturity. When I asked
him what animal he'd like to be, he named three—a lion, who
wouldn't have to get smashed around, a cat, who'd have fur
and be petted and loved, and a tiger, who wouldn't be pushed
around and would be left alone. That seemed to pretty much
sum up his feelings then.

His three wishes came with no hesitation. He wanted a crane,
a bike, and two switch trucks, adding "That's all I'll ever need."

Tony cooperated well with me, but it was difficult for him to
sit quietly. He was always moving in his seat. I found him very
verbal and appealing with those dark eyes of his.

I made some notes about information he volunteered about
his father, which may be of interest to you. He said, "My Dad

doesn't like noise. He's always yelling, 'Tony, you're too noisy. Be quiet!' He doesn't hit me. He yells at me all the time.'" As you know, his dad was 62 at the time and out of work. I guess he was quite ill.

In my conference with Mrs. Petri, she told me Mr. Petri lets Tony do whatever he wants, saying he can't make him do things so he has quit trying. For example, the father will complain that Tony won't go to the store with him, so he, Mr. Petri, ends up not going either.

I felt Mrs. Petri was unable to cope with the situation, and I recommended counseling plus a medical-psychiatric evaluation of Tony and perhaps a neurological, if the doctor felt it would show anything.

You have revived my interest in lonely Tony. Please let me hear from you again.

Sincerely,
Mrs. Emma Dern

Diana scanned the Wechsler Intelligence Test record form that Emma Dern had enclosed and was not surprised to see that, in this first and probably most untainted-by-rebellion of Tony's IQ tests, he had scored as high as 119 in verbal skills and 106 in performance tests. Certainly above average. Even more revealing were the ranges of scores on each of the subtests. Looking at his equivalent IQ scores in each of the areas of intelligence being tested by the Wechsler, Diana discovered that Tony had scored from a low of 79 in coding to 138 in vocabulary—the top of the Superior range! She pondered the irony of that high score. The vocabulary subtest, like the early readiness test he had taken in kindergarten, was supposed to be a great predictor of school success. The other test scores verified the kinds of strengths and weaknesses she had seen and she loved Emma Dern for taking the time to supply her with this essential evidence. She would save it to compare with his later testing.

She placed the papers in her file marked THERAPY, since Mrs. Dern had recommended it.

Therapy. Diana pondered the meaning of this word that would have been so foreign and mysterious to the uninitiated Petris. Therapy—for the deeply private, increasingly guarded, then-unemployed Ann Petri. Therapy for the dubious, minimally educated, chronically ill, still-unemployed Johnny Petri. Therapy for Tony at seven and a half, described by Mrs. Dern as confused—inattentive—fidgety—lonely—failing to achieve, but "cooperating well." Needy but reluctant candidates for therapy, these three.

Ann Petri had felt offended by Emma Dern. The negative feelings took years to be released, but release them she finally did one day as Diana was questioning her.

"That woman told me some things about Tony, and then I discussed them with him," Ann said. "She got mad at me, said those things were private and told in the strictest confidence and I wasn't supposed to discuss them with Tony. She talked down to me and to Tony too. She wanted us to be so secretive....Well, what she didn't understand was, Johnny and I, we never treated Tony like a child. We talked to him like an adult. After all, I was thirty-seven when I had Tony. It just wasn't in us to baby him or to hide things."

Had Emma Dern been aware of Mrs. Petri's extreme sensitivity to criticism? School psychologists, so overworked, so tightly scheduled with test after test, conference following conference, reports to be filed, scores to be computed, rarely have the time to intuit or search for such guarded sensitivities.

In that after-test conference, a message was transmitted to Mrs. Petri. The message, never stated by the professional but felt by the worried mother, was: something is wrong with your mothering.

Ann Petri was somehow unable to arrange any further meetings with Emma Dern.

Ann Petri had managed to avoid more contact with the psychologist, but what she couldn't avoid was the advice about therapy. The words fermented in the mother's mind all summer, as her waking moments were haunted by her son's Wrongness.

In September, she was hired to work as a checker in a discount store. She marked the end of her six months of unemployment with a decision: she dialed a help-seeking call to the family guidance clinic connected with her medical center and took the first available appointment.

Riding up the elevator to the seventh floor of the high rise building, Mrs. Petri felt the changes come over her body—the clammy wet-cold in her hands and the prickling sensation in her scalp that maddened her with wanting to scratch. It maddened her more because she refused to scratch, refused to give in. She'd tried so hard to control her life, this super-responsible being, but even her own body sometimes eluded her control. Body and mind both resisted facing yet another prying stranger with yet another list of personal questions.

She tried to rehearse what she would say in that first therapy hour, to decide just how much she wanted to confide. She needed to confide but she feared being judged. What should she say? What would a therapist consider important? What did she feel ready to tell? The silent debate rumbled in her until she found herself in the waiting room of the clinic.

She rummaged through her purse for a comb to freshen up a bit and spotted the folded report she'd received from Tony's first-grade teacher at the end of the school year. No need to unfold it. She'd already memorized the edict: "Tony has shown almost no achievement. In fact, his work has deteriorated since September, with no academic gain. He shows no span of attention, even when playing. He is squirmy in his seat—overactive and jumpy." No academic gain. Work deteriorated. Over the whole year. What was that tutoring doing? Should she tell the therapist this? Would he think Tony was a dummy? Why wasn't the boy learning?

She thought of some of the things Emma Dern had said. She had recommended another physical. There it was again. Something physical. What did they suspect? Was it his eyes, or his hearing? His hearing seemed fine to her. He certainly heard what he wanted to hear. She thought again about Tony's birth and that doctor and the forceps. Maybe it *was* something neurological. Tony'd never had a neurological exam because they always just hinted about things like that and never suggested to go ahead and have it done.

Ann felt her palms' fluids begin their work again. She kept hearing Mrs. Dern's voice talking about Tony's power at home and how the family must stop denying their problems. Didn't that woman know we wanted help? Dear, sweet Jesus, just help my boy learn like other kids..."

"Mrs. Petri?...Ann Petri?!"

The sound of her name cut through her concentration. A youngish man with a tieless shirt, pleasant face, and the kind of hair that always looks shaken rather than combed, was calling her. She felt somewhat eased by his warm manner and his casual, unscrutinizing acceptance of her.

Walter Sand introduced himself as the therapist who had been assigned to her family by the clinic.

She followed him into a small office, cluttered with shelves of toys, games, test kits, and stacks of paper, none of them squared off at the edges. For just an instant, she wondered how Walter Sand's mother felt about *him*.

Mr. Sand offered her a choice of seats—an old, overstuffed chair at the side of his desk or a molded, orange fiberglass one directly across from it. She chose the latter one and sat as she might have on the benches in church—attentive, careful to avoid too much comfort.

The therapist offered her some coffee, but she declined. She didn't need caffeine. Her body was producing its own tension-manufactured stimulants.

Then the questions began. Why was she seeking help? What was the nature of the problem? Mr. Sand kept the questions broad, acknowledging the awkwardness, the delicacy of first sessions in therapy.

Mrs. Petri was characteristically cautious in her cooperation, but even in that first hour she couldn't hide from the therapist's trained ears that she was exhausted and overwhelmed by the total responsibility for the care of herself and her child. She focused on Tony whenever she could—his development, his disastrous school history, and his behavior at home. She also tested these strange waters of therapy with a few asides, hints at her own frustrations, particularly with her mate, with respect to finances and their disagreements about Tony. When Mr. Sand urged her to expand on the issues, she withdrew; sensitively, he didn't pursue the effort. He recognized that she would have a difficult time learning to trust this stranger whose life's work was to listen to people's most private pains.

The hour's end surprised Ann. She hadn't noticed the passage of time. Perhaps she was feeling comfortable with this man? He helped soften the closing moments by rising and extending his hand. Not wishing to expose her wet palm, Ann kept the handshake brief. They scheduled the appointment for Tony's evaluation with the consulting psychiatrist, exchanged thank-yous and good-byes. On her way out, Ann realized, surprised, that her palms were no longer wet.

91

The family guidance clinic used a team approach for their psychological and educational evaluations. Tony would first be seen by a consulting psychiatrist whose job was to interview clients, rule out mental illness, and to select the staff therapist best suited to each. That staff therapist would, in turn, request additional services and testing by other team members as these were indicated during the course of therapy.

The consulting psychiatrist met with Tony and concluded that he was very much in need of a male therapist. He felt that Walter Sand, who had already been assigned to the Petri parents, would also be an excellent choice for Tony and he recommended that the boy be seen once a week.

Mr. Sand received the psychiatrist's report and made notes about his new client: Anthony Petri—at least high average intelligence. Appealing. Curious. A gift for technical skills and information. Fearful of expressing any aggressive feelings. Yearning for companionship, lonely.

The "lonely" was the only surprise to Walter Sand. Hadn't Mrs. Petri said the father was always home? Lonely, but not alone, the therapist hypothesized.

In September of Tony's second grade year, they began what would be a year of psychotherapy. They would play together, this man trained to listen and this boy used to hiding. Hopefully, when they played, they would talk. Mr. Sand would see how Tony played, how he planned on winning or whether he cared to win, and how he dealt with loss. The early games were checkers and cards. Tony was used to those, comfortable with them because he'd played them so often with his grandmother. Gradually, checkers and cards gave way to Monopoly and then to noisy war games. Congenial Tony was always a good loser. Too good a loser, noted the therapist. Rarely, ever so rarely, the boy would brave some fleeting challenges to his new friend, but even the challenges were done in a safe, respectful way.

"How's school, Tony?" Mr. Sand ventured one day.

"OK."

"You doing OK these days?"

Tony didn't want to discuss it.

"I got some faulty wiring somewhere," was the boy's only comment. Wiring was a world he understood. He understood less about grown-ups and fighting. He didn't like to talk about such things. In passing, only occasionally, he'd mention his

92

parents, commenting that they were "always yelling," but usually wouldn't venture a guess about why.

Sometimes he'd come into the office saying, "I had a lousy week." Then, no follow-up, no details, no why. The job of why, of course, was the therapist's. It would be no easy job with this constrained, already-wounded young boy.

During those early months of therapy, Tony's second grade teacher, a concerned young nun, took it upon herself to call Mr. Sand. She described Tony's difficulty with working independently and his tendency to quit unless she assisted him constantly. However, she was beginning to notice a brightening in his attitude, his behavior. So were the Petris.

By January, there was an air of optimism that the therapy's advantages were taking hold.

Then it was February.

In February, Tony was promoted to A2—the second half of second grade. To a new teacher, one of the few lay teachers hired by St. Jude's from outside the religious order. Her name— Loreen Hinkle.

In February, Mr. Sand noticed an unexplained restlessness in Tony. A new evasiveness. The boy was still friendly, but with a distance now. He rejected the old games, was suddenly fearful of making errors. He began instead to paint—great, huge paintings of rockets and giant people with radiating antennas and enormous ears that emitted smoke-like clouds. Tony responded to Mr. Sand's encouragement of his painting, but he now seemed to doubt the sincerity of his new friend's praise. Shortly after that, even the painting became too threatening. He stopped it. Mr. Sand brought in plastic models, having learned that Tony was genuinely proud of his dexterity with these.

The change had been dramatic, puzzling. The self-doubt had become extreme. Tony made no mention of school. No mention of his change in classrooms. No mention of his new teacher, Miss Hinkle.

Not surprisingly, Mr. Sand presumed something significant had been happening at home, something more than the tensions previously described. He had been meeting sporadically with Mrs. Petri. As the weeks turned into months, she had tried to steer the discussions away from feelings—hers or Tony's—and to focus more on Tony's school problem. She, not Tony, wanted to talk about school. Tony didn't want to talk at all. No insights could be gained from John Petri, who had appeared only once, in September, and who was so preoccupied with his health that he didn't return.

Walter Sand found himself becoming troubled and confused by this family, presuming that they were withholding or denying some crucial information that could explain Tony's behavior changes.

Food and gifts had begun to consume Tony's thoughts during his therapy hours. And suddenly there was anger, soft anger, anger never allowed to surface before. A toy got crushed—"accidentally." A pencil turned spear and unexpectedly punctured the middle of a rocket picture. The first time Mr. Sand said "No more" to the plastic models, Tony erupted out of his chair, his hip thwacking the table edge as he rose. He tried to leave the room in furious protest. The models had served their purpose for revealing both Tony's skill at building them and his manipulation of the therapist to provide them. The models had become just another diversion, helping him to avoid talk of feelings. Mr. Sand was catching on.

A major goal of Tony's therapy had been to provide a safe place for the expression of his locked-up anger. While the expressions of anger became more open, however, the causes remained hidden. Tony still avoided the topic of school. The therapist was growing frustrated. His questions were becoming more and more direct.

One day, out of annoyance with Mr. Sand's questions about school, Tony blurted, "My mom knows the secret why I do bad in school, so stop asking me!"

Mr. Sand followed up the suggestion. Mom had been surprised by Tony's comment, but her interpretation of this "secret" seemed to tie into her own conflict between her working and mothering roles. She felt sure, now that she was working again, that Tony missed her terribly, and that this was the reason for his poor school performance.

By April, optimism began to fade in the lives of the Petri family. Ann Petri quit her brand new job the day she learned Johnny had received a work offer. How deeply she wanted Johnny to be a working person again! And she was sure Tony would be thrilled to have her home.

Her hopes were in vain. The job failed to materialize for Mr.

Petri. This time Mrs. Petri couldn't mask her supreme disappointment when she spoke to Mr. Sand. The therapist concluded that the triple strains of unemployment, uncertainty about financial survival, and the failing health of Mr. Petri were the obvious sources of Tony's increasingly disturbed behavior.

Contrary to his mother's predictions, her return home did not "thrill" Tony. Tony was not thrilled about anything during those post-February therapy sessions. He grew more sullen, uncommunicative. His "secret" about why he kept failing, both in his classroom and in tutoring, remained unspoken to the therapist. There was no mention of ear-pulling or hair-pulling, of frustrations over recurrent mistakes. There was no hint of the helplessness and suffering engendered by the teacher whose mere name would evoke Tony's rage eight years later.

Nor did Tony discuss his tutoring sessions. Why should he? He had been in tutoring since the beginning of parochial school. It was a constant fact of his life.

No need to tell Mr. Sand that the tutoring group was reading its first hard-backed book. All but Tony, that was. No need to say that the other kids were getting better while Tony was giving up completely. Furtively, the overgrown youngster would take his tutor aside and, in a half-whisper, ask when he could catch up like the others. She felt his frustration along with her own and concluded that "only individual tutoring can help Tony at this point."

Her recommendation was sound; the Petris' resources were not. The change was not possible. In desperation, the tutor started Tony in one of those new programmed workbooks where he could, as the brochure proudly proclaimed, "work at his own pace," separate from the group. The program: Phonic Sounds. Once again. Under a new cover.

By the mid-year of his second grade, Tony's self-consciousness about making errors was already part of him. School had become non-success on all levels. He had no frame of reference for anything but failure. Could an eight-year-old know that it didn't have to stay that way—that to be helped you had to ask for help?

CHAPTER 10

*"That therapist didn't know about
our marriage. Sure, we have our arguments,
but who don't? At least we were always home...
that should count for something. Being there."*

The testing room at the family guidance clinic was small, but the eight-year-old client wasn't bothered by its size. The room was cold, sterile, somewhat dark from the foggy light of the May day, but the tester tried to compensate with her personal warmth. She was a psychologist, one of three on the clinic diagnostic team. The team had been asked by Walter Sand to do a complete psychoeducational evaluation of Tony after this eighth month of his therapy.

The teacher introduced herself. "Ellen" was the only name she offered.

Another grown-up, Tony thought, trying to pretend that tests were games. Within minutes, she'd know about him—know he couldn't read. Know he got mixed up with his right and left. Did they think he didn't notice they wrote things down whenever he'd start something on the wrong side?

Here it comes. The boxes. Those little green suitcases filled with all that stuff. And pages of questions. All those questions. What's the difference between a bird and a dog. Dumb lady. Everyone knows that. All you have to do is look.

"How are iron and silver the same, Tony?"

Boring. Who cares? "I don't know...I don't like this." Fidgeting. Wiggly, like a guppy under water.

Then Tony heard the number stuff again. He remembered it from Mrs. Dern, only now it was Ellen asking him to repeat the numbers, "just like I say them, Tony—4-1-3."

"4-1-3," he mimicked.

"7-2-9-8."

"I can't figure that out. Can I go now?" he said, surprising her by getting out of his chair and heading for the door. Four times during that hour he would make escape gestures.

Ellen jotted her note: "He gives up if the task is even mildly difficult." She tried to cajole, to reassure. "I know it seems boring and sometimes too hard, Tony, but we need to understand more about how you learn so we can help you. Just try. Please. Try to tell me what these words mean. The first one is 'pity,'" and she started on one of the vocabulary lists from the intelligence test.

He surprised her with a splinter of effort. "In 'pity' you're not in very good luck. You're gonna get in trouble." Pity me, he squirmed. Let me out of here. *I'm* in trouble.

"Compare." She read off the next word before he could retreat.

"Like, I compare my train with another kid's train and see if mine is better than his."

The kid has a vocabulary, Ellen realized, pushing.

"Revenge," she called out.

"Someone did something to you and you want to get back at them. There. Can I go *now*? I gotta go, they're waitin' for me." His face was pained with the pleading.

"Who's waiting for you, Tony?"

"Just some guys."

"Well, if those guys are your friends, I'm sure they'll wait for you. You're doing so well here, let's just do a few more. Then we'll take a break, OK?"

No answer from Tony. Trapped by grown-ups.

Ellen persisted with more words from the fourteen-year-old word list that had reflected the eight-year-old's capabilities. To the next word, Tony responded "I don't know." To the next a softer, "I don't know."

Tony shrugged at the next. Often in that hour, Ellen noticed, he communicated with gestures, withholding language altogether.

The test instructions required five consecutive errors. Ellen tried one more word, realizing she was testing his limits rather than his vocabulary at that point.

Tony became openly angry then. "I don't know, I don't know these words! Can I go now?" He reached for a small box from the open testing kit on the floor and began to rattle its contents. The psychologist knew it was time for a break.

At break time, Tony was transformed. No more fidgeting and squirming. No more darting from each object that caught his eye. The youngster who moments earlier had shown such poor powers of concentration was now sitting motionless on the floor, playing with the Lego blocks he had longed to touch when, in the middle of the counting test, he had spotted them across the room. As he snapped the colored plastic parts together, he responded to Ellen's informal questions and talked about his pets, collections, and hobbies.

But, in spite of the new flow of conversation, Ellen felt a continued fearfulness and distrust. The more she showed a genuine interest in his play, the more Tony's replies reflected discomfort. She had never before experienced this combination of verbal openness and emotional retreat. The closer she got, the more troubled he seemed by the closeness.

After the break, Tony's former distractible, restless, fidgety self reappeared and he began a tactic to deliberately irritate Ellen. As she would introduce a change in the test directions, he would respond by following the previous ones. If she said, "Tell me these numbers in reverse order," he'd tell them in the same order as before. If she said, "Now count by 5's," he'd continue to count by 10's.

Ellen suspected that the behavior was deliberate and not caused by a thinking disability. How could she determine if, by mocking the test, he was hiding the true difficulty he had for remembering sequence? The ploy was ingenious.

Ellen followed her hunch and let Tony know he was irritating her.

He smiled again, the first real smile of the day. Caught. "Oh, I'm just goofin' around."

Just goofing around. Dumb like a fox, Ellen thought to herself. Tony was self-critical, but his style was different from those of other kids she'd tested. Most kids feel shamed by their failures, but not Tony—he seemed comfortable with his, at least in this testing situation.

His pattern was consistent, even with tasks that didn't look like school work. When Ellen asked him to draw or build something, or to construct a puzzle or design, he'd speed through it without care, without effort, without concern for quality.

Ellen disarmed him briefly by an unexpected behavior of her own. When she presented him with some words on flash cards, she gave him no time for the "I-don't-know-can-I-go-now" response. She beat him to it by telling him immediately what each word said. He was so surprised at the change of rules that he paid attention, and when she asked him if he could read them back he read every one correctly. She mixed them up and tried again. By then he was kind of pleased to be showing off, surprising himself as much as Ellen by the revelation: Tony Petri was able to learn whole words by sight.

Diana studied the document prepared by Ellen and the other two team psychologists, eager to compare its findings with those of Emma Dern from the previous year—the year prior to therapy. She was impressed by the thoroughness of the evaluation and by its insightful, provocative conclusions. It had assessed perception, intelligence, academic achievement, and emotional components. The psychologists unanimously felt that Tony's intelligence ratings were depressed by emotional factors. They remarked on his erratic willingness to pay attention. No more "cooperating well" as he had for Emma Dern.

As she skimmed the three separate evaluations, she noticed the word "hostility" mentioned frequently in each. Repressed hostility, the examiners had said. Tony had said it less clinically: just sucking it in. Well, Tony, by eight and a half you weren't sucking it in so well. Trained eyes, and not just Walter Sand's, were beginning to notice.

The concluding statement both troubled and excited Diana. It read: "Tony Petri's underachievement is primarily due to the effect of very difficult family relationship problems, resultant immaturity, strong passive resistance to learning task demands, and preoccupation with internal stress."

Diana felt troubled that, once again, a family had been proclaimed primary culprit for a school failure. Or so it seemed, to these professionals, at that moment in time. Neither the testing team nor Mr. Sand had any knowledge of Tony's school realities.

She was excited, however, by the diagnosis of "strong passive resistance to learning task demands," appearing in print for the first time. The report verified her growing suspicions: passive resistance, a way of controlling angry feelings, was setting in as Tony's mode of operation as early as age eight.

As she closed the report, Diana felt grateful for access to such insightful documentation of Tony's early behaviors and disabilities.

By June, a month after the testing, Mr. Sand recognized the subtle signals—the beginnings of withdrawal from the therapeutic process. Both Johnny and Ann were minimizing their marital problems, focusing on Tony rather than on their marriage, and choosing not to discuss as a couple what each had confided to him in individual sessions. Tony had completely stopped talking about his family. Restless and fidgety during his therapy hours, he scorned the equipment in the room and was unwilling to play anything. His only conversations, meager and infrequent, centered on the family's new kitten, creating an effective smoke screen against involvement.

That same June a call came from the school principal, saying she believed St. Jude's was too competitive for Tony. It was the call Ann Petri had so feared. St. Jude's was giving up on her son. She felt a sense of personal failure. Mr. Sand tried to intercede in their behalf, but it was too late. Tony's failure was complete in all academic subjects. But, tellingly, he had received a "B" in citizenship. Tony had been a "good boy" in Miss Hinkle's class. He had indeed been "just sucking it in."

The principal recommended a private—and of course unaffordable—remedial school for Tony. With the choices narrowed to one, the Petris were resigned: come September, Tony would return to public school.

Shortly after the forced decision, Tony's reports from the tutorial service came home. At least they had been consistent, Mrs. Petri thought. After two years of phonics under different wrappings, Tony was now testing two years behind his peers, at the achievement level of a child just leaving kindergarten.

The closing comments of the tutors' final report were more than the truth could bear: "Tony is still showing enthusiasm for the new workbook materials, where he works with beginning consonants, short vowel sounds, and final consonant sounds. We feel Tony is much more outgoing now and is to be complimented on his accomplishment."

Mrs. Petri read this and wept.

Something snapped in Ann Petri that summer following Tony's second grade. The insulting report from the school's tutors with its words of hope after hope had died freed her from

100

her earlier "expert worship." That summer, the mother would challenge the experts.

Ann Petri had tried.

She'd tried harder than her son to get involved in this therapy thing.

She'd tried to believe Mr. Sand's suggestions. She'd tried to believe that Tony's improvement in school depended on his parents' resolving their marital grievances. But every night she came home to a husband who questioned the whole notion. She found *herself* asking questions about therapy everywhere she went. She began polling the opinions of her friends, family, strangers she would meet on the bus. She was drawn to articles about therapy in magazines and newspapers and was especially influenced by the ones that were were critical of it. Doubt was breeding.

They had come to therapy seeking help, approval, answers to their questions about Tony's school problems. Their growing sensitivity to questions, even questions asked with care and compassion, made them feel increasingly uneasy—as though they were somehow to blame for Tony's troubles.

The Petri parents vented their feelings about the past more and more openly with Diana as she grew familiar to them. She became privy to dialogues they had never dared in front of Walter Sand. So many years had passed. The pains were more remote.

"I got so sick of that man," Ann Petri groaned. "He kept implying it was something between Johnny and me that kept Tony from learning. I told him, I suppose we have fights or a few beers or we play cards, but we're no different from any other couple, in my knowledge of family and friends. We like different things. Me, I love laughter and music, but Johnny—he doesn't need either one. Oh, yes, he listens to those sad concertos and operas until the tears come, but honestly they make me want to throw up. All that heavy music. He likes to cry. I like beautiful, happy music. But our household life wasn't any different than anybody's I knew. In fact, it was better than a lot. Sure, we fight, but...."

"We do *not* fight," Johnny Petri said, breaking his usual silence on this issue.

"We do fight, a lot," Ann responded, but without anger. With a smile.

John persisted, eyes twinkling. "We do not *fight*. We argue!" He chuckled at the disclosure of what was obviously a family joke.

Then Mrs. Petri laughed aloud and said, "Well, I tell him to leave. He won't. He tells me to leave. I won't. After all these years, why start over again? Where you gonna go? So here we are. Together." She looked away for a moment.

Mr. Petri wasn't done. "That therapist didn't know about our marriage. Sure, we have our 'arguments,' but who don't? Why, Annie's right. Our marriage is a lot better than some others. At least we were always home, where the average person wasn't. That should count for something. Being there."

All that talking and analyzing just wasn't John Petri's style. "Being there" was his style.

As Diana listened to the Petris' verbal jousting, she was reminded of her own parents' contests and her difficulty as a child in understanding why they disagreed. Only as she grew older could she hear the loving that lay underneath, just as she heard it from these two now. Why, she wondered, did grownups work so hard to hide their tender feelings for each other?

Listening carefully, Diana realized that the therapy had yielded an ironic result. Even though they had been seen, either separately or together, a total of only twelve times, this couple had made one radical change during those months. They had begun therapy divided in their view of their marital problems and personality conflicts, but the months of therapy had united them. It united them against therapy, against the feeling therapy gave them that something was wrong with their family.

Did the guidance clinic's evaluation team sense anything different about Mrs. Petri when they called her in to discuss their test findings and recommendations? Did they notice she was no longer able to hear? All those scores and numbers and big words were repeating what she already knew: there's something Wrong with your child. Untrained, Mrs. Petri couldn't have recognized the astuteness and significance of this particular testing—couldn't have realized the worth and urgency of the team's recommendation. Disenchanted, Mrs. Petri had stopped trusting.

She steeled herself for the advice, knowing in advance what it would be. More therapy. More tutoring. She was right.

The evaluation had been honest, realistic, and accurate in assessing Tony's inner strengths and deficits, in spite of all his maneuvers to hide them. But, as she read through the team's list, Mrs. Petri attended to only one recommendation: the one calling for a complete eye examination. She wrote it down. She had always felt there was something with his eyes.

A small class setting with lots of individual attention from the teacher, high quality remedial assistance, and supportive therapy to deal with his emotional needs were recommended as "right for Tony." To the doubting mother, they were more bug dust. Ten months they'd had. That was enough.

She listened politely, smiled politely, thanked them politely for their efforts that day in the conference room. She never mentioned that Tony was being tutored at that very moment by student volunteers at the Teen Center near her home. She never mentioned that she had withdrawn him from St. Jude's tutorial service. She'd given that group two years. Maybe the teens wouldn't do any better, but to the disillusioned woman, they couldn't do any worse. And the cost was only two dollars an hour.

Mrs. Petri closed her eyes to the fact that, at two dollars per, the teens had no training whatsoever and that Tony became just one of the mob of kids who were there primarily to keep one hand on their academics over the long summer. She pretended not to notice that all Tony was working on that summer was the alphabet. Reciting the alphabet. Writing the alphabet. Reading the alphabet. Tony was still leaving out the u and v. Sometimes. But he was getting his consonants, said the novice teens. Well, except for d, l, n, r, and p. Sometimes.

And they wondered, those well-meaning tutors, why Tony's progress varied so much, why he seemed so moody. "Sometimes he's cooperative and sometimes he refuses to concentrate," they wrote to the concerned parents.

Refuses to concentrate.

Three years of school failure. Two years of tutoring. Ten months of therapy. And now this big, bright, proud eight-year-old was once more reviewing the alphabet.

The teen center's reports never mentioned any misbehavior or disobedience. That summer, at least, Tony was still "sucking it in."

The summer closed with the guidance clinic relocating its offices thirty-five miles farther from the Petri home.

Tony Petri failed to appear for his next appointment.

Mother and son appeared together for the following session. The hour was strained. Both seemed mildly depressed, saying that things were not going too well. They chose not to expand or give details.

Mr. Sand asked Tony's feelings about his pending change to public school. Tony expressed no concern, ending the discussion. Mrs. Petri talked of only one reality—Tony's diagnosis, by her union optometrist, of a visual problem severe enough to require prism-lens eyeglasses. She had high hopes that the new eyeglasses could well be the answer to Tony's problems. No other topics proposed by the therapist could elicit any response.

Tony failed to appear for the last two appointments in September.

Mr. Sand called Mrs. Petri to see what had happened. She said something about losing insurance eligibility. She said something about maybe resuming in December if the eligibility was renewed.

That was the last the guidance clinic ever heard from the Petri family.

As Diana organized the facts she had assembled about the Petris' experiences with therapy, she became aware of the advantages of hindsight. She read her list:

Fact one: The success of therapy depended on the guarded anecdotes of a second grader unused to discussing his feelings.

Fact two: Mr. Sand had been diverted by the crises at home.

Fact three: The crises at home had been constant since the beginning of therapy in September.

Fact four: Mr. Sand's reports recorded February as the time of marked changes in Tony's behavior.

Fact five: It was at school, not at home, that major changes occurred in February.

Fact six: Walter Sand was never told there had been a change of teachers—never even knew there was a Miss Hinkle.

Fact seven: Six weeks after the testing, the Petris terminated all contact with the guidance clinic.

Fact eight: The superb evaluation, with its detailed analysis and recommendations, never left the guidance clinic files, never found its way to the public school to which Tony transferred that September.

Fact nine: This crucial report, written at this crucial juncture, remained unseen—for seven years—by anyone who might have implemented its recommendations.

Diana decided to question Tony about his therapy sessions with Mr. Sand. Surprisingly, Tony became uncomfortable, superficial in his response. "I remember there was this smelly coffee," he said, wrinkling his nose. "It used to stink in there!" And the models...yeah, I remember building those models and I didn't have to pay for them," Tony the manipulator recalled. He didn't remember going as often as the records indicated, thirty-six times, but conceded, "It's possible...I dunno. I didn't trust the guy. I don't even remember what he looked like. Maybe he was tall, about six feet tall...I dunno." He shrugged and fell silent.

Diana waited. Nothing more came out. That was it. A year of personal therapeutic interaction dismissed with a shrug. Not even a name. No emotion recalled. Just models and smelly coffee.

Walter Sand had become a fading ghost in Tony's memory while Loreen Hinkle loomed as an indelible effigy. Diana puzzled over this inconsistency until hours later one of Tony's past comments pushed its way into her consciousness: "It's so hard to remember the good ones." Curious comment, she'd thought at the time. Judging by the scarcity of memories, Walter Sand may have been a "good one" on Tony's scoreboard.

CHAPTER 11

Tony the Gopher: "It must be
something with his eyes…"

"**W**ow! Look at Tony….Hey, Tony, wh' happened?
You look like a gopher!"

"Yeah. Tony the Gopher, Tony the Gopher!
Nyeh, nyeh, the Gopher." His gang on the block contrived the
chant the day Tony arrived home wearing the thick, prism-lens
eyeglasses. He grabbed Billy, the biggest pest of the bunch,
and squeezed his arm 'til he howled. Even at eight, there were
some advantages to being big. But big wasn't always enough.
Kids were cruel. Strong-arm stuff only worked for the moment.
And Tony Petri didn't plead. Not with anyone, not for anything.

So he'd be The Gopher that year. He'd adjust. They could
call him Gopher. He learned not to hear it. Not to react. In less
time than it took the ice cream man to finish his route that
day, Tony the Gopher regained his position as leader of the
neighborhood gang. After all, he was still Tony Petri, the idea
man for adventure. Only difference was, now the leader wore
lenses.

To the Petri parents, especially mom, the lenses had a very
different meaning. For the first time, someone had found a
definable physical malfunction in Tony. He had a condition.
Dr. Gary Frank, Mrs. Petri's union optometrist, had given it a
name. Hyperphoria. It had something to do with one eye moving
wrong, sort of like a crossed eye, only Tony's went up instead
of in. That was why he kept switching off, the doctor said, using
one eye first and then blinking and switching to the other,
because when he tried to use them together he'd see double.

Dr. Frank had invited Mrs. Petri into the examination room
so that he could demonstrate the behavior for her. He explained,
"A child with this condition would naturally keep trying to use

106

both eyes together, but then he'd be under terrific stress, visual stress, because he wouldn't be seeing clearly. And," he added, "hyperphoria can be worsened by emotions."

Well, Tony certainly had emotions. Could emotions be worsened by hyperphoria? Could emotions be worsened by thick eyeglasses that made an eight-year-old into a Gopher?

Prism lenses were different from regular eyeglasses— thicker, and the size and thickness would have to keep going up as Tony grew, said Dr. Frank. Prism lenses would bend light rays at an angle to make up for the incorrect angle of his upturning eyeball. One problem though. His eyeball only turned up once in a while, not all the time. But he was told to leave the glasses on all the time.

Within five days, Tony grew totally dependent upon the lenses. Adolescent Tony didn't recall his eyes particularly bothering him before he got the glasses. But he vividly recalled what happened once he got them. If he took them off, he couldn't see. Scary. Then bad headaches if he tried not to wear them. He solved that problem. In the morning, when he'd wake up, he'd squeeze his eyes tight-shut, groping blind as he felt for the glasses, never opening his eyes until they were securely on his face. He was afraid to open his eyes without them. Once he'd knocked the lamp off the bedside table. The Old Lady had come rushing in, but he never opened his eyes. He knew she got real upset at him groping around like a blind guy, but he had to do it.

Then they made the glasses stronger and that was even worse. How he hated those damn things! Every time he'd move they'd fall off, and they were always dirty or something. He hated but needed them. He hated needing them. He was terrified of losing them, because, once he'd started wearing them he was "just no good if I didn't have 'em on."

The glasses made no difference in Tony's ability to read. Or to catch a ball. But Mrs. Petri felt they gave him more self-confidence, made him more calm. And the way he groped for them in the morning meant, to her at least, that he really needed them.

The optometrist's "three-diopter right hyperphoria" had been a great relief to Ann Petri, coming as it did at the end of the fruitless year in therapy. She was not seeking controversy from anyone on that diagnosis.

Annette Ellis was adorable. Her persimmon-red hair gleamed under the fluorescent classroom lights and her green eyes sparkled with the optimism of youth. The kids all loved the Playboy-bunny medallion she wore around her neck daily, given to her by her number one guy. She answered their where'd-ya-get-its right off the bat. Up-front lady. Tony liked that.

Tony liked her. He hadn't expected to. Not after Miss Hinkle. He hadn't expected to like the new school either, but so far things looked like they might be OK. The teacher's enthusiasm was infectious.

Annette had high expectations for her third grade class, Tony included. No reason not to include him. No records or reports about Tony ever arrived to prejudice her thinking. Nothing from St. Jude's. Nothing from the guidance clinic either. The law said Newberry School should have requested them and St. Jude's should have sent them. Something didn't happen, so Tony was able once again to have a fresh start.

The young teacher sensed a specialness in the new boy. He was much larger than the others, but there was more. He was reluctant to socialize, even though the kids seemed to like him and tried to include him. To her, Tony seemed like a satellite, often circling the group but never part of it. Hers was a bright, driving group of third graders, but she felt a need to protect them a bit from what she described as excessive pressure from their "pushy parents." Miss Ellis believed in realistic demands; she did not believe in making kids nervous.

The first days were busy with getting acquainted, organizing the classroom, getting supplies and materials. Seduced by Miss Ellis' tender spirit and, as yet unexposed by any academic failure, Tony began, in a surprisingly short time, to seek her company and share little confidences. He impressed her with his verbal adeptness. For the first time, he felt admired by a teacher. Encouraged by her interest, he began to confide in her while the others were on the playground, telling her elaborate stories of things that happened to him away from school. She had difficulty knowing which of his stories were "for real." There was always lots of talk about space and rockets, and Annette observed that in all of his stories he was very involved in being of some use to someone. Unusual for such a youngster, she thought. He told her one story of collecting supermarket carts and returning them to the store. She felt that rather than working for praise from others he wanted to feel worthwhile for *himself.* Tony had shown Miss Ellis more of himself in a month than he'd revealed in thirty-six sessions of therapy.

The class began their schoolwork with the usual beginning-of-the-year review, and Miss Ellis quickly learned that Tony had other kinds of specialness. He couldn't read, not even from the first grade phonic reader. Six weeks into the semester she began to inquire at the office whether information about Tony Petri had arrived from St. Jude's, but it had not. Not knowing what was wrong, she presumed Tony had one of those perceptual problems she had read about; and yet, he wasn't exactly reading in reverse, which was what she expected to see when a child had such a problem. He had a terrible time sounding out words, and wouldn't even try words with more than one syllable. Tony became increasingly dependent on her and seemed to be unable to work on his own.

She finally asked him to choose his own book—whatever interested him—and she was pleased to notice he began to do much better. He still needed lots of help, but he could learn-whole words by sight and remember them once he was told what they said. Suddenly Tony's fertile mind had a purpose for reading. Annette Ellis was untrained in learning disabilities, but instinctively she was on to something.

She noticed that his writing contained reversals. Sometimes he'd go right to left, so she'd take his hand and show him where to start. His printing was unusually large and she thought to herself, "Maybe it's because *he's* so large," laughing at her unscientific conclusion.

In spite of her frustrations with his education, Annette Ellis genuinely liked Tony and felt he enjoyed her. She was puzzled, though, by his continued isolation from his peers.

At home, in the neighborhood, however, Tony the Gopher continued to enjoy great popularity and leadership except, of course, in sports. On the ball field, his powerful swings moved only the air, never the ball. He used to duck when he saw the ball coming at him, but he didn't think it was because of his eyes. He just thought he was clumsy. Uncoordinated. By staying away from the games, he stopped risking being the last chosen for teams. He told himself he wasn't interested. Who wants a donut on Donut Day again. At Newberry, even though he had a fresh start with a whole new group of kids and a chance to assume any role with them he chose, he chose no role.

Most likely, the third grader chose to isolate *himself* at school. In that way, he could avoid comparisons and competition with other kids. He had his gang at home; he didn't need this bunch. The risk was too great.

Tony's outstanding ability to express himself verbally had tricked Miss Ellis into believing, wishing, dreaming that he would magically learn to read those self-chosen books. But the numbers of words in his sight word vocabulary were still limited to the numbers she had the time to tell him. Independent reading was an impossibility. Instinctively, Annette Ellis had come close to the NIM approach that would have helped him put everything together; but she lacked the time, had never heard of the method, and had no one available to help or advise her.

Her concern only increased her frustration. She even asked Mrs. Petri to see about putting Tony in the Opportunity Class, but the placement never happened and she never knew why.

Though their meetings were often brief and on-the-run, Miss Ellis felt the love behind the mother's quest for answers. At their final conference of the year, Mrs. Petri told Annette Ellis she thought the problem was "something with his eyes." To the young teacher, Tony's thick lenses added credibility to the mother's words. It must be something with his eyes.

As Diana compiled more facts, she became obsessed with the question of Tony's eyes. Just how big a role did they play in his failure? Should he have had surgery when he was little? Did those prism lenses really help? How much stress was he trying to overcome? Was the stress visual or emotional—and which caused which? There was so much controversy. The medical and non-medical eye specialists never saw "eye to eye," she laughed sadly.

She had been paying close attention to Tony's eyes when she worked with him at the junior high and was aware that they sometimes seemed out of alignment. She decided to ask him if he still had trouble.

"Yes," he answered, "when I'm struggling to do something, and especially to read something, but it's not real bad. It's like my eyes are...strained," he searched for the word. "They don't particularly *do* anything. I'll just rub them or cover up one eye or put my hands over my eyes, or do different things like that to read something. Sometimes I'll see two images, one on top of the other, and I'll have to blink my eyes to make one go away, but that doesn't happen all the time."

The description sounded very much like Dr. Frank's explanation of the third grader's visual problem. So. It was still with him.

Diana contemplated Ann Petri's reverence for doctors. Gary Frank was a doctor. The title "DR." was on his door, on his card, on his stationery. He had given Mrs. Petri her first piece of certainty. She wanted no more opinions after that. Diana had to know more about the meaning, cause, and treatment of this condition called hyperphoria in order to answer the questions on her growing list.

She headed first to her "answer man" on eye questions, ophthalmologist and personal friend, Dr. Sam Henry, professor of neuro-ophthalmology at the local university. His thoroughness and commitment to his profession had always gained her respect. She had learned, however, to expect his ire if the word "optometrist" came up in a discussion. Clearly, the "DR." on an optometrist's door was a source of gall to him.

Diana shared Dr. Frank's findings and some general information about Tony. As she had expected, Sam found a point on which to challenge the optometrist's opinion. "Hyperphorias are *not* worsened by emotions," he quickly declared, then conceded, "but trying to get the eyes to work together could cause *physical* stress.

"A phoria is a tendency for the eyes to diverge upward. We all have a phoria at certain times, like when we have too many martinis," he said, winking. "Some hyperphoria is perfectly normal, and most of us have it, but our fusion mechanism controls it and there are no problem symptoms. However, when that fusion mechanism breaks down, what was a phoria becomes a tropia."

Diana listened hard. For one awful second, she flashed on the Petris trying to decipher such an explanation. Sam went on to apply his phoria-tropia-diplopia-fusion talk directly to Tony's case. The rhythm of his words could have made a great jump rope jingle, Diana thought as she did a quick mental translation of his "ophthalmologese." Tony's eye movements upward came and went; usually his eyes held together, but sometimes the vision split. When his right eye remained turned upward, even for a few seconds, it gave him double vision, with images riding piggyback on each other. The coming and going of this double vision caused stress.

Diana always came away with answers from Sam. And with new questions. Can one have physical stress without its becoming emotional? She decided to seek more opinions, as Ann Petri had been forced to do, and plunged into the world of the vision experts.

Ophthalmologist Dr. Don Washburne explained that most hyperphoria is congenital, which means hyperphoric individuals have never experienced any other kind of vision. "This condition isn't rare," he commented, "except for five- or six-diopter hyperphoria, which is extreme and unusual."

Diana noted the word "congenital"—from birth on. "If you don't know any different, you just accept that's the way it is," Tony had said about having been his own caretaker as a young child. Most likely, he had never known anything different in his visual functions either, Diana realized.

Next she investigated diopters. Dr. Walter Brownstein, non-medically trained optometric researcher, recent graduate of the university with the most prestigious training in his field, patiently explained that a diopter is simply the unit measuring the bending power of an optic lens. The number of diopters required to straighten the eyes at the time of testing would be the number given to Tony's hyperphoria.

But Dr. Brownstein gave her a warning about all these numbers—a warning that would soon echo back to her, eventually clarifying the inconsistencies in Tony's visual diagnosis and treatment.

"Don't be surprised if different doctors come up with totally different diopter measurements on your boy. The measurement of this condition can be altered by all kinds of things: how much the person relaxes during the exam, at what angle the doctor does the exam, and whether or not eye drops are used. Eye drops should never be used for this kind of test because they tend to blur the image, and the image must be sharp for measurement of hyperphoria."

Wagging his finger at Diana with the passion of expertise, he continued, "The most important measure is the fixation disparity measure, because it measures how much stress is on the system. Ah, there's the key—how many diopters of hyperphoria Tony can pull together *on his own.*

"You see, if I covered Tony's eye, and while it was in the dark the eye began to move upward, but when I uncovered it it began to straighten on its own, I would want to find out how much he had corrected it *by himself.* The part left over, the part he couldn't pull together, would tell the amount of stress he was experiencing. This amount of stress would determine the lens strength. If he had four diopters of hyperphoria and only two diopters of stress, we'd just prescribe a two-diopter lens."

Diana suddenly realized the high risk of error in this business. And the high risk of using only one source of information. Or was it a higher risk to have too many sources?

Dr. Brownstein spoke expansively now, "Lots of people have phoria *without* stress, but Tony's kind of phoria, with the eyes pulling upward, is more closely correlated with stress. Yes," he emphasized, "vertical phorias can cause tremendous stress."

Tremendous stress. The words kept recurring in the expert testimonies like an occasional comprehensible English phrase overheard in a foreign land.

Tremendous stress.

Fidgety little boy. Always moving.

Could this have been why?

Dr. Frank had mentioned stress but never given the *amount* of stress when he first diagnosed Tony. Dr. Brownstein clarified that mystery quickly. Measurement for fixation disparity was relatively new and probably unheard of by Dr. Frank eight years earlier.

End of the line. Diana would never know the degree of visual stress Tony was experiencing during those first school years. She would never know if his lenses were correcting for stress only or if they were, in fact, overcorrecting and increasing the stress.

Over the next two weeks Diana sought and questioned seven eye specialists of assorted disciplines. As she tallied their opinions about treatment options for Tony's condition, she knew they would have spelled utter confusion for any parent.

For surgery: two in favor, one optometrist and one ophthalmologist.

Opposed to surgery: one ophthalmologist.

When to do the surgery: one vote for the very early years

and one vote for any age, depending on the circumstances of the case.

For prism lenses: a strong six votes, acknowledging the value of these lenses, but two votes of debate concerning the factors that determine the strength.

For orthoptics and/or vision therapy: one loud ophthalmological No! and one maybe—if fusion was intact. One soft optometric call for attempted vision therapy and one optometric acknowledgement of the slim odds of its effectiveness.

She decided to wind up this part of her investigation by returning to the indomitable Dr. Sam to get his opinion on hyperphoria as a cause of learning disabilities.

Once again, she found him unburdened by any doubt. To him, the eye problem was clearly *not* the cause of Tony's academic failure. "The woods are full of Ph.D.'s in English history who have poor fusion and who function fine, with no learning disabilities," he discoursed with conviction. "I myself had reversals as a child, and I still have stress in reading, but I had no learning disabilities. I don't feel that vision problems—other than blindness, of course—in any way impair learning. I've never seen a child with erratic, abnormal eye movements whose eye movements would have had anything to do with learning disabilities!" he expounded. "All that talk about visual perceptual problems and eye movement problems—well! As an ophthalmologist, I see no scientific information on the subject and our whole professional association has come out with a formal statement to that effect. Yes, a child may have bad vertical muscle imbalance, but lots of people who have this do just fine in school!"

He blew out a long breath, calmed himself, and glanced at Diana sheepishly, realizing she'd raised his ire again. Smiling, softening then, this friend she loved to challenge added, "There may be some visual-sensory *contribution* to the problem, but I don't believe it's the cause."

At Diana's request Tony was given one more ophthalmological examination, in his fifteenth year, by Dr. Sam Henry.

In true Dr. Sam fashion, he wrote his findings: "Examination showed visual acuity to be 20/20 OU without correction. Tony was orthophoric in the primary position, with full duction, and no pathological nystagmus. Convergence was excellent. He fused for distance and near. On Wirt stereo targets, he identified nine out of a possible nine correctly. Undilated fundascopy showed normal discs, vessels, and maculae OU. Impression: Normal ocular examination."

In short, Tony at fifteen showed no signs of hyperphoria, no problems with fusion, depth perception, or sharpness of focus.

On that day, in that office, in that doctor's opinion, Tony Petri's eye functions were completely normal.

On that night, in her journal, Diana wrote: "Regarding the question of the role Tony's eye function played in his school failure, this investigator remains thoroughly confused."

The guidance clinic team's report had shed some light on Tony's oft-diagnosed "perceptual problems"—another issue pertaining to his visual function. Ellen and the other examiners acknowledged eight-year-old Tony's directionality confusions and letter/number reversals, but they felt that these behaviors and Tony's failure to correct them were related more to stress than to neurological problems. The report read: "Compensation for mild perceptual difficulty has not taken place due to a lack of effort combined with anxiety."

With that statement, Diana's main question about the severity of Tony's perceptual problems was answered. His perceptual difficulty was mild; he should have adapted and found other ways of learning the required skills. Why hadn't Tony compensated? Was that a separate line of inquiry?

Wondering how much the parents had understood about this possible aspect of Tony's wrongness, Diana decided to question them. She found that after more than eight years, the Petris still felt confused about the meaning of the term 'perceptual problems.' Their bewilderment had in fact grown for some very common reasons. At times they'd been too intimidated to ask for explanations. When they did ask, the explanations were too confusing and they found themselves nodding their heads, pretending they understood. Inevitably, they stopped asking.

Diana hoped she could do a better job during a meeting she arranged for that purpose. "Perception is simply the brain's giving meaning to all those messages and signals repeatedly sent to it from the eyes, the ears, all the sense organs," she explained to the curious Petris. "It's the process of getting to know your world—to know all about the things, events, people, sensations that surround you. Just seeing or hearing or smelling or touching or tasting is not the same as perceiving. It's the brain that perceives that luscious smell as freshly baked bread even though no loaf is in sight. It's the brain that gives meaning to objects you touch as you grope through a dark room in the middle of the night. If you go to the top of a tall building and look down at the street below, your brain knows what your eyes don't. It helps you understand why those cars look so small from that height. Or have you ever had the experience of searching for some object that may be right in front of you?"

The Petris nodded.

"That's a temporary perceptual problem because your eyes get distracted by all the other objects and keep your brain from perceiving the one you wanted. The same thing can happen with sounds. Perhaps you've noticed we can tune out what we don't want to hear? Any parent of an adolescent knows that!" Diana smiled.

The Petris laughed knowingly. Tony was proficient at tuning out. Diana explained that, unlike Tony, some children have no control over hearing what they want to hear and can't tune out competing sounds.

"Perceptual problems related to school tasks come in many different forms too," Diana said. "Some youngsters may start to read a page and then lose their place, skip a word or even a whole line. All of a sudden, they've lost the meaning. They feel confused, but if they try again, they usually leave out some other line. Then comes the embarrassment, the dread of reading aloud."

Diana studied Mr. and Mrs. Petri to see if they were still with her. They were. She went on.

"The most common perceptual problem for school kids and the one that gets the most publicity is the one involving reversals of words and letters. You know this one, I'm sure. It was the cause of that first call from Tony's kindergarten teacher. There's a reason why reversal is such a common problem. Look at this chair," she said, rolling her desk chair in many different positions. "I can turn it all different ways, even upside down, and the image your eye sees keeps changing. But no matter how I turn the chair, your brain still tells you it's a chair. It doesn't matter if I show you a big stuffed chair, a modern chair, an old-fashioned chair, or even a broken one. Your brain has learned something about all of these objects that makes them be chairs—let's call it 'chairness.'

116

"When kids start school, though, the rule that makes a chair be a chair or things be things no matter how they're turned doesn't work any more. In school, perhaps for the first time, the child is exposed to the world of abstract symbols like numbers and letters which have their own rules. For the first time, a ball and a stick, depending on how they're positioned in space, have a different name and a different function. The letters b, d, p, and q are visually identical—they all have a ball and a stick. But, depending on where we put the stick, they're all different. That never happened with the chair!

"The sad fact is that when they start school so many kids aren't ready to remember which way that b or d goes or which way the numbers turn. Some can't even copy them correctly while they're looking at them. The eyes and the brain play tricks on them."

"Tony certainly had those problems. He still gets confused," Mrs. Petri confided.

"Well, he isn't alone," Diana continued. "Most kids learn the directions of letters and numbers by themselves, but about a fourth of all first-graders in our country aren't mature enough perceptually to master the symbol tasks of first grade. That means about a fourth of the kids are set up to feel failure at the beginning of their school careers. Some of those kids will 'grow out' of their problems, but others will go on failing, and failing youngsters find their own ways of handling feelings of failure. Tony may have had a very common perceptual problem, but he was not a very common boy. He was a bright boy and I'm just beginning to find out some of his rather unusual ways of handling those feelings."

"So you think this perceptual problem was the reason Tony couldn't read?" Mrs. Petri asked, hoping for a clear-cut answer.

"I think," Diana answered, "that Tony definitely had mild perceptual problems and some confusions between left and right. I think these were major factors in his feeling that something was wrong with him. I think he had some visual problems too. On top of that, Tony was bright, strong-willed, proud—he'd been the star in your household. You know how upset and confused you were when the teacher said something was wrong with him? Well, that little boy got the same message and we will probably never know exactly what he thought. You can be sure, though, that he was doing his own brand of thinking and figuring it out.

"Mrs. Petri, you told me how Tony used to spend long hours building airplane models and mechanical projects. You said they were neat, well put-together. That kind of ability doesn't fit for a seven-year-old with severe perceptual or attention problems. The psychologist, Emma Dern, said Tony was constantly moving, with no attention span. Why was he suddenly so wiggly and inattentive at the end of his third semester of first grade? Was it his perception, his eyes, his frustration, his will or pride, his distrust? There are so many factors."

Diana begged the Petris' patience with her investigation. It was too soon for simple answers. And, deep down, she didn't believe the explanation of Tony's severe academic retardation would ever prove to be simple.

CHAPTER 12

"What's his name? I'll go back and
talk to him now. I'll show him how hopeless
I am. I'll back over his face with a truck!"

Tony grinned. "I remember her. Yeah, the red hair, and she used to wear that Playboy bunny thing around her neck...." The grin slowly remolded into a sneer as he remembered more. "She thought she could help me. She tried. She was right to wonder about all those stories. I made 'em up. I was really great at snowing her. I could snow everybody. Why, I could still tell you things; even now—straight faced—I could lie and I could convince you." Tony at fifteen was spewing more disgust with the dark side of himself, condemning even his third grade imagination.

He was right about one thing. Miss Ellis' good intentions hadn't been enough. Four months into third grade, in spite of all of her efforts, Tony was going nowhere with his academics.

Inevitably, somebody ordered an evaluation on the eight-year-nine-month-old third grader—a complete test battery identical to the one done just five months earlier. Newberry School and Miss Ellis had remained in the dark about Tony's past. Tony, true to form, said nothing of that other testing to Carolyn Honeywell, the newest addition to his collection of psychologists.

The Gopher who met Miss Honeywell was different from the Tony of guidance clinic days. This boy had a teacher he liked. This boy was wearing eyeglasses. This boy was becoming a behavior problem. This boy failed one of Miss Honeywell's tests on "auditory memory for meaningful information." This boy, whose auditory memory had always been outstanding, was suddenly not wanting to remember what he heard.

Two things hadn't changed. Tony was still restless, inattentive. The eyeglasses hadn't changed that. And he was falling farther and farther behind his peers in school.

Following the testing, Ann Petri found herself sitting in another office waiting to hear another test report. After that elaborate report from the guidance clinic, the day she'd decided to ignore such things, she'd thought she was finished with these terrible ordeals. But what would the principal of Newberry have thought if she hadn't made an effort to come in? "The mother doesn't care about her boy"—that's what they'd think. She had to come. Once. She'd give Newberry School one chance.

Miss Honeywell seemed pleasant enough, and there were all the tests and numbers again. Ann was amused by Tony's portrait of himself dressed as a spaceman whose gigantic body dwarfed the rocket next to him. The untrained mother gave the drawing no psychological interpretation, but if she'd thought for a moment, it would have been easy. Tony now weighed 100 pounds and was 57 inches tall, standing seven inches above the average-sized boys in his class and outweighing them by 40 pounds.

Mrs. Petri vaguely listened to the psychologist talk about the intelligence test and Tony's highs and lows again.

"...is university material." The last words of Miss Honeywell's spoken paragraph registered late.

"Excuse me? What was that you said?" Mrs. Petri thought she had misheard.

"Why, I was just saying that Tony does have something wrong, but he has a fine mind and if he ever decides to learn I really believe your son is university material, Mrs. Petri." Then she added, "Whenever you break whatever it is that's holding back his learning, he'll be a marvelous person. I can't tell that to all mothers, Mrs. Petri. It should make you very happy."

The burdened mother had been totally unprepared for such a prophecy. She'd made herself so strong, so ready for more Wrongness, more advice for tutoring, for therapy. The one contingency she hadn't planned for was an ally.

In her joy at finding someone who recognized the potential of her son, she overlooked Miss Honeywell's other statement—"if he ever decides to learn." The implication was that Tony had *chosen* to stand still and that he could choose to climb out of the hole and head for the top of the academic mountain. Mrs.

Space man

Petri couldn't have known that the outcome of such a climb would depend on the depth of the hole, the strength and will of the climber, and the equipment he possessed.

Fulfilling the bureaucratic requirements of her job, Carolyn Honeywell officially declared Tony to be "1.8 years retarded in reading and spelling and .9 years retarded in math." She concluded, "There is not sufficient discrepancy [sufficient discrepancy was two years' difference] between achievement and grade placement to warrant EH [special class for educationally handicapped] referral at this time. This child is emotionally involved in a home-centered problem and needs a family-centered approach to ameliorate." Tony missed the qualification by two-tenths of a year.

The bureaucratic guidelines also required a list of recommendations for the amelioration of Tony's problems. The list was written and recorded in his file for Diana to find years later.

Diana read over the yellowed pages, wondering who else had seen them, and what they had meant to other readers. She pondered the odds, at that time and place, for implementation of any of the recommendations so sincerely prescribed. Like "kinesthetic activities." Who knew what that meant? Who was going to administer them?

"Strengthen visual perception"—was Miss Ellis supposed to do that? True, Miss Ellis had suspected "some sort of perceptual problem," but she had no experience with the remediation of that often-diagnosed-but-little-understood disorder.

"Praise and encouragement" had been listed. Any teacher could provide that, but praise and encouragement are empty, lost, suspect, to a bright child who knows too well that his work is a disaster.

Who would do what to build up and *maintain* "adequate self concept"? A Herculean request for one-to-one therapy; an impossibility for a teacher with 35 other students.

Surely Miss Ellis could not meet the demands of this list. All roads for help seemed to be leading to Miss Honeywell's final recommendation: referral to the PTA guidance service.

Could Tony now become "involved in guidance" after a year of resisting it?

Diana aimed her investigation at this newest hope—the PTA Family Guidance Clinic.

None of the Petris could remember the name of the man called "therapist" at the PTA Clinic. But they'd never forget his prophecies.

He had seen the Petris for four sessions—the full course of therapy for this facility, whose flyer described it as a short-term, crisis-oriented program, designed "to try to reduce stresses and pressures at home so the child can perform better at school." The standard method for achieving that goal: an interview with the parents alone, then with parents and child together, next with the child alone, and finally with the parents and child together once more.

At four different times during their year of contact, Ann Petri told Diana about the "stress-reducing" therapy. "The man told us Tony was hopeless." The mother looked furious. "A hopeless boy—unless we did something right away….But all he recommended was that Johnny get Tony interested in sports. Sports, of all things! I couldn't think what that had to do with anything, but we even believed him for a while. Well, he was a specialist, and the school had sent us and all. So we tried. Johnny would take Tony and they'd practice ball in the backyard," Ann Petri sighed, clearly troubled by the recollection, "but Tony just couldn't get himself to catch. And that man! He just didn't believe we were trying. I'll never forget his words. Never…never," her lips pursed while she mimicked, verbatim, the guidance man's curse: "'You're going to leave here and keep trying to talk this boy out of things, but let me tell you this. If you don't get control of this child now, when he's fifteen he's going to tell you to go straight to hell.' Can you imagine him saying such a thing? Well, you see," she said feistily then, "he was wrong. Tony's passed fifteen and he's *never* told us to go to hell!"

Relief and triumph showed on her face. But the weight of the curse must have been enormous, as this devout believer waited, watched, year after year, for the words to come true.

"I was so confused, so discouraged," Mrs. Petri continued. "That nice Miss Honeywell had just told us that Tony was university material. To have her wonderful words followed by that man's warning—I just didn't know what to think." She paused then, but went on to admit a private doubt: "I guess Tony showed his bad side to that man."

Even through her hurt and resentment, Mrs. Petri had still granted a shred of credibility to the specialist who had based his dire prophecy on four hours of contact.

John Petri wasn't as charitable. Usually the master of disengagement, forgetter of details, he neither forgot the man nor was intimidated by his manner or title.

"*That* guy?" The mild father suddenly exploded. "He was a goddamn liar. I don't know how that guy got a job. Tellin' us the only reason Tony can't read is because we have troubles at home and we don't control the boy. Well, Tony was a *good* boy—didn't make trouble for us *or* the school. He just couldn't read was all. I think that therapist needs reexamination himself. Tony didn't like him, that's for sure."

Tony didn't like him. For Tony, the PTA Guidance Clinic was another Miss Hinkle story. Only this time Tony didn't bother to censor or temper his responses. He let the expletives fly.

"That guy? He's an asshole, man. I'd still like to kick him. I hate the guy—he was a prick! He was so full of shit. He used to tell the Old Lady not to let me have a leather jacket. And I used to wear pointed shoes, and he said not to let me have those, or I would turn into a ruffian. I'll turn into a ruffian if I see him again! You know, I spit on that place every time I pass it."

Diana interrupted his outburst, needing to know if Tony had somehow provoked this man, had "shown the man his worst side," as Mrs. Petri had said.

Tony protested instantly. "No! I really didn't! *He* messed *me* up. For a while there, I was really messed up. He really freaked me out! I was no good after I saw that guy. I just remember that one session about the leather jacket. I never even *had* a leather jacket....What was I then, about eight or nine? Isn't that ridiculous? He didn't even *know* me—he just saw me once or twice, looked at my shoes, and started to say all these things would happen. What's his name? I'll go back and talk to him now. I'll show him how hopeless I am. I'll back over his face with a truck!"

The winter of Tony's third grade was no exception. Mrs. Petri followed the pattern that had begun after Tony's kindergarten fiasco. Every time he began a new therapy or suffered a new test battery, she would schedule him for a physical at the health clinic. Simultaneously with the family's exposure to the PTA Guidance Clinic came the winter physical.

By that time, Tony had developed a seasonal allergy pattern. Diana reviewed the medical records and learned that Tony had "slight wheezing," a colorless nasal discharge (an allergy symptom), frequent nosebleeds (common accompaniment to allergies), glasses "for hyperphoria," "visual-motor perceptual difficulty," and general obesity. There was no mention in the chart of referral to an allergist.

Only one prescription came out of that physical exam of the "hopeless" boy whose only comfort was food—a calorie chart.

By mid-year at Newberry School, Miss Ellis had decided to recommend retention. She'd tried everything, gone through all the available procedures—the evaluation, the referral to PTA Guidance—and made her own start with Tony in the classroom. The tutoring that Miss Honeywell recommended be "considered" had never materialized. If Miss Ellis could just keep Tony with her for the full year, she was sure she could achieve a breakthrough.

Mrs. Petri was less sure. Another retention would place Tony a full year behind. And he was so big. But the teacher seemed to care about him and was so interested. Didn't the teacher know best?

Mrs. Petri gave her consent. No consideration was given to the emotional toll on Tony as his classmates went ahead to the next grade and, as he phrased it, "All these little punks came in. Nobody could tease me very much," he testified, "'cause I was always bigger than them, but I felt even bigger than I was!" And little kids can chop you down without ever saying anything, if you know what I mean."

That winter, Tony stopped confiding in Miss Ellis. He quietly, totally stopped working. He never said anything to his parents about school. He just woke up, groped for his glasses, sneaked into the kitchen, gobbled goodies unlisted on the calorie chart, meandered tentatively to school, outlasted the school day, and came home in the afternoons—always the first one out of class.

One of those afternoons he arrived at his kitchen door and found it locked. Mrs. Petri was home, scrubbing the kitchen floor, and she yelled at him not to come in. He complained, but she persisted, asking him to wait.

He had been waiting all day. Waiting for recess. Waiting for lunch. Waiting for school to end. He rattled and pulled impatiently at the handle of the locked door, his fury silently building.

Then Mrs. Petri heard the crashing. The startled mother, sliding through the suds, was impeded in her efforts to rush out and see what was happening.

Outside, Tony had picked up a heavy rock, aimed it at his toy dump truck, heaved with all his might, and shattered the sturdy toy in that first blow, the rock rebounding off the truck and slamming into the wood fence. In a frenzy, Tony went after the rock and threw it again, then a third time, determined to demolish the toy that had been a prime source of after-school joy.

By the time Mrs. Petri got to him, Tony, tears streaking his dust-coated cheeks, was silently pulling apart the pieces of the truck. His mother was stunned. She had never seen him like this. He wanted no comfort from her, spoke no words of remorse; but she, believing he would be very sorry about what he had done, gave him a stern lecture. She couldn't recall her exact words—only her moral: that when you show your anger and hurt something, you hurt yourself more. Tony's nine-year-old strength and potential to destroy must have frightened them both.

Ann Petri couldn't recall seeing him destroy any other toys again. She later worried, in fact, about what had become of his anger and whether she might have been too stern with him.

Summer came. John Petri was recovering from another major surgery. Tony combed the neighborhood in search of jobs to help pay for his burgeoning mechanical hobbies. That summer was his first at mowing lawns. Mowing lawns brought good money, especially for a nine-year-old, but this nine-year-old was allergic to grass.

Tony arrived at school that fall more listless than usual after sleepless summer nights of respiratory distress in his room without air conditioning. Mother marched him back to the pediatrician once more. The doctor took another brief history from the mother only, drew his conclusions, and advised accordingly: remove the feather pillows and get rid of the cat.

With just a few more questions, the doctor might have diagnosed grass allergy without ever doing skin testing. The doctor never asked. The nine-year-old didn't know to tell.

Diana's review of Tony's medical records showed a pattern of visits to the pediatrician during other springs and falls. There were always comments on the charts about wheezing and nasal discharge. In spite of the fact that Tony's allergies were seasonal and obviously pollen-related, in spite of his history of school failure, there was no mention in the charts of referral to an allergist. Cost could not have been a factor because the medical clinic provided prepaid health services for all its members and had an allergy department on the premises.

Seven years after that third-grade year, when Diana's investigations brought her to Tony's former pediatrician, she asked the question: why had he never made the referral?

"The results of desensitization are not that good," the doctor stated with conviction. He granted that Tony had some symptoms, but since he'd been able to suppress them with medication he reasoned, "Why subject the child to all those years of weekly shots? Besides, Tony was doing quite well and the shots were not indicated."

The pediatrician's final comment rang in Diana's head. Quite well. Quite well at what? Tony's symptoms were fatigue and inability to pay attention. According to both mother and child, the medications to treat the symptoms also created fatigue and inability to attend. That meant both the illness and its "cure" were interfering with his ability to learn.

Having observed Tony's reaction to hemp that day at the junior high, Diana no longer doubted the effect of allergies on his concentration powers. She'd never seen the effects of the medication on him because he had long since refused to take it, saying it made him "too sleepy to function."

Diana kept wondering about this little-understood subspecialty called allergy. Why did it seem to be the ignored, disrespected stepchild of medicine? She'd often heard pediatricians question the effectiveness of desensitization. She'd wondered herself about its value and decided to seek some answers from Leo Ben Ami, a scholarly allergy professor who was in the throes of rewriting the basic textbook in his field.

Dr. Ben Ami was delighted to share his knowledge with her since he was even more concerned than she about the misinformation and prejudice that plagued his specialty. Acknowledging its scientifically shaky beginnings, he explained that, while the causes and characteristics of allergies were first uncovered in the 1900's, the process of giving injections for building sensitization wasn't available until the 1920's and 1930's.

Diana was puzzled and asked why the medical profession was taking more than fifty years to endorse desensitization.

"Well, Mrs. Cotter, unfortunately, there were no good research studies until 1960, so that meant, for thirty years, allergists' methods lacked professional validity. And it's easy to be suspicious of allergy treatments because of the nature of allergy itself. You see, an allergy is simply an unusual body reaction in people who are sensitive to certain substances. The automatic part of the nervous system makes the body respond automatically, causing the allergic person to lose control over bodily responses. But there's one other complicating factor. Emotions also are hooked up to that same automatic, or autonomic, nervous system. Consequently, people often believe that allergies are fake, or 'all emotional.' Since allergies and emotions share the same 'wiring,' so to speak, strong emotions like anger, fear, resentment, worry, and even lack of self-confidence all increase the probability of an allergic response. Mind and body really do work as partners in the allergy business.

"Unfortunately, early prejudices die hard. Our profession simply had to prove itself. Finally, by the mid-1960's, a number of excellent validated studies confirmed the value of the desensitization procedure. Those studies in the sixties—I guess your Tony would have been a preschooler at that time—verified for the first time that desensitization could really do what we claimed it could do. We were getting an 80% to 90% success rate. You can imagine the elation among my colleagues."

"But you must have published the results in the medical journals. Didn't other specialists hear about the findings," Diana inquired.

"The results were heralded in all the right journals. But you must understand that changes in attitude don't come easily in the medical world. Many doctors have no time to read outside their own specialty. Many of them had learned nothing about allergy in their medical schools, and of course, that's where attitudes are formed. For those and I'm sure other reasons the old pre-research mythology still dominates. Perhaps Tony's pediatrician was one of those who remained suspicious," Dr. Ben Ami conjectured.

"Suppose the doctor *had* been trained in allergy," Diana asked. "Was there a way Tony could have been treated without experiencing fatigue from medication?"

"First let me explain that there are three ways to treat allergies—by medication, by elimination of the substance causing the allergy, or by the desensitization procedure. I believe Tony could have been treated because desensitization is especially helpful for the types of allergies he suffered—the respiratory ones, particularly asthma and responses to seasonal pollens. Desensitization involves injections. If Tony was reacting to grass pollens, we would inject minute amounts of grass pollen and gradually his body would produce its own blocking agents against the trouble-producing substance. We'd start by giving these injections once or twice a week for a few months and then decrease the frequency to once a month, if he was responding well."

Diana interrupted. "There's the problem, Doctor. The big complaint I've always heard is that these shots have to go on for your whole life and this is why so many people seem resentful— like they're never cured and have to keep depending on their allergist. And they resent the cost too, over such a long time."

Dr. Ben Ami smiled fatalistically. "There's more mythology, I fear. You see, if the patient is truly a candidate for desensitization then the full course of treatment should take no more than two or three years, with an occasional booster later on if there is some special circumstance. That's *not* a long time, I feel, to have a life free of suffering. So few people realize the truth. I guess our specialty really needs a PR director," the academician laughed.

Diana thanked the doctor for the thorough explanation and left. As she mulled over her new understanding of allergy treatment, she realized that the Petris would never have initiated and followed up a desensitization program for Tony without the guidance of a doctor devoted to the value of the procedure.

The Petris never encountered such devotion. Tony had remained untreated.

"Playing hookey" was pretty innocent stuff in third grade. With Miss Ellis struggling, and failing, to determine his needs, Tony managed to be absent twenty-two days—more than a fourth of the total semester. Sometimes he pleaded exhaustion from his allergies. Sometimes his absences were more creative and were unknown to his parents.

Ann Petri discovered one of these by accident. The discovery provided her with some rare laughter in those days.

"I had dropped Tony off at school and I was half-way to work when I realized I had forgotten something at home," she related. "So I went back and there he was, home again. How he got there so fast I'll never know. I heard real loud music, and the front door was double-locked, so I came around to the back door thinking, 'What is going on here?' I knew Johnny had gone to visit some friends that day. Well, I walked in and there he was, dancin' to beat the band, stark naked, in the livingroom!" she chuckled. "Scared the liver out of him, seeing me there. Oh, that boy. I don't know how many times he came home like that, because I was away at work. But that was the only time I ever caught him."

Miss Ellis, meanwhile, was unconcerned with absences, either creative or authentic. She had bigger worries. By mid-semester, she admitted she was in over her head with Tony Petri and recommended a private tutor. Mrs. Petri, grateful for the teacher's supreme effort, respected her advice and pursued the referral.

On their first visit to the new tutor, Ann Petri was impressed by the great number of students pouring in and out and believed that was surely a sign of the lady's competence. Every half hour, new groups would arrive and be set up at different "study stations" in the house, as the tutor circulated from one to the other doling out the daily assignments.

After just four weeks, the tutor called Mrs. Petri to say that Tony "just isn't trying" and it was a waste of her time and his.

Tony's description of this abbreviated experience took Diana behind the closed door. He laughed devilishly as he said, "She had a guarantee. Can you believe that? She actually guaranteed that with her stupid games I would learn to read. She lost! I remember making the Old Lady think I was doing so well. She was so pleased, thinking I was making these great improvements. I would cheat so good. Ha, I was such a liar. The tutor would walk out of the room and I would look at the answers and copy 'em. She'd leave the answer book sitting right there; it was so easy. She used to call me 'Larry.' I'd say, 'My name is Tony.' She couldn't even remember my name and she used to give me someone else's homework. The best thing about that time was the Slurpies the Old Lady bought me afterwards, 'cause she thought I was trying."

Miss Ellis really *had* been trying, but her three-semester effort was coming to an end. She wrote her final comment on Tony in his December Cum: "Below grade level academically, though possesses much verbal information. Is being tutored in reading and has shown some improvement. Tries hard. Likes responsibility. Had made enough strides to be dismissed by PTA psychologist."

A tragic testimonial to public-school misinformation. The teacher had no idea that Tony had quit the tutoring after only weeks. She did not know that he had been dismissed as "hopeless" by the PTA psychologist, was given no meaningful therapy, and had had no opportunity to make any "strides." The mere referral to the PTA clinic brought an assumption of help to the teacher's mind. She so badly wanted something, someone to help Tony. She obviously had no knowledge of the clinic's operation or four-session method of functioning.

Were teachers informed about or expected to know about such things? Perhaps *not* knowing was the only way they could maintain an illusion of hope.

CHAPTER 13

*"If I ever do that bad again,
I'll go to a Home."*

"**R**ead each of the following sentences. Use brackets and the symbol NP to show where each noun phrase in a sentence begins and ends. Remember that noun phrases may also be part of the predicate of a sentence. Then decide which words are included in the verb phrase. Use brackets and the symbol VP to show where the verb phrase begins and ends. Put an X on all the helping verbs *in that verb phrase. They are verb signals indicating the main verb is to follow. The first two have been done for you.*"

For 10-year-old, older-than-his-peers Tony Petri, fourth grade was academic death.

For most of the kids, fourth grade was stomach-ache, nervous tic, I-don't-wanna-go-to-school time. No more time to acquire skills; time to apply them. Independently.

Fourth grade became a world of directions. Oral directions, long, rapidly delivered. Written directions, complicated, with weird, unfamiliar-to-nine-year-olds words and language. Fourth grade assumed that reading was to oneself, that writing was by oneself. Reports, outlines, letters, poetry—all to be executed in handwriting now, please.

Fourth grade brought the introduction of The Textbook. *Our Beautiful State. Our Wonderful Nation. Exploring Our World. Our Amazing Bodies.* Pages of text, camouflaged with pictures that were meant to entice. Nine-year-olds are rarely enticed, alas, by a fourteenth century reproduction of Marco Polo kneeling at the feet of the Great Khan. Chapter after forbidding chapter ends with little blue-outlined boxes entitled "To Help You Understand" or "Another Look at Unit III."

In short, the fourth grade curriculum presumed—rather, *de-*

manded—proficiency in reading, spelling, speaking, and writing.

With his reading score of "grade 1.5," fourth-grade Tony Petri was completely out of the ball park. He had only one objective—to survive each day as invisibly as possible, and get back to his neighborhood, where real life began.

In the previous semester, Sue Rosenberg, a fourth grade teacher who made no bones about her preference for high achievers, had joked with Annette Ellis over lunch one day about that "clutzy kid" she had noticed—who could miss him?—on the playground. Annette wasn't surprised when Sue candidly confessed that she hoped she "didn't get him" in her upcoming class.

She got him.

Mrs. Rosenberg wasted no time. Two weeks into the new semester, she did her job of "informing the parents," thus officially returning to them the responsibility for finding remedial help for Tony. She told Mrs. Petri that her son was doing absolutely nothing.

Something in the teacher's manner and words outraged Ann Petri that day. "I could tell what she thought about Tony. She thought he was dumb! I said, 'My son is not dumb, you know. I know he's not dumb, because he was tested right here in your school and they told me he had a very high IQ.' I even asked to see the records so I could prove it to her, and she had the nerve to tell me, 'You're not allowed to see them.' That woman! I didn't like her and she didn't like me. And she certainly didn't like Tony! She implied he was too dumb to learn."

Mrs. Petri became immobilized by this latest wound to her hopes. She found herself saying, "Tony, you're just not trying!" and him, never saying yes or no, and never getting mad—just staring at her kind of strangely and not saying anything at all.

Tony endured. He made it through a whole semester in relative happiness in Sue Rosenberg's classroom. She was busy with "the stars." She didn't understand or respect him, but she didn't torment him. He just kept his low profile, made no waves, did nothing, and was as invisible as a hundred-pound, fourth-grade "clutz" could be. And the months passed.

On the last day of that semester, Ann Petri entered her house to find no one at home. She called out for Tony but he wasn't around. Then she noticed an envelope on the dining room table.

Inside was Tony's report card, his dreadful report card, the final one from Sue Rosenberg. Propped up alongside the envelope was a note from Tony. A first. Ann was astonished. He had never even tried to write a note before. Of course, he couldn't spell, and it was a funny-looking thing, but it was a note and she could make it out.

It said, "If I ever do that bad again, I'll go to a Home. Tony."

That was how he signed it. Just "Tony."

The mother dropped her head into her hands and sobbed the uncontrollable silent tears she allowed only when no one was around.

It was a warm day. The classroom had been left open in search of an occasional cooling breeze. Instead of a breeze, the open door brought in the sounds of the custodian as he swept the paper, gum wrappers, and smashed milk cartons from under the benches nearby. The clatter of the gigantic rubbish bins finally caught the teacher's attention.

"Tony, maybe you should go out and help him," the teacher began, innocently enough. "The exercise would do you good." Ella Koontz laughed to lighten the barb.

Tony countered instantly with a lifeless "OK, I'll go," keeping his face a mask, hoping for a chance to get out of the classwork and away from this insulting person.

"No. Ohhh, no. You'd just love to get out of your work, wouldn't you, Tony? We can't have *that* happen now, can we?"

Every day it was something else, but there were no surprises any more. Not since the first time, in the first week of his promotion to Miss Koontz' upper fourth grade class. The first time really shook him. The intercom from the principal's office had jarred the class with its intrusive buzz followed by a voice requesting a student to run an errand. He hadn't been prepared for her comment.

"We have to give that job to Tony because he's the fattest one in the class and he can use the exercise. Right, Tony?"

He didn't know how to answer. He longed for the invisibility of his days with Mrs. Rosenberg.

"Looking back, I should have killed her." Adolescent Tony had the words for Ella Koontz now. "She was a mean, insulting person who shouldn't be allowed to teach." His voice quivered as he recalled some of the daily remarks she'd made in reference to his "fatness."

134

He described the husky woman with her orange-ish hair pulled up in a bun. "She always wore these things that looked like house-dresses and they were always too tight. You could see the buttons pulling, you know what I mean? Like she was stuffing her size 16 body into a size 12 dress. I used to just watch those buttonholes pulling and wish, just once, they'd pop right open. I couldn't figure out why she made such fun of *me* being fat when she was so fat herself! Maybe someone made fun of her as a kid and she had to hand it back to me.

"I'll never forget this system she had. She'd give out colored slips—white and red and blue and black. Black was for the worst. I always got black, of course," he said, his tone oozing resentment.

So Miss Ella Koontz was the lady with the colored slips Tony had mentioned with scorn in those early therapy sessions.

"What was the point of those colored slips, Tony?" Diana inquired.

"That was her own special stupid system for if you were a good student or a bad student." The "stupid" spat off his tongue. "You'd get a slip each day to show how you did on your work that day. You know how they do it, all those stars and stuff that teachers give. But she had all these colored slips. She never gave me anything but black. Not ever," he repeated.

He picked at an already bloody, bitten-to-the-quick fingernail. "I either tore 'em up or, if I brought 'em home, I'd light a match and burn 'em. I remember, the old man was asleep and the old lady was still at work, and I'd go into the kitchen and hold that black bugger-slip in my fingers, burning, 'til it just about burnt me, and then I'd drop it in the sink 'til there was nothing left but ashes. Ha! 'Take this home to your mother,' that creep said. No way.

"That Miss Koontz was something. I remember one time I had to stay after school, and I had a paper route and I wanted to get out really bad. She had these two girls there and she started talking to them and I said, 'Can I have my slip now?' and she said, 'Just a minute,' and—it really clicks now—I can remember I sat in the chair for one-and-a-half hours while that big fat-ass talked to those girls. I wanted to get out of there and finally the girls left and she said, 'Oh, do you want your slip now?' Here you go.'" He mimicked her high-pitched, sugary tone.

"I learned pretty quick never to talk back to her, because I realized, even when I was that young, that she *wanted* me to talk back, that she was just setting me up for some other insult," said the boy some had dared to call dumb. "I wouldn't give her the pleasure, so I just took it from her and didn't say nothin'.

"I did have one way of bugging her, though," he said, grinning at the thought. "I used to wear those hard black shoes with taps—you know, the ones with the pointed toes that bugged that guy from the PTA clinic? Well, those shoes made a real loud clicking noise on those hard floors, and I'd walk over real slow and loud to the pencil sharpener or someplace, and she'd always harass me about the noise, but there was nothing she could do about it. I never answered her fresh or anything—just clicked around in those shoes."

Then Tony described his spelling and reading lessons in the Koontz year. "I knew she considered me stupid, and whenever something had to be read out loud she always called on me first, just to embarrass me. If I'd screw up on a word, she wouldn't let it go or tell it to me. Oh, no that'd be too quick. She'd make me stand there in front of everybody and tell me to keep trying, pointing out how wrong I was. Over and over. And you know those spelling games they always used to have? Well, I used to try to hide. I didn't want to play at all because I knew I couldn't spell. But she'd wait 'til all the teams were set and then she'd find the best team with the smartest kids and she'd say, to the whole class, 'We'd better put Tony on this team to balance it out.' I didn't talk back, but I think I should have. I should have hit her as hard as I could, but I always backed away from things. I've just always figured that everything will come back to those who dole it out. Just like Miss Hinkle with that brain tumor. Yeah, it all comes back." He nodded, seeming relieved that his prophecy for ultimate justice had actually come true, at least in one case.

"Miss Koontz picked on me the most, 'cause I was the farthest behind, but I wasn't the only one. She tried to make examples of everyone. She was always proud to announce bad grades. 'Oh, you got another F,' she'd say. It was an interesting thing, though, about the other kids in that class. When she'd try to humiliate me while I was reading, the kids wouldn't laugh. In fact, there was always a kind of eerie silence, like they knew something was wrong—with *her*. By that time, I had a lot of

136

friends. I mean, they liked me, even if I didn't play their games and stuff. I guess they felt protected with me because I was so big and they knew I wasn't a bully, so they just hung around me a lot, especially the real little ones. We all knew something wasn't right about Miss Koontz." The sixth sense of school children.

The other faculty knew about Ella Koontz too. Her behavior was no secret among them. Privately, confidentially, they described her as "very disturbed." She had been pressured to retire early because of the insidiously destructive way she dealt with students. The teachers had learned to ignore her remarks, including the constantly negative comments about Tony. They were ashamed that she had been licensed into their profession. Unfortunately, her retirement came too late to help Tony.

"Oh, Tony Petri. Yes," Ella Koontz said over the phone. Diana had sought out the retired teacher, curious to know if she remembered Tony, eager to hear the teacher's perceptions of this boy who felt so victimized by her. "He was one of those who just put in his time but was never really interested." The midwestern nasal accent came through the receiver. "There were even times he showed he *had* some intelligence. He did have one fantastic ability—for making money. That he certainly could do. As I recall, he helped in the cafeteria." She paused, then added, "It was a puzzlement to me as to why he never did his work. It was a family thing, I believe. Something about his father and mother—I think that was the problem."

Diana thanked her for her time. There was nothing else to say.

Tony was assigned to a second semester with Ella Koontz. A full academic year.

"Tony's worst year of all," as Ann Petri perceived it. But she never knew why. She would try to find out why he was always so short-tempered and cross those days, but he wouldn't talk. At dinner on the nights when he would bring home a bad paper or would refuse to bring home any work at all, she often found herself parroting, "Tony, you're not trying!" and then hating herself for joining the ranks against her own son.

During that traumatic year, Mrs. Honeywell, the school psychologist, called Mrs. Petri and recommended Tony be considered for an EH classroom. Mrs. Petri, believing the "EH" stood for Emotionally Handicapped rather than Educationally Handicapped, vehemently opposed the idea.

"Tony was *not* emotionally handicapped," the mother explained to Diana. "I went and observed those classes, and some of those children were so pitiful. It would have turned Tony completely off to be put in that classroom. My boy was not retarded and he didn't misbehave and act wild. I suppose they didn't like what I said, but I had to say 'No' to the EH class. Whenever I went to school, Diana, I always had that awful feeling they were saying, 'Oh, oh, here comes the mother and she's not quite "all there" and she thinks her child is absolutely perfect when we know he's dumber than…sin.' It's sickening. You know, when he's six years old, it isn't so bad, but after the ninth or tenth year you about give up."

Tony's school system had 700,000 children. By state law, two percent of them—approximately 14,000 students—could qualify as educationally handicapped. The EH program had been in operation for only five years, with 300 classes, ten students to a class. That meant that of the 14,000 students in need, only 3,000 could be served—the 3,000 most severely troubled, of course, the ones most desperately in need of removal from the classroom.

Tony was, by fifth grade, clearly and significantly "behind his peers," but not yet a "desperado."

The year of Ella Koontz was the year Tony began "roaring." He would come home from school, say absolutely nothing about his day, eat quantities of junk food to salve his soul, jump on his bicycle, and roar—up and down the street and around the corners, jumping over curbs and performing high-speed "wheelies" over homemade wooden ramps of varying heights. The slow, lethargic, indifferent giant of Newberry School was the roaring, hot-rodding race-driver of Hodgkins Street. Mr. Petri, often at home in some state of convalescence, would hear the screeching of brakes and sliding of tires as Tony circled round and round the block, all afternoon, every afternoon. His vigor was so intense, his desire for constant increase in speed and daring so strong that even the broken wrist he suffered one day, when he skidded too far and hit a wall, didn't deter him from this new outlet for his frustrations.

That year, Tony met Danny Travaglini, who was to become

his best friend, on one of his roars around the block. Danny was half a yard shorter than Tony and had a rare eyelid deformity that forced him to look at the world through eighth-inch slits of light. But, incredible though it seemed, Danny could read. Tony served as Danny's eyes, Danny's muscle. And, in return, Danny helped Tony to read. Tony was Danny's best, and only, friend. Danny, too, was a roarer and a bike-freak during those fifth grade afternoons. Both boys had customized their bikes, and their admiration for each other's inventiveness was the factor that drew them together.

Danny described Tony as the instigator for everyone on the block in those days. If Tony would add some new device to his bike, everyone else would too. His size, air of maturity, and mechanical abilities gave him a presence never seen in the classroom. On Hodgkins Street, Tony reigned. He reigned without being an athlete, without playing on teams. On the block, it made no difference that he couldn't read.

Totally fascinated by mechanical things, the Rube Goldberg of Hodgkins Street was always engineering something new. He had the only ten-wheel "truck trailer" wagon in town. He'd rigged together two wagons with ten wheels on four axles, added a tail-gate ramp that worked on pulleys and ropes, and hooked up the whole contraption to the back of his bike so that his legs became the power source for the entire mechanism. He was constantly refining the fold-down tail-gate, modeling his revisions after the lids on the dumpsters in the back of the supermarket. This extraordinary "truck" became his work machine for loading and hauling his garden equipment as he moved around to his neighborhood jobs.

Danny Travaglini described how Tony financed his inventions. "He'd con his mom to buy him everything, and he'd promise her a great house when he was rich and famous some day. He was such a total fibber—you never know, to this day, whether to believe him or not, and his mom was such a sucker for him. He was always fantasizing and telling these fantastic stories. And he was so sure he knew more than anybody else about mechanical things, even when he was a little kid. He used to make bets with Jim Norris, our neighbor, about mechanical things—and Jim was a professional mechanic! Tony was so sure of himself, he'd say to Jim, 'I'll bet you, for your *car*, that I'm right.' We all laughed about it, but I think Tony really meant it when he made those bets."

Tony's rampages had pretty much "gone underground" since the episode with his dump truck in the backyard. He was still fascinated with destroying things, however. When Tony and Danny would be working on their bikes or on Tony's wagon and some part wouldn't work right, Tony would just take out the uncooperative part and heave it across the yard. He might have spent weeks building a plastic car model, getting everything perfect. Then he'd come home after a particularly bad day at school, pour lighter fluid on the model, and set it on fire, or take it out to an empty lot and blow it up with a firecracker that he'd saved from the Fourth of July. He seemed to *need* to tear things apart. A favorite target was always a stray beer can. Tony would crush the can under his heel, grinding it under his weight until it would crack. Then he'd pry it open with a stick and proceed to rip the entire can into little pieces.

Nobody but Danny ever saw him setting fire to his possessions. Nobody but Danny ever saw him heaving objects or ripping cans. Danny always laughed and said they both had the same kind of temper—sudden, furious, and over quickly. That's why they were such good friends.

The schools were changing from a semester system to an annual promotion system—no more B and A designations for each half of the school year. The new system meant that all students would enter a grade in September only and spend a full year in each grade. Tony had just turned eleven. After two semesters of no progress with Miss Koontz—the A4 and B5— Tony had few options for fall semester placement. He would have to repeat the fifth grade. Tony wasn't bothered by this, his third semester retention in five years; since the whole school was involved in this adjustment most of his class stayed with him.

His summer eye check at the union clinic brought another change in diopter measures. Up to five now, said the new report. Dr. Frank decided to strengthen the prescription, making the prisms thicker, thus magnifying The Gopher's eyes even more. However, the optometrist suggested there was no need for Tony to continue wearing his glasses all the time, since they were "only essential for schoolwork now."

How easy for Dr. Frank to say! Tony, now totally dependent on the glasses, was afraid to take them off even though he hated them. Seeing Tony's reaction, the doctor left the choice of use up to the boy, who continued to wear them from the moment of waking up to the moment of sleep.

"Come right in, young man," Harold Broder boomed, inviting the reluctant fifth grader into his classroom. Tony could hardly believe his eyes. A man teacher. He hadn't known there were any, had always thought teaching was a conspiracy controlled by females. Now he'd have a man—a tall man.

At home in his over-six-foot body, Mr. Broder moved confidently and sat informally on the edge of his desk. A full head of all-white hair belied his age, somewhere circling forty. The teacher's voice was masculine, pleasant-masculine, and his face offered easy smiles. He looked at kids when he talked to them, Tony noticed right away. He looked at kids when they talked to him, too. He listened. His manner, more than his words, told them he liked his job.

Very quickly, Harold Broder noted the early signs of puberty in this three-times retained fifth grader with the hoarse, changing voice. Very quickly, too, he learned of Tony's grossly inadequate reading ability. But he ignored it. He had a theory about kids like Tony. He believed that at some earlier time Tony had had an extreme frustration—had been unable to do something—causing him to develop what Broder liked to call "a block." He had often seen kids who blocked like that. Most of them had the trouble, he theorized, at around second grade.

Since there was basically no remedial help at Newberry, and little or no awareness of perceptual problems, Mr. Broder had developed his own approach to these kids. He took the time to find their strengths.

He found Tony's. Social studies. Projects and plays. Tony became Expert in charge of props, special effects, and murals. The other kids had a sense of wonder about him, didn't know what to make of him. They knew he couldn't read, but he could turn their ideas into realities. He became the classroom cameraman, and every electrical or mechanical problem became his bailiwick. Some of the kids even said out loud that he was "pretty smart." Tony Petri was suddenly acquiring some new descriptors.

Even though the other kids liked him and sought his advice, Tony stayed cautious, a loner. He never pushed himself into a situation, but quietly basked in the praise he got, particularly for his mural work. That was how he liked it.

Years later, Diana Cotter was able to find Harold Broder, still teaching fifth grade at Newberry. His recollections about Tony were clear, his attitude accepting.

"Tony was remarkable," Mr. Broder began. "Even though his reading level was first or second grade, I found that, if I could verbalize with him, he knew and understood every concept. I geared his work down. At that time, we had begun to group kids and use multiple texts instead of one basic text for everybody, so it wasn't a problem to have him working at his own level—I mean, it didn't have to be embarrassing.

"There was a beautiful teamwork that grew up in that class. The rest of the kids happened to be outstanding in writing ability, so they would write the plays and Tony would implement them. It was quite extraordinary. If you took the printed page away from him and got into the world of ideas, he was great. He didn't confide in me, but I understood that. It's tough for us men to open up sometimes," the tender man chuckled. "But he was an awfully nice person to have around. He had a placid disposition and could never do enough to be helpful." Then, matter-of-factly, Mr. Broder said, "He used to do wonderful book reports. I'd read the book to him, he'd tell me what to write, and I'd write it."

Diana felt her skin prickle. How casually the man spoke of this minor miracle. A book report from Tony Petri!

"His mother really cared and realized his inadequacies," Mr. Broder gave yet another unique perception of a Petri. "I think she, too, realized his abilities and was frustrated by the disabilities."

Harold Broder was the first teacher to get Tony to publicly expose his strengths in a *school* situation. The strategy: believing in the boy, respecting him, and adapting the curriculum to his strengths.

Fate plays strange, cruel tricks in the lives of humans. Just as Tony's fortunes at school were turning, something was happening at home that would seriously diminish Harold Broder's effectiveness that year. Ann Petri developed cancer.

142

In February Ann Petri endured a unilateral radical mastectomy, followed by six weeks of recovery at home, then six weeks of radiation therapy.

Nobody ever really talked to Tony about the nature of the surgery. Tony remembers that a girl in the fifth grade came up to him and said she was sorry, and he asked, "What are you sorry about?" He didn't know what was going on. The Petris never discussed such details of privacy and pain with each other. His mother had been too shy, too ill at ease to talk about it. But for the first time Tony saw the family's supporter and strength, who had never missed a day of work, suddenly bedridden, weak, pale, hurting.

Tony missed thirty-five days in the second half of the school year. He stayed home to help care for "the Old Lady." Sometimes his parents asked him to stay and help. Other times, if they didn't ask, he faked illness so that he could stay. "I didn't like school anyway, so I stayed home to help," he justified.

Actually for once, Tony *did* like school. But his allegiance to being where he sensed he was most needed came first.

Ann Petri discussed her cancer with her usual strength and economy of words. "I felt it was a trauma for Tony. I was all bandaged, and every day I had to stand by the wall and try to move this arm against it." She crawled the fingers of her left hand up the wall, elevating her arm slowly, demonstrating. "To be able to completely lift that arm by the end of six weeks was almost a miracle, but I had to do it. You see, it was important that I get back to work by a certain time in case they hadn't removed all the cancer, so that my job would still cover me for the medical care."

Diana could not believe the will of this woman she was slowly beginning to know on her own merits rather than through the judgments of others.

The professionals Diana had interviewed had each spoken with such authority about Mrs. Petri, but it seemed impossible they were all talking about the same woman.

"This mother was overprotective," one teacher had confided.

"This mother was rejecting of her child," a therapist had proclaimed.

"His mother was so crazy about him!" another teacher declared in sympathy.

"This mother was concerned and anxious. It was a helpless situation," said a tutor.

"This mother was exhausted and overwhelmed from what she saw and felt as total responsibility for the care of herself and her child." Another therapist.

"This parent-child relationship was not as it *should* be!" a tutor had condemned, a tutor who just happened to be single and childless.

"She seemed too soft and caring, almost spoiling Tony," a teacher remarked.

"His mother really cared and realized his inadequacies." This comment now, from the teacher Tony loved best.

"We couldn't get his mother to believe we could help him," a puzzled reading specialist had remarked.

"I felt his mother leaned on this 'perceptual problem' as an excuse more than a reason for Tony's lack of performance," said a teacher who admitted to no background in perceptual problems.

"This mother was the one who made all the things happen."

"This mother was..."

Diana pondered what it meant to be a "mother," with the flood of advice from society. The "shoulds" were everywhere—in magazines, newspapers, on television, in casual conversations with friends and family, in asides from doctors and strangers.

Ann Petri was one mother who tried to make all the shoulds come true. Her vulnerability to the fluctuating judgments of others had enveloped her in self-doubt and guilt, each imperfect act performed by her child driving her from one helping service to another.

Facing cancer, though, she needed help for herself. Strength. Recovery. Now Diana understood those dawn visits to the church. Morning mass must have provided solace when events seemed to move increasingly beyond her control.

By June, Mrs. Petri was indeed back at work.

In June, the fifth grade classes at Newberry School took the state achievement tests. Tony scored Stanine 1 in reading comprehension and math and Stanine 2 in reading vocabulary, language, and in spelling, which meant that somewhere in his state there were students functioning even lower than he, a reality Tony would have found hard to believe.

CHAPTER 14

*"My mom was such a pushover
for those kinds of guys."*

"**H**ey, Mrs. Cotter. I've got a great joke for you today." Tony clomped into the teacher's lounge, in high spirits that day. "Why does an Italian mother have such heavy arms?" he began the joke, positive she was longing to hear it.

"I don't know, Tony. Why does an Italian mother have such heavy arms?" she giggled, anticipating another of Tony's one-liners.

"From lifting dumbbells! Dumbbells! You get it?" He guffawed, delighting himself.

Diana laughed, too, pleased that he could laugh at a joke that might have come too close to home.

Then Tony opened his spiral notebook, tenderly took out an illustrated brochure, and placed it with care in front of her on the desk. "That's it. That's the one. They're holding it for me at Glenview Harley, but the Old Lady doesn't know."

Diana glanced at the fold-out cover picture of a moon-like desert landscape at twilight, a young man pitching his lean-to tent and a gorgeous cycle parked in the foreground, its chrome gleaming in the sunset. "HARLEY-DAVIDSON. THE GREAT AMERICAN FREEDOM MACHINES," said the red-white-and-blue print beneath the scene.

She opened to the text and read, "The SX-175. As tough a cycle as there is. After you've spent a day wheeling and dealing around on your SX-175, nobody will be able to tell you a thing about freedom."

Freedom. Tony didn't need to read those words on the brochure. The photo was seduction enough. Diana let him say all he had to say and then asked him to educate her about this particular bike.

Planning her timing precisely, she artfully captured the moment and guided him into a lesson.

"Hold on a minute, Tony. I want to write down your words. Dictate to me what you know about the SX-175 and give me the reasons you want this one instead of a different model."

"Hey. Pretty good trick." Tony knew he was being maneuvered. "Did you plan the whole thing?" he asked, not angry.

"Yeah." Diana knew he'd catch her, but that was her business. "If you want to grow up to be a rose instead of a weed, we've gotta do more than talk here, Mr. Petri. But go slowly so I can stay with you."

He talked and she wrote. He watched her write his words and say them aloud as she recorded them. She put it all down, even the part about his mom saying if he doesn't quit school when he turns sixteen, she'll buy him the motorcycle.

When she finished writing, Diana asked Tony to read back the words she'd just written—just as she always asked him to do when they worked on dictations. He read perfectly, and she beamed.

"You're getting pretty good, fella."

"Yeah," he allowed a half-smile. "Just keep it to yourself."

Not ready to go public yet. She respected that. Comparing the new Tony to the old one was fine, but the standard expectations for a ninth grader were another story.

Tony changed the subject quickly then, asking her if she knew of any place that taught teenagers to stop smoking.

"I didn't know you smoked, Tony," she expressed her surprise.

"No, it's not for me. It's for Ginny. This girl I know."

"Somebody special?" Diana asked spontaneously.

"Naw...well, not really. Well, yeah, I do like her. But I *hate* smoking and she knows it. Now she's started lying to me about it, and the other day I caught her sneaking a smoke and I got so mad I really scared her."

"Where'd you meet her, Tony?" Diana asked, intrigued to see the beginnings of interest in the opposite sex, a topic that had never before been able to compete with the machines in his life.

"Oh, at a party. Some friends I ride bikes with had this big barbecue party. They had it all planned but never told me I was being fixed up. Boy, were they surprised when I showed up with Danny Travaglini. That'll teach 'em to surprise me like that!" He laughed at the thought of their faces when the "odd

146

couple" showed up at the door. "Anyway, that's where I met Ginny, and she'd be all right, for a girl, if she'd just give up that smoking crap."

Diana wrote down some places that advertised they helped people stop smoking, but she wasn't sure if they took teens. Then it was her turn to change the subject because she needed that hour to pick Tony's brain about the questions that kept arising out of her investigation.

"Tony, I found out that in the sixth grade you went to a vision therapist—a Dr. Hartunian. What was that all about?" Diana asked.

"Oh, that guy," Tony snickered. "Well, there I was, goin' into sixth grade and I still couldn't read or write, and the Old Lady was going nuts trying to figure out what was left for her to try next. She had some friend—*some* friend!—who told her about this guy Hartunian. Was that what he did—vision therapy? I never knew what you called it, but that guy was a real eager beaver. He was a little guy with glasses, but I remember the first thing he said to my mom, after he examined me, was that I had to stop wearing mine. And he wasn't fooling around. I mean, he came on so strong to the Old Lady, she really got scared. He said if I kept wearing them, they'd have to keep getting thicker and thicker for me to see out of them.

"The thing about that guy was he was so *positive* he was right, and my mom was such a pushover for those kinds of guys. She didn't know what to think, because I'd just had my prescription changed, and the new glasses *were* thicker, so she thought this Hartunian must have been right. After all, my eyes weren't getting any better from those glasses, and I sure wasn't any professor on my reading with 'em."

Diana had seen the reports from Dr. Hartunian about sixth grade, 12-year old Tony. He still drew a ball and a box from right to left instead of left to right, and his eyes turned inward and upward. Without his glasses, Tony saw double, off and on, and was "under great stress, especially when doing a task that requires concentration," said the report. There was the stress again.

Dr. Hartunian had demonstrated all of this to Mrs. Petri, who was impressed with his sincerity, his persuasiveness. But she was so confused about the "double vision" part. Just the summer before, Dr. Frank had told her there was *no* more double vision. Strange. Dr. Hartunian had mentioned surgery for Tony's problem, but felt that such a drastic step was not advisable without first trying vision therapy.

So Tony began vision therapy. Once a week, at $25 per hour, with follow-up exercises to be done at home nightly.

Tony admitted to Diana that he cried when he was told to stop wearing the glasses, complained for days that his eyes hurt, and got headaches without them. But he did as he was told. After about a week he stopped complaining. He obeyed, he said, not because he loved the doctor, but because he hated being the Gopher. He, too, was scared by his dependence on those glasses. And, this time, he was not being given a choice.

The doctor had told Mrs. Petri the therapy would take "from four months to three years," depending. Depending on Tony's efforts. Depending on his eyes' responses to the exercises. Just depending.

Dr. Hartunian had lost his certainty when the question came around to "how long." From four months to three years? What on earth did that mean? Ann Petri weighed her uneasiness against the doctor's enthusiasm and decided to begin.

Tony worked with Dr. Hartunian from August to November of his sixth-grade year. Once a week, in the doctor's office, he would work on eye movements and directionality. Every night during that eleven-week time span, he would lie on the floor at home and do his Marsden ball therapy.

"I would tie a string to a ball and watch it with my eyes as my mom would make it go around and around over my head. Or I'd sit in his office and look all around the ceiling. Real interesting things like that. He had a whole flock of fun machines that did stuff like that," Tony ridiculed, his tone of voice revealing his disdain. "We both felt dumb doing those exercises. I thought they were worthless and I told the Old Lady not to spend all that money. They just weren't helping me that much. I know she wondered about it, too—it seemed so stupid. We didn't do it very long. Pretty soon after that, we quit."

Tony's memory was correct. After the seventh session, Mrs. Petri announced to Dr. Hartunian that they were quitting. As always, she felt obliged to furnish an excuse. She told him that she'd been sick, unable to work, couldn't afford treatments anymore. Not so far from fact. But the real reason was a new kind of growth in her—the cancer of doubt. She was beginning to expect to lose if she didn't see results immediately. Even the mystique of "doctor" had lost its hold. Tony was showing no improvement in school, and the family couldn't afford a $25-an-hour uncertainty.

The option of vision therapy ended abruptly.

Diana sought out Dr. Hartunian, not knowing what to expect. After listening to Dr. Sam's tirades about vision therapists, she had conjured up an image of a fast-talker who would peek through a hole in the door and send her away when she told him the true reason for her visit.

She was wrong. Rather than fearing her, Dr. Hartunian welcomed her, gave her unlimited time, a tour of his facilities, and expansive conversation about the case of Tony Petri. He put lenses on her, altering her vision to duplicate the way the doctor believed Tony's world must have looked to him in those early years. Dr. Hartunian's passion for his specialty was convincing, enticing. He described the hows and whys of vision therapy, demonstrated his techniques, and strongly impugned the over-use of lenses. Diana found her usually suspicious, professionally trained self nodding her head in agreement with his conclusions.

Dr. Hartunian's zeal fed on the limitations of traditional corrective procedures, on the doubts everyone has about what is "right" for their loved ones. Improving vision without lenses—what an intriguing, seductive idea!

"I gave the mother the Marsden ball exercises to keep her happy and involved," the doctor explained then. "I need parents to help me diagnose because they observe the child so much more. Mrs. Petri was really conscientious, but she did not thoroughly understand the extent of the visual and educational handicap Tony had. She expected a miracle to solve his problem with limited time and budget. She had no patience to stick it out."

No patience. If this man only knew about Ann Petri's patience.

Patience was not the problem. Credibility was. Dr. Hartunian had failed to apprise himself of his client's past searches and battle wounds. Even more, he had failed to prove, in the limited

149

time the mother had granted him, that he could do what he claimed he could.

Diana had the same question. She asked the doctor for literature about his field. He gave her some position papers and tracts from the Association for Vision Therapy, a professional society to which he belonged. He had no research papers available and no exact references, but he implied that these existed.

As Diana scanned the tracts, clauses that could have been describing Tony jumped out at her: "...such a youngster must use excessive energy and efforts just to keep the eyes pointing at the reading distance...he would rather not do anything difficult...would rather look out the window than read...often labelled as having a short attention span, not trying, having a behavioral problem, or being just plain dumb...human nature dictates that what a child doesn't do well, he would rather not do...often gives up and develops a strong dislike for school..."

Then came the conclusion: "There is an absolute direct relationship between the child's ability to team his two eyes and his ability to learn to read successfully....Many children have a directionality problem," said the tract, "which, we feel, has the more direct relationship to the reading problem....Vision therapy, which is directed towards establishment of a firmly established left-to-right direction pattern, will produce more positive results in a shorter length of time."

The descriptions of behaviors were precise, perfect. But Diana knew that the conclusions were the cause of all the flap among eye specialists. Vision therapists concentrated on eye movements and directionality, but had correction of those problems, *in isolation,* proven to be enough to turn non-readers into readers?

She searched the library for scientific evaluations of vision therapy but was unable to locate any of the research to which the doctor had alluded. Instead, she came upon the joint statement issued by the American Academy of Pediatrics, the American Academy of Ophthalmology and Otolaryngology, and the American Association of Ophthalmologists—the famous position paper Dr. Sam Henry had mentioned regarding visual training for the treatment of learning disabilities. That three medical subspecialties had combined on this issue gave the paper tremendous power.

Diana noted the essentials of the oft-quoted document: Learning disabilities, she read, require a multi-disciplinary approach—including medicine, education, and psychology—in their diagnosis and treatment. Children with learning disabilities have the same incidence of visual abnormalities as children who are normal achievers and are reading at grade level. Underlined for emphasis was the following statement: *"Eye care should never be instituted in isolation when a patient has a reading problem."* The report claimed that "Studies had shown that there was no eye defect which produced dyslexia and associated learning disabilities....Eye defects do not cause reversals of letters, words, or numbers."

The document attacked the lack of scientific support for claims that gains in academic abilities can be achieved solely by visual training or "neurologic organizational training," such as laterality, balance board, or perceptual training. The report charged that such training has "frequently resulted in unwarranted expense and has delayed proper instruction for the child."

The unnecessary prescription of glasses, which "may create a false sense of security that may delay needed treatment," also was challenged. Except in cases of truly correctable visual defects, glasses have no value, the report indicated, in the specific treatment of dyslexias or other learning problems. The charges were a strong indictment of vision therapy.

The position paper concluded with a clear call for cooperative effort by the multiple professions to improve an educational problem whose ultimate remediation would be the responsibility of educational science: *"Ophthalmologists and other medical specialists should offer their specialized knowledge...[to] assist in bringing the child's potential to the best level, but the actual remedial educational procedures remain the responsibility of the educators."*[1]

Dr. Hartunian had not recommended educational therapy in conjunction with his vision work. He had been devoted to vision therapy as *the* answer for remediation of Tony's learning disabilities. The doctor had failed to address one crucial question:

---

[1]Jennison, M., et al. *The Eye and Learning Disabilities.* Joint Organizational Statement of American Academy of Pediatrics, American Academy of Ophthalmology and Otolaryngology, and American Association of Ophthalmology, June 30, 1971.

even if the boy's eyes and directional sense had been magically made perfect, wouldn't Tony still have emerged from vision therapy an illiterate academic failure, one more year behind his peers?

Diana would never know the value of vision therapy for Tony. Mrs. Petri's rapidly fading ability to trust ended the experiment prematurely.

The mother started something new that November—using professionals to check on professionals. She'd abandoned Dr. Frank, given Dr. Hartunian seven sessions with her son, and then gone to a brand new optometrist to check on Dr. Hartunian. But the new doctor got new diopter numbers again—something about a "4 right hyperphoria at distance, 7 right hyperphoria at near." He said Tony saw double at a distance but not up close.

And what was this doctor's recommendation? Stop all vision therapy and get a complete evaluation at an educational therapy center.

The family had come full circle.

One door was closing.

There was a quiet time that followed the last eye exam. A resting time. A time to think.

Terry and Janet Robinson didn't know it, but they would be the last private source of help ever sought by the Petri family. Mrs. Petri came to see them, in that sixth grade year, after finding an advertisement for their center in the *Daily News*. She had discarded all her old rules about finding experts. The newspaper seemed as good a source as any to her now. Why not? Lately, more and more articles on dyslexia and learning problems had been appearing in the paper. She read everything hungrily, often learning things she'd never heard from any professionals. When the Robinsons' ad appeared, she clipped it, adding it to her bulging file on Tony, and called for an appointment.

Terry and Janet Robinson had just finished their training. Their youthful optimism bolstered the flagging energy of the formerly determined mother. Ann Petri went through the initial interview in a foggy state, too tired to question, but she found Terry Robinson "a most charming man" with his bright blue eyes and trimmed goatee. He must have been charming indeed; the leery mother signed a six-month contract for Tony to attend

152

a half-hour remedial session once a week. She understood that Tony was to follow up the sessions with a series of recordings to be used nightly at home.

The Robinsons' center was furnished for very young children. They hadn't expected to begin with a pubertal twelve-and-a-half-year-old. Tony sat there in his 5-foot 10-inch, 187-pound reality, tragicomically overlapping their primary-school chair, his legs doubling back under the miniature table so that when it was time to leave he limped for a minute until the circulation returned. Tony tried not to notice the juvenile posters and alphabet cards that decorated the walls. After going over sounds and perceptual exercises for his scheduled half hour, Tony was expected to go home, sit at the kitchen table, and repeat phonic sounds and rhyming words back to a tape recorder. Phonic sounds and rhyming words. His sixth year of them.

Tony sat at that kitchen table by himself, not wanting anyone to see him engaged in this babyish, insulting task. The tapes commanded him to repeat. And repeat. And repeat. By the third repeat, the repeat was a shout. He was shouting at the machine.

His parents listened from the next room, helpless.

Janet Robinson sat behind the reception desk in her combined role as receptionist, secretary, clerk, welcomer, and—when time permitted—remedial specialist. She moved about with an athletic self-assurance. She greeted Diana warmly, and the two of them went into a small office for privacy.

Janet remembered the Petris clearly, especially the parents, who took turns bringing Tony. "I talked a lot to Mrs. Petri in the reception room," she told Diana. "Our hardest problem was getting her to believe we could help him. I guess she'd had help earlier and stopped it in midstream." Diana nodded.

"She told me she stopped because Tony didn't seem to be moving fast enough, or wasn't interested. I never thought the reason for stopping was finances. I think she just had a hard time accepting that her son had a *major* learning disability and that that kind of thing doesn't change overnight. I had the impression she had dabbled here and there in the hope that somebody was going to do magic—you know, touch his head one day and say, 'Ta-da, your son reads!'"

153

"What about Mr. Petri?" Diana asked. "How did he feel about things?"

"He was different," Janet said. "When he brought Tony in, he seemed very hopeful and encouraged the boy. Mr. Petri saw progress and mentioned it to us, but his wife just didn't see any. Tony seemed to have absorbed some of that magical thinking of his mom's. Sort of, 'I'm here. Fix me,' like there was no work necessary. Oh, he'd do the homework sporadically, and when he did we praised him highly.

"Of course," she admitted frankly, "we were just beginning then, ourselves. Now we would want to see him two or three times a week, not just once, with the kind of severe problem he had. It took a long time for my husband to form a working relationship with Tony because Tony would carry over this authority battle he had going with his mother. Their rapport was not good. She was always down on him and he always acted indifferent to her. Then he'd be angry in the sessions."

"I'm sure it was hard to have time, in one half-hour session a week, to get that relationship going," Diana said, feeling burdened by too much knowledge of this family to do much more than listen.

"Yes, of course, and apparently Tony rebelled strongly against doing things at home. When he didn't do his homework Mrs. Petri would say to me, 'Ha, I told you he wouldn't!' She just seemed to know he wouldn't try, and if she tried to help him he became very negative. She just didn't know how to handle him, and she expressed her anger at him freely. There was *no* praise. Just put-downs. She said he used to shout along with the tapes, which upset her, and she was angry at him for doing that, too. I felt maybe he was getting back at her by not learning. One thing was sure: the family needed joint counseling."

Diana was particularly interested in one piece of Janet Robinson's testimony—the part about the mother's anger. Finally, Ann Petri was being human, susceptible. Tired and confused, she had expressed her anger—in public—at the failure of all her efforts. Angry at her unfixable son, angry at her unfixing self, she was hoping for some magic. Was there ever a woman more entitled to feel anger?

The sadness of this interview overwhelmed Diana. The Robinsons had no idea of the source of this family's frustration and anger with each other. They lacked the experience to look

154

beyond their test scores and their packaged electronic method to question whether their brand of remediation was the most appropriate for Tony at that moment in his life.

Although the Robinsons made no contact with Tony's sixth grade teachers, Mrs. Petri gave all three a printed sheet explaining perceptual problems and updating the school on Tony's remediation.

The sixth grade teachers decided that Tony would no longer receive "report cards" in the conventional sense. Together, they'd prepare a quarterly joint statement to the parents, re-marking on their "good boy" who "obeys his teachers, is willing to try, participates in oral discussions, and makes valuable contributions."

Of course, he was not reading. Or writing. And his math, they said, had suffered from his twenty-five absences. In the mid-year statement they noted, "We are delighted to know that you and Tony are making progress in overcoming his difficulties. We'd appreciate being kept informed as to his progress with the Robinsons and will do whatever we can to help."

"And now for my right-hand man. I'd like to call Tony Petri up to the stage." Ted Barnett, principal of Newberry Elementary, stood at the podium with a small, neatly wrapped gift, scanning the graduates, spotting the head towering over all the others.

The youth stood up slowly, privately proud as the applause burst spontaneously, first from his peers and then from their parents on the lunchroom benches or standing outside on the hot asphalt playground.

They were applauding for Tony Petri. A fine moment. He really liked it. Tony's memories of it were disjointed. The words—kind, caring words—from his "out-of-sight" principal and friend, saying something about how he couldn't have made it through without Tony. The whole school was there, and this sort-of-girlfriend that Tony liked...his first....Freak-out, hard to handle, glorious moment. Inside, rockets of good feelings....Too few of them in his life.

They graduated Tony Petri from elementary school that day. They *had* to graduate him. The law required it. At 13 years and 3 months, he couldn't be held any longer.

In the departmentalized sixth grade, Tony had had three

teachers who loved him for his helpfulness and were baffled by his mysterious academic problem. There had been a qualitative change in their reactions to him. There developed a mystique about this silent, strong, helpful boy, and because of the mystique the teachers, principal, and other staff had begun denying the severity of his problem. They came to believe that somehow Tony would "work it out."

The magical thinking had become contagious. Each expressed his own version of the fantasy that Tony would somehow be a successful adult. The office clerk pictured him as a building contractor. The math/science teacher saw him in a job with people working under him because "he has that kind of leadership, a way with people, and a way of getting jobs done." Then she added, "Maybe he'll get the academics someday, or maybe he'll never need them."

Tony's reading teacher had been impressed with his sophisticated head for money matters, the side of him that even Ella Koontz had found remarkable. She'd shared his frustration, embarrassment, and boredom with the third grade book he was reading and allowed herself to be seduced away from reading tasks and into discussions with the interesting, unusual sixth grader.

The science class had been a different matter—a bright moment in his academic day. The science text that year was so extraordinarily difficult that the entire class was incapable of reading it. To help them all, the teacher organized the science period as a discussion-and-experimentation class. Tony had become a star, volunteering to do all the experiments. He'd been in his element then—translating the teacher's explanations into mechanical or experimental realities. One day they'd had a discussion on drug abuse. Having been tenderly "tutored" on this timely subject by his teenaged biker friends on Hodgkins Street, Tony was a minor expert on the drug culture. He knew all the terminology and had left his classmates and teacher open-mouthed at his knowledge.

Tony listened carefully as Diana read him all the fine comments his sixth grade teachers had made about him. But, unable to accept the "good strokes," he had to reverse the praise.

"You know, I used to go out of my way for that school and for Mr. Barnett. But you know why I did it?" His tone was full

156

of self-disdain. "It was mostly so I could be important. That was why."

"Nothing wrong with being important, Tony. We all need some of that," Diana interjected.

"You don't understand. Everybody was so nice to me. But they never saw my bad side. In my neighborhood I was real different. Just the threat of me was enough to stop all but the very foolish." He allowed a momentary smile of pleasure at his choice of words, as he prepared to counteract the compliments with a horror story about himself.

"See, after a while, all the kids knew me and knew about my problem, especially after that insulting Miss Koontz, and they all left me pretty much alone about it. But in sixth grade there was this new 'tough guy'—he thought he was tough. One day he followed me home and said something about my reading. I didn't say a word, just ignored him and walked home and into my garage. But he stood out there, calling out names and teasing me. Boy, was he surprised when I came shooting out of that garage with a lit blowtorch and started chasing him. Of course, I didn't catch him, but I never had any trouble with him again."

He avoided Diana's eyes as he said, "Yeah, those teachers at Newberry all used to believe in me. I really had them fooled. One of these days they'll find out just how crazy I am."

Tony Petri spent eight years passing through the elementary school. No remediation had ever been provided at public expense from kindergarten to graduation. The only help he ever received was accomplished through his parents' efforts and funds. And both of those were diminishing.

The day Tony graduated from Newberry Elementary School, Ann Petri made a private pact with herself. Her end of the job was finished. From then on, Tony would have to find his own way.

157

CHAPTER 15

"If he feels he's been wronged,
this boy can strike out."

"The Grasshopper," Tony's pet name for his seventh grade math teacher, ended it before it got off the ground—crushed Tony's embryonic effort at "making it" in junior high.

"Right from the start, I thought he was a little strange," Tony testified. "He was about knee-high to a grasshopper and he kept buzzing around, pointing to everybody and saying, 'You got a U, you got a U.' Weird. We were all new to the school and kinda freaked out, but I was doing really good in math, so I didn't care. I had a little book, and I was doing all the work and getting 100 percents on all the tests, and I figured, 'Wow, I ought to be getting a C or even a B.' But then the grades came out and he gave me a D-minus! D-minus! I said, 'What *is* this? Why did I get this?' and the little creep said, 'Well, you did so bad before, so I had to give you that.'

"Well, that just wiped me out. I mean, I'd been doing everything so perfect. I took all that time. It was my *best*. You know what I even did? If I didn't finish in class, I even took it *home* and did it. That was a completely new thing for me—I never worked so hard in all my life...and I got a D-minus! I just thought to myself, 'Shove it up your nose, man.' I never said it, but I thought it. Every time I saw him, I said the same thing to myself—'You're an asshole, Man!' After that I just quit."

He did quit. Mrs. Petri had said Tony would have to find his own way now, and he did. Tony's way became the way of minimal visibility, just passing through the halls, through the doors, through the hours, days, months as obscure Tony Petri. The teachers all saw the same nondescript person he allowed them to see—not very bright, absent a lot, big and quiet, a floater, no trouble, no backtalk, no effort, no work.

Diana Cotter's investigation shattered the two years and two months of obscurity by drawing sudden attention to the Petri case. As a result of that attention, the school program coordinator made a surprising move in November of Tony's ninth grade year. He decided to change Tony from a low-track to an average-track history class.

The change was subtle.

The first hint of it surfaced the day Diana asked Tony to reschedule their appointment to a different hour the following week. She hadn't been notified about the new history class.

"Just don't come during fourth period," Tony requested. "I don't want to miss history."

The comment was straight, non-sarcastic, and came from a boy who just a few months back had said, "You could take me out of any class in the day and I wouldn't be missing anything."

Diana couldn't hide her smile.

Tony responded with one of his own, acknowledging recognition of the change. He hadn't intended to change, but he had. Not only did he not want to miss history, but he was even beginning to develop an allegiance to the teacher.

The unlikely object of this new emotion was Edward Aldrich, a man universally disliked by the other students because of his odd personality and his "totally out-of-it" teaching methods. Tall, painfully thin, short-haired, and bespectacled, Edward Aldrich was a nervous, unassertive man with an eye tic and a speech defect. He lapsed into a painful stutter when under pressure, and pressure was what this class exerted constantly, as students exploited his handicap and ridiculed him when he looked the other way.

"So, right there I decided I was going to like him," the maturing Tony explained. "Of course, he didn't need me for a friend 'cause there wasn't much I could do for him. But I look at somebody and figure, 'Why is he like he is? And why is he treating us like assholes?' Well, I looked at those guys in class, and they were all treating him like an asshole, so how could he help doing the same?"

In spite of their bad manners, the students in this middle-track class were accustomed to achieving. In spite of their contempt for the teacher, they were learning history and Tony immediately felt the difference in academic climate. Mr. Aldrich felt the difference in Tony, the boy he'd always thought of as a "rowdy-looking hoodlum."

In this changed environment, Tony became absorbed in class discussion and intrigued by the study of geography and its effect on a nation's history. He practiced his new reading skills on the funny words for the names of places on maps and applied his mechanical skills to the creation of colorful, careful map renderings for the class.

Tony enthusiastically shared with Diana his new knowledge—about Allende in Chile, about Russia, its tsars, and the meaning of communism. He even connected this book knowledge with his personal knowledge of a Nike missile base he'd discovered while riding in the hills. He informed Diana that those missiles were "all pointed toward Moscow." Whether or not his information was accurate, his awareness of Moscow and its context in world politics was change enough. Although he was, of course, unable to read the textbook, he confided that he "aced" the first test because someone in the class got hold of it the day before and gave all the kids the answers. That he cared enough to *want* to pass a history test, even by devious means, was a significant first.

His new attitude meant a change in the academic goals Diana had so smugly designed for him. Her two hours a week with Tony didn't allow for elaborate history review.

The problem was partially solved by an unexpected ally, Tony's advisor and current English teacher, Sarah Duffy. Sarah was a soft, sweet spinster in her late fifties who had a naïveté about her that made the kids say, "She's someplace else"—out of touch with their world. She had been Tony's advisor for his three years at Dalton and she was well-acquainted with the incredibly low scores on his Cum. She'd also taught him in three different English courses. Yet she knew the real Tony not at all.

Sarah Duffy had become increasingly curious about Diana's involvement with Tony. She questioned Diana about her methods for remediation and about the cause of Tony's severe problem. Diana apprised Miss Duffy, in small doses, of the Petris' exhaustive quest for help over the years. The advisor was fascinated and astonished.

Her curiosity activated her. On her own, Miss Duffy tried

out one of the guided reading methods on Tony during a conference with him. She was surprised that he was willing to demonstrate his skill, then impressed—but totally confounded—by his progress. She had never dreamed he was capable of learning.

When she heard of Tony's interest in history and Diana's wish for someone to guide his reading in his history book, she did an extraordinary thing. She purchased a small tape recorder with her own funds, asked a student volunteer to tape readings from the book, and surprised Tony with the entire package. Moved by Miss Duffy's new concern, Tony tried listening and following in the book. Unfortunately, the class was moving through the book too fast for the fledgling reader to keep up; but more important than the outcome of the lessons was the change in Miss Duffy's attitude about his potential.

Who would have dreamed that the typically indifferent, unresponsive Department of Motor Vehicles would have made a special provision? Who would have believed that the ability to read was *not* a requirement for becoming licensed to drive in their state? An impersonal government agency had dropped the bottom out of her reading-and-writing curriculum for Tony Petri. The truth was that he would have a choice: he could take the written test or the oral one given for illiterates.

She waited for two days, debating. Should she listen to her own inner voice or to the voice of Ann Petri, who begged Diana not to reveal the option to Tony. The driver's license had a separate meaning to the mother: it was to be the reward for his learning to read. It was her only way of inducing him to enter and finish high school.

As Diana listened to Mrs. Petri's reasoning, she knew what her decision had to be. "Mrs. Petri," she shared her thoughts, "I have to confess that I, too, thought about lying to Tony when I first heard the news. But we can't do it. He's not a child any more. We can't spare him life's realities. If we don't tell him the truth, somebody else will."

Mrs. Petri didn't answer right away, but then, reluctantly said, "I know you're right but I'm just trying to get some hold on him. Just last month, I told him he couldn't quit high school 'til he was eighteen, and then some boy at the cycle shop told him he could quit at sixteen! It made me so mad, but I guess I can't keep these things from him anymore."

"It's a sad fact," Diana agreed. "We can't trick him or force him through high school any more than we can make him listen to something he doesn't want to hear. We've got to give him all the facts we have and begin to trust his judgment. He's got to start being a part of the decision making and learn about the consequences of his choices. Otherwise, it's too easy for him to blame everyone else when things go wrong. I know it's scary," Diana sighed, "but I think your son is pretty terrific, and it's worth taking the chance."

She stopped talking a moment, but hearing no response, she went on. "As for me, Mrs. Petri, I just can't lie to him now. If I do, it'll risk all the trust we've built up so slowly, and that's too big a price to pay. Tony doesn't build trust easily. You know that.

"Of course, you and your husband must decide if you want to give your permission for the license." Diana paused again, then shared an after-thought. "You know maybe if Tony is a driver he can finally help lighten *your* load. Why don't you think it over, Mrs. Petri, and let me know what you decide?"

As Diana hung up the receiver, she thought about one of her comments: "It gets too easy for him to blame everyone else when things go wrong."

The more she learned about Tony, the more she saw him fall into a pattern common to failing adolescents. When they can't learn like others, they begin to withdraw. Then they quietly resist. Finally, in the last stages, they project their awful feelings about themselves onto others and blame outside causes for their troubles. The animal instinct—to protect and defend—reigns.

When Tony learned that he was failing Mr. Thorne's math class, he "didn't know why." Diana knew why. He had stopped putting out the effort for Mr. Thorne. His school-time energy—more academic energy than he'd expended in his past three years combined—had been consumed by Mr. Aldrich's history studies. Tony had thought he could coast with Mr. Thorne. After all, math was his "best subject."

When the fail notice came, Tony was shocked, said he'd ask for an Incomplete and "do the whole book over on his own and show that guy." But Mr. Thorne said "No," no second chance, no special treatment. Tony had been given a block of time defined by the class rules. He was capable of doing the work, but he had chosen to use his time differently. If he was ever going to learn success, he had to begin to acknowledge his part in the failures.

On the following Monday, not knowing what to expect, Diana told Tony about his choice of drivers' tests. When she spoke she was unable to resist deliberately describing the oral one as the "test for illiterates."

Proud Tony took the bait. Without hesitation he chose the written test, confirming the value of all their work together. The young man didn't need an easy way out. At least, not this time. Something new was happening. Diana felt like singing.

With their goal reaffirmed, they raided the trash baskets at the DMV for their "textbook supplements"—the multiple forms of used drivers' tests, which they studied using guided reading techniques. Tony had already learned many of the words from their study of the vehicle codes, and they practiced the new ones in preparation for the exam.

Meanwhile, something new was happening at home. Tony was beginning to sneak-read. He'd been subscribing to *Popular Mechanics* magazine for two years but until that time had "read" only the pictures. Now, for increasing periods of time, alone, in silence, he'd sit in his room and read captions, headlines, and even some paragraphs. His concentration was so intense he didn't notice his mother observing him.

Tony never mentioned his reading to Diana. He was testing her to see if the tricks she was teaching carried over to "real reading." Something must have carried over, because, according to the mother-spy, he spent more and more time with *Popular Mechanics*.

Bob Long was the last name on Diana's list of junior high teachers to interview. Mr. Long, the P.E. teacher, had been identified as having important firsthand information about the Halloween revenge incident so briefly mentioned in Tony's Cum.

It was the day after Halloween, Bob Long remembered, and there was a crowd of kids gathering. He heard shouts, angry sounds, and walked quickly over to see what was going on.

"There must have been thirty or forty kids there, and Tony had this kid, Charlie—the one who had shot him with a fake bullet—up against the wall. I looked at the size of Tony and I thought 'My God, he could break every bone in this kid's body.' You know, it just surprised me, seeing Tony like that. He'd always been such a quiet kid in my P.E. classes. When I first saw him, I figured we might groom him for football, but he never seemed interested. He wasn't a jock or a cruncher, if you know what I mean. Some kids are sort of hungry to crunch flesh and crash into each other. Tony wasn't like that. He came to class and was never any trouble. Just put in his time.

"Well, when I saw this scene, all I could think was, if he feels he's been wronged this boy can strike out. He was pinning Charlie there and everybody was shouting and egging him on, but he was waiting. He may have been hoping someone would stop him...but maybe not." The teacher furrowed his brow, speculating about the outcome of that incident if he hadn't happened by.

"I *couldn't* hit that kid." Tony filled in the other side later that day when Diana asked him about it. "The other guys kept saying to punch him, and I'm sayin' to the kid, 'Look, I don't want to hit you.' Then the punk says to me, 'You can if you want to.' I guess he figured he had it coming for that dumb stunt he pulled. But I *didn't* want to. The whole school was sayin', 'Kill him, kill him,' and I didn't want to....I couldn't!"

Tony began sweating as he talked, diverting his eyes from Diana. She'd never seen him so physically overwrought. "I've never really hit anybody...I mean, never *really* punched 'em out." Then, reconsidering, "I do have a mean temper—God! I'm really dangerous." His repeated self-condemnations were becoming familiar to Diana. "I hate to think just how crazy I get, and the stuff I've done. Like the time I almost killed Danny." Tony suddenly needed to finish the story he'd begun and aborted months before, about his near-fatal attack on his best friend.

"That was a bad day. Just a bad day, and everything was going wrong. I was working on my truck in the garage. Everything was a mess, the engine just wasn't working right, and then Danny kicked over some oil and that did it! I just picked him up and pushed him into the wall. We both laugh about it now, 'cause there's still a dent in the wall, and I tell him it's a bodyprint, like they have in those cartoons. We just started yelling and getting into it, and then I threw a stool at him. Lucky for him it missed him, but it broke through the garage door. If it had hit Danny, it would have broke his back."

164

He wasn't laughing when he finished the story. He looked at Diana and came back to the story about Charlie. "But I just couldn't hit that punk at the school. First of all, I wasn't really mad anymore. And mostly I figured, 'Well, the kid made a mistake.'"

The kid made a mistake. He could forgive a peer an act he understood. The "crimes" of his teachers he would never understand.

Diana asked how Tony would have ended the incident if it hadn't been stopped. He shrugged and finished the whole conversation with, "It was good Mr. Long came by."

She had noticed Tony's eyes looked particularly red that Monday and she asked if he'd been out riding on a dirt track that weekend.

"Hey, you're gettin' to be a detective. How'd you know? I took Ginny this weekend. Had to do a lot of fancy talking, because she's not really a motorcycle lady, if you know what I mean. I borrowed an extra kidney belt and helmet for her, but she looked at all that dirt and those bumps and she was absolutely terrified. She kept sayin' 'Gee, I really don't think I oughta do that.' I guess she only went under pressure, because her cousin Betty and her boyfriend went along and Betty loves to ride. They really pushed hard on her, but I was more persuasive. More cool, y'know. I promised her I'd go real slow and be real careful. She learned about me, that I keep my word, and y'know what?" he laughed. "After a few minutes, she even told me I could go a little faster! I'm usually pretty fearless—kind of a daredevil, you might say—when I'm alone, but if somebody else is afraid I try to respect that when I take people ridin.'"

The former killer-and-bad-guy was now Mr. Chivalry. Diana was getting used to his dramatic shifts.

"Sounds like you and Ginny are becoming pretty close," Diana said.

"Yeah. We talk a lot. It's pretty easy for me to talk to her. She's shy in a group and she's embarrassed about her dancing, but me, I'm just the opposite. When I'm at a party with my real friends, I just horse around and talk and joke. And I love to dance. I guess my style is 'wild man'—that's what Ginny says. I just kind of fly around the dance floor with my arms and legs going." He demonstrated by flinging his appendages. "But she gets so worried that she's not graceful on her feet, so

I just pick her up and swing her around 'til she laughs so hard that she can't be worrying about what people think of her dance style.

"She's still pretty worried about cycling though. Maybe when I get my new Harley, I'll find out about sidecars and she can just ride along with me that way. Some models have them, but I'm not sure if my new one will take a sidecar."

"Hey. That's an idea. Let's write to Harley-Davidson and find out about sidecars, or whatever else you want to ask them."

Write a letter to the Harley-Davidson Company! The revolutionary notion shocked Tony. He had written only one "letter" in his life—the barely legible note to his mother about "going to a Home" when he was in fifth grade.

After the initial recoil, Tony became excited. He *would* write the letter. The thought blew his mind. He dictated, copied, recopied, and perfected the precedent-setting document and even accompanied Diana to the mailbox to post it.

Within two weeks of the posting, much to his surprise and delight, Mr. Anthony Petri of Hodgkins Street received a cordial reply from the Harley-Davidson Company of Milwaukee, Wisconsin. On that day, he experienced the power of the written word. With spirits elevated, ready to test the new power, he enlisted Diana's aid in drafting a second communication to the famous motorcycle manufacturer in protest of poor service and unavailability of parts at a local Harley dealer. He wrote requesting a specific part and even enclosed the catalog number.

His second letter was never answered.

Lesson number two: the power of the powerful to refuse to respond. Tony knew about quiet refusal to respond, but he couldn't hide his disappointment when it was used on him. The positive effects of the first letter quickly soured.

At home, he began to resist doing guided reading with his mother, telling her he "didn't have time." What he didn't tell her was that Ginny had begun to help him study for his drivers' license. Tony was developing a new tactic—withholding his academic successes from his parents. When he worked on a map for history class, he told his mother he was "just coloring something," never sharing the excellent finished product. It was his own brand of adolescent rebellion against parental control.

On March 18, dressed in his "Mafioso costume"—an abused

brown fedora, mirrored sunglasses, and denim vest over his white T-shirt with "No. 1" emblazoned in bold metallic blue across the front, the sixteen-year-three-day old Tony paraded into the room with new authority, threw down a long rectangle of paper on the table in front of Diana and said, "Take a look at that!"

"Wow! Happy birthday, Tony Petri! Fantastic!" Diana squeezed his arm in delight as she realized the significance of the paper in front of her. Only in that moment did she learn that the Petris had granted their permission. Scrawled on top of the test, just under his name, was an enormous "100%." Elegant underlines were added by its recipient, who preferred something classier than the scoring marks used by the DMV. He had indeed achieved a perfect score.

Diana was thrilled for him. "What a way to celebrate your birthday! I'll bet your folks were pleased. Did you go out for dinner?" Diana knew his parents had planned to take him to a restaurant for his big day, but she wanted to hear it from Tony.

"Naw. We just stayed home," he sounded despondent.

"Tony Petri, you did *not* stay home, so stop bullshitting me. I talked to your mom and she told me you were going to a restaurant, so what is all this stuff?"

"Caught me, hey? Well, I'll tell you, if you had *seen* that dinner, you'd have known it was like not going out at all."

They both burst out laughing, cherishing a moment of shared pride and friendship. They had really grown to know each other.

CHAPTER 16

"Tony will be going to Olvida High...
that is *his district, you know."*

From an educational therapist's standpoint, the months from April to June are strictly high risk. Spring fever prevails. For Tony, spring fever came in March, the day he got his license.

He grew increasingly impatient with the "geeks" who came into the gas station where he worked. One day he decided he had taken too much abuse from customers, and smugly quit on the spot, knowing that he had a job waiting for him at Glenview Harley. The element of power in that job switch pleased him.

His teachers were expecting more and more of him at the very time he was ready to give less. Miss Duffy had assigned a final project, a report, which would determine whether he could qualify for June graduation. Another first, if he'd do it. Too bad the assignment came in the spring.

Armed with his new dictate-and-copy method and prodded by Diana to keep his attention on work instead of riding, Tony began an epic on motorcycles. He dictated pages and pages of information that had been stored between his ears for years but had never before committed to print. Their plan was for him to dictate the entire report to Diana and then copy it during his English class, study hall, or at home.

One day he came into the teacher's lounge looking totally exhausted. His unshaven face was marred by an angry flare-up of acne. He was not in the mood to communicate. With no real expectations, Diana started him on a writing lesson, offering to give him a model to copy. At first he said nothing. Then he grabbed the paper and insisted he was going to try to write from scratch. Enough of this copying crap.

Tony struggled painfully over the virgin sentence, hiding his paper from Diana. His slow writing motions gradually became interspersed with rapid pencil scratchings, as he crossed out the rejects. He grew tense as the scribblings increased. Inevitably he erupted, crushing the paper into a ball and flinging it to the floor.

"It's the b and d again! The frigging b and d. I just can't get it! Forget this whole asshole thing! Forget it, man!" He flung his pencil across the room, lumbered over to the sofa and collapsed into the cushions. He closed his eyes and flopped his head against the wall.

Diana waited until his breathing returned to normal and said softly, "Want to talk?"

No answer.

"Hey, Tony, we all get tired some days. That's not the best time to test yourself to the max."

The eyes stayed closed.

Diana said nothing, letting them both be soothed by the space of the silence.

"It's this asthma—this asshole asthma!" he blurted. "I can't sleep. I just toss around all night and sit up trying to suck some air and there isn't any. Then I take some of those stupid pills from that stupid doctor and I get so shaky I can't sleep from shaking! Well, last night was it, man! You know what I did last night?" He didn't wait for a reply. "I put my fist through the wall! Right through the bedroom wall like a damn apeman. That's what I am—an apeman!"

He blew out a long breath and went silent again.

Diana waited once more, then said, "That riding in the hills in spring can be pretty tough on you, Tony. Everything's blooming and all that fuzz seems to find your lungs, doesn't it?"

"Yeah," he wheezed the answer. "The doc wanted me to get rid of Louise, but he's not the problem."

"Who's Louise?"

"You know, my cat. He's a boy, but he's a little strange, so I named him 'Louise.'"

"Makes sense," she giggled, knowing laughter meant recovery for Tony. "Look, Tony. You had a lousy night, you're feeling exhausted, and even when you're feeling terrific, writing is not your best sport. One day, when you're feeling your best, I'll show you every trick I ever learned for keeping the damned b

169

and d straight. If you give me all your attention, I'll bet you'll learn it in only one lesson and we'll never have to deal with it again." The mirror twins had come to represent everything that was wrong about Tony.

"Show me now."

"What?" She was surprised.

"Show me the tricks."

"It would be better if you were rested."

"It's OK. Show me."

Diana proceeded to show him the favorite tricks she'd used over the years to help kids see the differences between the maddening pair: coloring in the "b" that was hiding in the "B," because very few kids ever reversed "B"; the word "bed," (making its b in red and its d in blue) which she turned into a picture of a bed for him to visualize in his mind, with a body resting its head on the pillow over the "b"; and the sequence a-b-c-d, showing him that by closing the c with a stick it *became* the "d."

In spite of his exhaustion and turmoil, Tony gave her his total attention.

To the end of the year, he never again confused the two letters.

On that most unlikely day, another question had been answered for Diana. When he chose to pay attention, Tony Petri was neurologically capable of correcting his perceptual errors. But he had to *want* to learn.

For the remainder of the year, they set most of their goals with caution. There would be less disappointment that way.

Tony's history efforts were increasingly confined to elaborate map-making. The textbook had gone the way of all the others— book-bagged for carrying but not for reading.

Then the belated birthday gift arrived: the SX-175. The seduction of the incredible new "toy," and the challenge of his job in the parts department at Glenview Harley were too much competition that May. Mr. Aldrich's introduction to the history of India didn't stand a chance.

Diana faced a dilemma. As Tony's trust had grown, his increasing need to share personal information had superseded his desire to expand his academic skills. For a boy who had so long been silent and private, he needed to be heard. Diana weighed her dual obligations—to push the academics and to provide a much-needed ear. That May, the ear won out.

Someone had to listen, to reflect back to Tony the immense

satisfaction he felt about his system of locating parts from the volumes of catalogs at the cycle shop. He had developed a unique method of using the numbers and illustrations without ever having to read the words.

No one rushed him there. No one else in the parts department knew how to read either. In fact, Tony was the only one who made an effort to find unusual parts. His work buddies simply told the customers, after going into the back room and having a smoke while they pretended to look, that they were "out of that part." Diana half-jokingly suggested to Tony that, if he could only learn to read, he could be the king of all the parts dealers in business.

Someone had to listen, too, as he described his plans for entering the serious racing world. First, he'd decided to lighten his bike. Listing all the parts he'd removed, Tony estimated the weight of each and added their total—an impressive 112 pounds!

His inspiration had come from a racer he'd seen on the weekend. Following the race, he'd gone to the shop and stripped down his cycle, intricately diagramming the miles of wiring he pulled out so he could rewire it after the streamlining was complete. He brought Diana the wiring diagrams, pointing out the superfluous wires in an ignition system that just cried out for simplification. He even talked about lightening himself, cutting out the Cokes and "crap food."

His friends from the Harley shop watched, horrified, as he removed parts and ripped wires from his brand-new, still under warranty cycle. They called him crazy, advised him to wait for the shop mechanic, but when it came to his motorcycle Tony waited for no one. He knew what he had to do, he did it, and it worked.

Diana was impressed with his guts and his success, but she became increasingly uneasy. She knew his English report was coming due, as well as a history test whose grade would stand between Tony and graduation. After his Fail in Mr. Thorne's math class, he couldn't receive another Fail grade and be allowed to graduate. High school required that diploma. She confronted him with these realities and with her growing personal dilemma.

"What about it, Tony? How are we going to get you out of here? I'm not going to kid myself that I can get you to read at home about the history of India when you're so high over racing. You're close to getting this diploma, but the distractions in your life are just too much for both of us," Diana admitted.

Tony agreed. He was excited about his real world. He didn't care about high school. It was just for the Old Lady that he even talked abut high school.

"Don't throw it out too fast," Diana cautioned. "If there's any way you can get that high school diploma, once you have it no one can take it away. And that's power. I see how much you crave being your own boss. Someday, you may look at this diploma thing differently."

The word "power" caught his attention for a moment, but he was honest with himself and Diana then. The power of certainty in his world of "grease" was the only power that had relevance to the Tony she faced at that moment. He knew he could never last three years, full time, in any high school. Maybe a trade school. Down the line. He'd see.

Something was happening in Diana's life that May—a personal crisis in her family involving her own pain and distraction. She had to cancel some sessions. Then, when she was ready to return, she had to change the appointment day. When Diana showed up on Tuesday, he had come Monday. He'd never got the message from his dad.

She paged him from his classroom and he walked out slowly, saying nothing. Diana asked if his dad had given him the message and Tony just shook his head no. She apologized. She explained her crisis. It was Tony's turn to be the listener. He listened well, offering his sincere counsel for his friend's pains. Then, without any notice, he took out an illustrated map of India "by Tony Petri." He had completed it on his own.

"I got tired of waiting for you so I did it myself."

"Well, I can see you don't need me for that." Diana was pleased.

"I'm learning not to count on you for anything." With the one-line zinger Tony let her know his hurt, but then he felt sorry, knowing she had tried to contact him.

"Anyway, I got some stuff that should cheer you up," he said as he opened the notebook that was no longer empty. Inside the front cover was a framed, blown-up, black-and-white photo of a motorcycle racer, his shirt blaring the giant number "88."

"Terrific photo, Tony. Did you take it?" Diana had missed the significance of the surprise. The identity of No. 88 was a mystery behind the goggles and helmet.

"It's *me*, you turkey!" The proud racer lost his cool. "Can't you see that's himself in there?"

"No! That's really you?!" Diana put her face up real close and still couldn't tell it was Tony until she spotted the pointed shoes. "By golly, that really *is* you, Ton! Fantastic! How was the race? How did you do?"

"Came in third," he grinned. "Not bad for my first try in the Big Time, eh?"

"I got something else to show you. Knowing you, you'll probably like this even better." He pulled out a light blue binder and handed it to Diana.

"Is this what I think it is?"

"Just open it up." He tried not to grin.

"You finished it, Tony. You did it without me. Oh, wow! Am I proud of you." Diana spoke softly, spacing each word for the impact of her full pride. Tony had completed the motorcycle report. He'd spent every hour in English and all of his other classes meticulously copying the pages of information. At home, he had labored over gorgeous detailed renderings of the engine and close-up views of specific parts. He'd included wiring diagrams. The final product was an effort of extraordinary merit.

"Tony, it's fantastic. What did Miss Duffy say?"

"I haven't turned it in yet. But while you were gone, I did some thinking and decided, after Mr. Thorne and all, I wasn't gonna fail anything else. Not ever again. I think I even have a real good chance to pass the history test. Mr. Aldrich says he'll read me the questions. That'll be a piece of cake then, 'cause I know all that stuff."

"What do your Mom and Dad think of all this? How'd they like the report?"

He didn't answer. Then she realized he'd never shown it to them. Diana knew that her next goals for Tony had to include improved communication with his parents. If there was time.

Someone, somewhere decided not to let Tony Petri out of junior high school without one more battery of tests. Someone, somewhere needed more numbers to see if he qualified for a special program at the high school level.

Agnes Terry, a new school psychologist whose only previous experience had been with elementary school children, came to Dalton to do the testing. Tony would be her first adolescent subject.

Agnes Terry was visibly rattled by Tony Petri, but not because of anything he said or did. The source of her unease was his Cum. Comments delivered once, in confidence, at a vulnerable moment, and typed into permanency in that folder altered her objectivity about this family. She felt unspoken expectations of her for expertise in this case.

During their first meeting, she asked Tony to draw an illustration of his family—The Draw-A-Family Test. Tony, feeling a new self-confidence from his recent school and racing achievements, cooperated well. He drew a poignant and tender group portrait of the three Petris, sitting together on their living room sofa, shoulder to shoulder, with the long draperies framing them, the coffee table in front of them, and an idyllic painting of a mountain scene at sunset directly behind their heads. All were smiling, and mother and son each had an arm reaching to touch the father. Johnny Petri had a hand gently placed on his son's knee. Tony drew himself as a tall, powerful, benevolent figure, dressed in his "No. 1" T-shirt. He had obviously taken great pains with this drawing. It was a drawing of closeness and dependence, with Dad as central figure and mother and son both supporting him. The surrounding table and curtains placed them almost in a protective box against the world. Tony had created a superb pictorial synthesis of the Petri family situation at that moment in time.

Miss Terry had been looking for rage and hatred, conflict and calamity. Tony had done it again—confounded another professional and made her fearful of committing herself to any opinions. She nervously administered the intelligence test, forgetting to ask for two answers with each question that required two. Even with her administrative errors, though, Tony scored 106 on the WISC IQ test.

In her final report, Miss Terry avoided any attempt at test interpretation and simply wrote, "Because Tony is receiving individual help in reading at the time when he is beginning to realize the need to learn to read, and his reading teacher is seeing some success, it does not seem wise to make an EH placement at this point."

She recommended, "Continue individual help and alert high school teachers and counselors to his problem so that he might be placed properly in high school classes that will utilize his mechanical talents. Re-evaluate at a later date if necessary."

Diana would soon appreciate the outrageous naiveté of the novice tester's prescription.

Tony had kept his promise to himself. He had not failed any more of his classes in ninth grade. Miraculously, he had qualified to graduate from Dalton Junior High. Second-grade-reader Tony Petri had made it through three years of junior high with only four Fails. He'd pulled it off by taking lots of shop, service, and work-study courses and by maintaining near invisibility in the low-track academic classes. His grades during the final semester of ninth grade reflected the fascinating phenomenon of change in teacher expectation.

All the teachers had been informed of Diana's work with Tony, and she'd communicated to each of them her impression of his remarkable intelligence, pride, and embarrassment with his illiteracy. The teachers, except for Mr. Thorne, had become sympathetic listeners.

Diana knew the limitations of her remediation efforts. During their eight months together, Tony had made great strides in many areas. But the breadth of his problem called for daily work, daily commitment. She was the first to acknowledge that he still remained, by definition, a functional illiterate—testing below fifth grade in reading competency.

His teachers, on the other hand, ignored this reality that semester. Tony's final grades for his graduating semester in junior high school were three "C's" and two "B's"—his finest in ten and a half years of schooling.

The week before Tony was to graduate from junior high, Diana sought out Sarah Duffy for information about his high school placement plans. She presumed Miss Duffy was the logical person to be making all the arrangements, since she had been Tony's advisor for three years and had become so involved with his progress and the details of his case.

"Oh, Tony will be going to Olvida High," Miss Duffy informed Diana, obviously pleased that a definite decision had been made so promptly in a system where fall placements often were left until opening day of the new school year.

Diana, too, was pleased at the authority with which the teacher/advisor spoke. "Do they have a special program for him there?" she asked.

"Why, I don't know..." her eyebrows and voice rose simultaneously, revealing that the question had never occurred to her, "...but that is his *district,* you know."

Diana felt herself stifling a scream. She waited for something more than the silence that followed.

Nothing else came. She couldn't believe what she was *not* hearing. No words could form on her lips.

Meeting her silence with a vacuous smile, the oblivious Miss Duffy turned, mumbled something, and scurried off, totally unaware of Diana's state of shock. Totally unaware that Tony Petri was in need of a program, a plan, and, most of all, an intermediary to communicate his needs to the senior high school.

Diana moved from outrage to inquiry. Three days of investigation confirmed her worst fears: there was no requirement for school counselors to be even minimally informed about prog-

176

ram options at the next level of schooling. There was no district policy on the matter. No training whatsoever. No inter-level communication at all. Even more alarming was the realization that Sarah Duffy had spent 27 years in the system and had never felt the need to inform *herself* about the programs to which she would be sending her students, particularly those functioning at drastically substandard levels.

Tony's school assignment had been unofficially recorded in the files, making it a *fait accompli.*

He would be sent to Olvida High because that was his district.

CHAPTER 17

"School has always been the only place
I've felt really worthless."

The curt secretary knew her job well. She used her best institutional monotone to protect her boss, Mr. Bastion, head counselor at Olvida High, from all the people vying for pieces of his time. The school year was ending, after all, and counselors-can-see-no-one-now-about-something-that-will-happen-next-year-and-would-you-please-stop-by-in-July?

No. Diana couldn't wait 39 days for an answer. She could wait 39 minutes or even an hour, maybe a little more, but she had to see Mr. Bastion that day. She handed the secretary her card and expressed her intent in her most assertive voice.

This office was the third stop of her shuttle among schools, counselors, and the district office trying to learn about special programs that might be appropriate for Tony. This role of ombudsman was always a test of her patience, but she'd gone too far with Tony Petri to leave his tenuous high school future up to chance. Maybe she could find one dynamite teacher in one particular class, she dreamed, and buy a little time for the cause of his literacy.

She felt a tap on her shoulder.

"Mr. Bastion says you can come in now," the curt secretary announced.

Diana entered the tiny office and faced a broad-smiling man who looked more suited to selling insurance than to juggling students' schedules. Gregarious. Charming. Pleased to see her. Even during this madness. How could he be of help? What was the boy's name? Tony Petri? He jotted down the name on the yellow pad that occupied the center of his desk blotter. Did they have special programs? Yes, of course. Two—the EH class and the Special Day classes. You've heard about them from the district office? Fine. Please be assured that the school will plan the best placement for Tony, Mrs. Cotter, and now, I beg your understanding—he echoed the curt secretary—that nothing can possibly be planned before July. Please come back then. Thank-you-so-much. Rising from the chair, he extended his hand to let her know that-was-it-for-today.

Outside, Diana burst out laughing. The wait on the bench had been longer than the interview. So much for personal assertiveness.

Diana waited thirty-nine days.

On the thirty-ninth, she started again. Back to Olvida. Past the curt secretary. Reintroduced to Mr. Bastion. Oh, yes, he did vaguely recall the matter she wished to discuss. So many students. Would she please refresh his memory—what was the name again? "Tony Petri" was again inscribed on the yellow pad.

Diana capsulized Tony's history, describing his successes in Mr. Aldrich's history class, his budding but fragile motivation, and his fine intelligence. Mr. Bastion then told her about the EH class, whose students stayed with one teacher for all subjects. Diana didn't mention the whispered warning she'd received at the district office that the EH classes were "filled with the wildest, most acting-out behavior problems in the county." From the gist of her questions, though, Mr. Bastion sensed that she knew the truth. He shifted his focus to the Special Day Class program, designed for students who were lacking in basic skills but who could still be mainstreamed for certain classes.

After listening attentively to more detail on Tony's strengths and needs, Mr. Bastion strongly recommended the Special Day Class for Tony. He praised the reading teacher in the program and suggested Diana talk to Steve Pearly, a health/science teacher and race-car buff. If he was willing to absorb Tony into his course, they could finalize the schedule immediately.

Diana expressed her pleasure at the proposed plan and Mr. Bastion led her to the room of Sally Arden, the special reading teacher, who invited Diana to join her for some coffee so they could talk in private. As they walked through the halls, Diana understood why they would have to seek privacy. Every few feet, a different summer student would call out, "Hi, Mrs. Arden," or come over to talk or reach out to touch. Sally Arden was surely a favorite at Olvida.

In the lounge they shared teaching philosophies and Diana's

179

concern for Tony. Diana liked this lady instantly; nothing she said about Tony seemed to scare Sally, who even offered to be available to answer his questions or just be a sounding board if he wanted to talk. Sally agreed that Tony didn't sound like a candidate for the EH class, and she urged Diana to go ahead and enroll him in her class before it was filled.

Then she introduced Diana to Steve Pearly, whose muscular body broadcast his dedication to physical fitness. When Mr. Pearly learned of Tony's homemade vehicle and his interest in cycle-racing, he was intrigued by the boy but skeptical about the placement. The low reading level frankly scared him; he had no training for it. Diana explained again the kinds of arrangements that might be made to guide Tony through the reading, and she offered to be available if he needed any consultation. Cautiously, promising nothing, Mr. Pearly agreed to try, saying he'd see about getting an aide in the class to help Tony.

By late afternoon Diana returned to Mr. Bastion, humming with satisfaction at her good fortune in finding not one but two teachers who were willing to take a chance with Tony. She officially requested the Special Day Class program with Sally Arden and the health/science basics with Steve Pearly. Mr.Bastion flashed his beautiful teeth and wrote it all down, assuring her that "this will be the plan." He urged her to call in the fall to remind him during the very hectic time of admissions.

She assured him he would be hearing from her in September.

On September 10, the day before school opened, Diana returned to the high school for final reminders. Steve Pearly and Sally Arden both remembered the agreement and were looking forward to meeting Tony the following day.

She headed for the head counselor's office but there was no way to get within twenty feet of George Bastion that day. Diana squeezed her way through the crowd to the secretary—a new one—who shouted over the noise that Mr. Bastion had appointments every 15 minutes until 5:30 that afternoon. Acknowledging the impossible, Diana decided to leave a detailed note with the secretary, reiterating the plan for Tony and leaving a phone number in case he needed to reach her. She felt a shiver of apprehension.

She left the school and called Tony to assure him his schedule was in order and his teachers were expecting him. She discussed

Steve Pearly's interest in racing and shared her good feelings about Sally Arden, giving him their names to lessen his uncertainty of the new situation.

Tony sounded almost interested. Maybe he would go tomorrow after all, he teased. Just to check it out.

September eleventh.

Tony got up early. Couldn't sleep so he might as well take a look at the place. It gave him somewhere to go on his Harley, anyway.

He pulled into the Olvida parking lot by ten of eight and watched all the arrivals. Though he recognized some faces, there were lots of new ones. This place seemed much bigger than Dalton.

He found a wall to sit on, right near the auditorium where the new students were supposed to meet to get their schedules and maps and all that "garbage." His new leather jacket and pointed shoes identified him as a biker. He sure didn't want anyone to think he was one of those fancy rich kids. Lots of 'em there, though, carrying nice new notebooks, wearing nice new clothes, and looking like they were glad to be there.

He wasn't glad. It was Ginny who'd pushed him to go, but she wasn't even there. She was at the alternative school. He'd check out this Olvida deal and then maybe go visit her over there.

A bell rang and the new sophomore class of Olvida High filed into the auditorium. Welcome to all, said somebody in a polyester green suit. Gangrene, Tony always called that color. Why would anyone buy a gangrene suit? Tony pondered the question as the Gangrene Man announced that there were 421 sophomores in the class that year. If he split now, there'd be only 420, he thought. Nice even number. He played with the notion, but didn't move.

Some teacher stood up and welcomed them, read off some basic rules and regulations, then divided the auditorium space into four sections and asked the students to move according to the first letter of their last names. Bodies surged up and milled around until they were all relocated by their letters. Tony moved himself to L-to-R. Then, in each section, someone began to call out names and distribute schedules.

The process began at 8:15 a.m.

By 9:30, Tony's name had not yet been called. He was told to wait.

By 10:37, there were only eleven students still sitting in the auditorium, only two in the L-to-R section. Tony's schedule was nowhere to be found.

By 10:45, a student assistant handed him a pink sheet of paper. On it was written a temporary schedule with classes randomly assigned—the classes that had proved hardest to fill.

On the morning of September eleven, Tony Petri never saw Sally Arden. Or Steve Pearly. Or the smiling Mr. Bastion.

By 10:49 a.m., saying nothing to anyone, Tony took the pink sheet and started walking. His shoe taps clapped on the concrete floor of the auditorium as he walked up the aisle, his fingers drawing the pink slip into his palm and crushing it inside his fist. He felt the blood rushing to his face as he rammed the pink ball into a trash can and walked, unnoticed, off the campus.

No more "sucking it in."

Tony gunned his Harley into the driveway, tires spraying gravel, brakes screeching. He bounded up the frail porch steps in one stride and exploded through the screen door. The flushed face, the clothes covered with burrs and grime, and the asthmatic wheeze all told the mother that her son had been riding in the hills again. He rushed past her in silence to his bedroom haven and locked the door. Within moments the muffled rhythmic thump of recorded rock music—his self-medication—vibrated through the walls.

When he emerged an hour later, Ann Petri knew from his eyes that he was finally ready to tell about his first day of high school. There was an expression about them, a controlled wildness, that always accompanied those slow, carefully chosen words, censored, she knew, so as not to offend his religious parent.

Diana listened to the mother's story, totally perplexed. After recounting the events of the day, Mrs. Petri meekly confessed—embarrassed that she hadn't trusted Diana to do the job alone—that she, too, had visited the high school and spoken to the administrators about Tony. She'd spent half a day waiting for a counselor, and related all the details of her story to him, only to be told that he wasn't sure if Tony would be in his caseload because he didn't yet know "what letters of the alphabet" he'd be assigned in the fall.

She'd returned a second time, by appointment, but no one saw her at all, she said, so she gave up.

Now she implored Diana to tell her what had gone wrong.

Diana dug for an explanation, feeling just as confused as the mother. "I can't understand it, Mrs. Petri. We both tried. The teachers *were* notified. They expected Tony. It was all arranged. I don't know what went wrong. It's always wild—you know that—and most kids expect it, or ignore it, or flow with it. They just wait it out, or they fight and shout their way into the classes they want during that first week."

But mother and teacher both knew that Tony was one of the growing number who had stopped caring, who didn't want to be there in the first place, who had grown to expect the undesirable, the irrelevant, the mediocre in classes and schedules. Tony had become an expert in expecting nothing—until the ninth grade glimmers of possibility.

"I'm afraid I've really hurt him, Mrs. Petri," Diana admitted. "I assured him he could relax this time—things had been taken care of. I let them catch him off-guard. I'm sorry. Look, we'll work it out, Mrs. Petri, but it'll take time." Diana felt sick.

There was silence, and waiting. Ann Petri needed more.

Diana tried for more. "I think it's just that nobody there has the time to follow anything through. I think they really mean what they say when they're talking to us, Mrs. Petri, but they just can't deliver. They'd have to talk to four or five teachers every semester for every kid who needs special attention. And they have so much paperwork and testing to do that they never have time for the greatest need—communicating."

Diana had forced herself to recite the usual rationale. Ann Petri sighed. "Yes, I guess I know all that. I'm just one mother with one child but they've got two thousand of them and every parent thinks his own is the most important," she said with such resignation that Diana realized she had been too convincing. After ten years of fight-and-lose, Ann Petri was willing to accept this explanation. Diana had wanted her to *understand* the realities but she hadn't wanted her to *accept* them. If kids were ever to stop hating schools, ever to start trusting, ever to start feeling any personal control over their lives, those realities had to change.

Time, talk, and patient negotiation had brought Tony back to Olvida after that disastrous first day. Ginny had been a big

183

help. She was a feisty, determined young lady, an independent spirit like Tony. She saw his anger at the system as well as his humiliation when he couldn't read. Wanting her man to be educated, she pushed for his return to school. Ginny could read and write just fine, but her breaking point was teachers and rules. She liked the mood at the alternative school and had tried to get Tony to switch.

As Diana waited for Tony at her office, she felt the mixed feelings that always come with goodbyes. This would be their last meeting for awhile. Tony had decided to try Olvida on his own, without her aid. She respected his grit, even though she knew he still needed so much help. She'd learned, in her near-year of working with him, that his progress was directly related to the amount of power he felt over his own life. He'd asked for one more session to discuss his plans and dreams for the future.

She heard the knock on the door just as the clock hands neared 7:30 p.m. His punctuality always intrigued her—a silent testimonial to his willingness to be there.

"Hi." He came through the door with his usual syllable.

"Hi. How's it going?" Diana returned her own.

"Pretty good. I've got a great story for you." Tony plopped down into his favorite side of the mohair couch and got comfortable. "You're gonna love this one."

"What evil have you been up to now?" Diana asked.

"This week, they decided it was time for us to have all those official tests again. Well, I decided to have some fun with 'em this time, so you know what I did? On the first batch, I marked 'None of the above' for *every* answer." He chuckled with obvious glee. "I was trying to prove that if you can't read good, you can't pass any of those tests. They got my message. They just couldn't understand what this kid had done. Boy! Did it screw 'em up! I was so proud of myself. I tried to read some of the tests, but it was too boring...well, you know better than anybody what my hang-up is.

"Two days later, they gave us some aptitude tests...that stuff to find out what you're good in. Well, I got 4% on one and 1% on another one. But the one I took yesterday was called Mechanical Reasoning, and you know what I did? I got 99% on it! The counselor called me in to tell me. It blew 'im away! Ninety-nine percent is about as high as you can get. There were sixty ques-

184

tions and I read 'em all. I only missed four. They were pretty much words I had seen before in *Popular Mechanics*," he said, forgetting in his excitement that he'd never told Diana about reading it, "or words we'd worked on. I felt pretty pleased with myself." He grinned with satisfaction.

"That's quite an accomplishment, Tony. Maybe when they see those crazy scores they'll let you go to the alternative school with Ginny." Diana knew he'd made the request for the change.

"Naw. At first I thought, 'That place is really beautiful—I can really learn there.' All that crap. Ginny was drumming it into me about how much I'd like it there. But then I said to myself, 'You don't like anything about that place. All you want to do is be there with Ginny and get out at 11:15.' It's just a place to screw off. The truth is, when you hear my plans you'll know why I can't screw around anymore."

"So talk. I can't wait to hear." Diana loved this mercurial kid.

"I started thinking about how I felt that first day at the high school. It just blew me away 'cause I realized I kept thinking, 'Why am I having to go here? I'm not gonna learn anything. It's just gonna be all these new people and I'm gonna have to prove I *can't* do it again.' I meant to say 'can,' but instead I thought 'can't.' Isn't that what you call one of those Freudian slips? On most things, I'll come close to drawing blood, I'll kill myself, to prove I *can* do things that people think I can't do. But my brain just slipped into 'can't' that day. Pretty strange, eh?"

"Not so strange. You've had lots of years of hiding out."

"Well, it's strange for me, because school has always been the only place I've felt really worthless. And I've got this habit—I guess you'd call it a habit—whenever I get upset I take off and talk to myself. Sort of like I'm two people having an argument. One is making me angry, but the other one checks me from being too hard on myself. Actually, it's pretty neat. I have my own built-in friend. Like, I'll say, 'Tony, you're fat. Really ugly and fat.' And then the other side of me says, 'Yeah, but you're doing something about it.'

"That day when they screwed around with my schedule I went up in the hills and I shouted to myself, 'They cut you to ribbons and you let them.' But then I said, 'You don't have to take that anymore. Get out of there. You're not a little kid anymore.' That's the kind of stuff that goes on in my head. And if I really do something dumb, it goes on for hours. Boy, if anybody heard me up there, they'd probably call the guys in the white coats for me, eh?"

"I doubt that, Tony. It's terrific if you can counsel yourself, as long as one side of you knows what the other side needs. The only problem comes if you're not sure what's right for you, or if you hold in the rage until it explodes some other way....But tell me something. Does all this mean you've decided to quit? Have you given up the effort to become a reader?" Diana asked.

Tony got quiet. Then, with a serious tone, he said, "Don't misunderstand me. I hate that I can't read—I mean, *really* read—everything. I wish I could pick up things I want to read and just read 'em like anybody else. Ginny and me, we'll be watching a movie on TV and all of a sudden they'll subtitle it 'cause they're speaking in a different language. I go nuts and start yelling at her—WHAT DOES IT SAY? It goes by too fast, and I get crazy. Then I ask her what all the print says at the end of the movie—you know, that itsy bitsy stuff that rolls up on the TV screen like your eyes are supposed to roll up in your head. Ginny thinks I'm nuts for asking, says it's just junk and nobody cares about that, but I want to KNOW it. If I know what it says, then *I* won't have to care about it, either.

"There's whole bunches of stuff that I'd like to read, and I see that even now, without making a whole lot of effort, I'm picking up more all the time. It's getting easier." He looked sheepish at the admission. "Yeah, even the street signs. I can read those better now, too. But all that health and science stuff in Pearly's class, and those reading kits, it really puts me to the test. I just can't get into it. I wanna read what *I* wanna read, and I know I have no discipline. You're not gonna believe this, but you know where I'll probably be in the next five years? In the Marines."

"The Marines?" Diana was really surprised.

"Yep. I want to join the MP's there." He waited for the shock to have its impact. "Y'know why? Because I want to be a cop. Yeah, a cop!" He loved dropping the two bombs in a row. "That's what I've been wanting to do for a long time, but I never told anybody. Is that a change?"

"Wow! Too much!" she responded, putting her hand to her head in a mock faint. "Tell me more."

"I've never had enough guts to tell anybody that. Then I

186

thought, 'Well, screw these people, if they don't like it, it's too bad.' You'd be surprised how many friends I've lost in this last week when I broke the news. My hard-guy friends are not big on cops, as you can imagine. I never told anyone before because I always said to myself, 'I can't do it, I can't do it, so why try?'

"But suddenly the other side of me started to say, 'Well, you can too do it.' I figured if I really tried, I could probably meet all the requirements for the police academy by the time I'm out of the Marines. I think I'll be able to read by then, and my physical condition has to be a little better. I have to lose all this weight. Actually, I want to get the hell out of here, and I can do that in the Marines too."

The Marines. Total discipline, Diana mused. No gentleness, caring, or sensitivity to what may be right or wrong. The ultimate blind acceptance of authority.

"They're brickheads, right? It's 'do it or get out.'" Tony responded as if he'd read Diana's mind, showing that he understood the challenge and was ready to accept that kind of discipline.

"I think I can handle it now, but...don't laugh," he warned. "Maybe I've got to finish high school first. I'll check it out. That's the part that may do me in. I talked to the Old Man about my plans and he thought they were pretty good. I told him not to tell the Old Lady yet, though."

Diana was fascinated by Tony's new confidences with his dad. "The plans sound terrific and ambitious, Tony. But what happened to the motorcycle world?"

His interest in "grease," he said, was over, outgrown. No future in it, no real happiness. "I really want to be more into helping people. I guess that sounds pretty weird, coming from me."

No. It didn't sound weird. Just new. Positive instead of negative. The hour had been full of surprises.

187

CHAPTER 18

*"Don't they know that
scared and angry are the same things?
When you can't cut it, you get scared."*

Ginny was jarred from her sleep by the start-and-stop cough of the Great White Wheeler's engine. Half-awake, she turned over just as the engine did. Instinctively, she reached for Tony, but the sheet was cold, the body gone. Then she heard the truck wheels roll down the driveway. Where was that man going at this hour? She forced an eye open to look at the clock. Not even 5:30 yet. Her head fell back in the pillow and she waited for it to decide what to think.

Her man. She worried about him a lot these days, but she couldn't let him know. He was so restless and jumpy since the accident and all that worry with Frankie. And now that insurance company—giving him a bad time. She was afraid he was about ready to lose his mind. She'd never seen Tony like this. Last week, her strong, silent guy let it out to his mom, of all people. On the phone. Told her how scared he was. Admitted his feelings. Finally. A few days later he got a letter from her saying it wasn't right for him to talk about how he feels, and that when he cries he should cry alone. The old macho rules. He was trying so hard to give them up, to find some new way to make it through. Kept talking about his friend, Montana, from the old neighborhood. When Montana first moved across from the Petris' house with his lady, the cocktail waitress, they sure shook up Hodgkins Street. They were so different and Tony was fascinated with the guy, not just because he was a hippie and a musician, but because he was so gentle. Never got upset.

Ginny smiled as she remembered her fifteen-year-old lover telling her he'd decided, after meeting Montana, that he had a

188

new philosophy about people. There were three kinds, he'd announced with authority: "Some people, if you slap them in the face, they punch you out, and some just can't help yellin' at you, but the third kind just face the other way." Montana was that third kind. That was how Tony wanted to be—just facing the other way when he got slapped.

Well, he was sure getting slapped now. But he was trying so hard to hold himself in and it just wasn't working anymore. He was so short with the kids, barking at them, spanking them for the least thing. Since Frankie's scarlet fever, the little guy needed more patience than ever. And Stephie—so quiet when her daddy raged and hollered. Nobody ever knew what *that* child was thinking.

As she lay still, twenty-year-old Ginny Shelton Petri thought she felt the flutter of new life in her womb and touched her fingers to her slightly bulging belly, waiting for more. Too early for much activity, but another little Petri was definitely coming. Not the best timing, lady, living on unemployment with two other little ones to feed.

Well, they'd manage somehow. Didn't need a lot of money to be happy. Always told themselves they'd find a way, and they always did, up 'til now. She loved being pregnant and each time got better. Easier. Had to be easier than the first.

The first. Sometimes she still had nightmares about it. Fourteen. She was just fourteen and scared about so many things. Boys and dating. Love-making, sex. She even thought they were the same things—tells you how dumb she was. And Tony. An "older guy"—fifteen—she laughed to herself. He'd seemed so safe. Just loved to talk and dance and sneak a six-pack of beer after the movies, and then talk some more. Boy, how they could talk! About everything. Parents, school, his job, his wanting to be a cop. She'd forgotten about that until just this moment. A cop. What a dream. She'd sure wrecked that one.

She loved the guy, fell for him so quick. She used to help him with his reading, and he'd help her to laugh and relax at parties, be a real person. But it was so hard for him to show affection.

Things were so crazy then. Everywhere you went, everywhere you looked, everything was sex—people talking about sex, watching it at the movies, reading about it, braggin' about it. Tony's friends were the worst—all they ever talked about was who was "getting it," and drooling over all those magazines.

189

The first time Tony showed her one, she about died. It was weird and scary and not what she thought of as love. Tony kept saying all those words to her about how much he cared, but she needed a touch, a hug, a sign of how much he cared.

What happened had to happen. In Tony's mind, there was only one thing a man was supposed to do to communicate his feelings for his woman.

When she'd said "yes" to him that night, it was her most precious gift. Because she was terrified. Terrified about inter-course. Afraid she wouldn't be good enough, not experienced. Afraid of Tony—his overbearing size and his wild kind of need once she said yes. And she was terrified about birth control pills—what they'd do to her body and what a guy would think of her if she took them. So she didn't.

After, he tried to comfort her. Knew she was afraid. Didn't know all the reasons, of course. She couldn't tell him all that.

After, things changed. Sort of, like he grew up overnight. Like he owned her—she should do what he wanted her to do. Stop smoking, for one thing. Use the pill, for another. But she refused. Well, he never used anything either. They were so young, so dumb.

She got pregnant right away. No doctor had to tell her. She knew it from her body changes.

Fourteen and pregnant.

Ginny's mind flashed once more to the scene she most often revisited in her nightmares. The Free Clinic. Huge room, packed with women—no, not women, girls, young girls, sitting on the floor. Waiting for pregnancy tests. Their conversations had horrified her.

"This is my sixth. How many for you?"

"Yeah? Well, this is my third." Not thinking twice about what they were saying or doing. Not thinking about it as "baby."

She couldn't say a word. Just listened, very afraid. And Tony was there, not making a sound, just staring at walls.

In the big room, someone gave a lecture to all the girls. About birth control—the different ways. Be thinking about it, girls, they'd said. Here's the prescription—take the pills—don't come back. That was the message. But lots of 'em came back. And back.

"Virginia Shelton." There it was. Loud. A gunshot. For everyone to hear. Then the move to the corridor, filled with beds, and the uniformed person telling her, "Strip down, get on the bed, put your feet in the stirrups and wait for the doctor."

Curtains around each bed, drawn curtains, but she knew that all around her was somebody right here and here and over there, all going through the same thing. Then her curtain opened and there was a doctor, saying "Hi" like it was a day at the beach. Closed eyes then and the doctor looking down there, up her insides. Wanting to disappear again, but no way to escape the words: "The cervix is dark and spongy, Virginia, and that means you're pregnant. Without even waiting for the blood test results, I know you're pregnant."

She hadn't meant to, but she felt herself smile. It just came. Elation. Elation at the thought of "baby." Not 'til the doctor said, "Get dressed and go back out in the waiting room and wait to talk to the counselor," did she feel any fear. Tony was out there.

Dressing slow then. Deep, heavy breathing. Walking slow. Calmly sitting down next to him. "It's yes." That was all she could say.

He was so quiet. Solemn. No more wishful thinking that "maybe she wasn't." She was.

They waited to see the counselor. Some words tried to come. Tony, saying something about having an abortion, her saying she didn't want one. Then him saying something like, "This is ridiculous, of course you do, you're too young—I'm too young, and I'm not ready to get married." Her saying, "Who said anything about marriage?" She'd already told herself she wasn't going to drag him in like that. She could make it on her own.

Tony stopped talking after that until they went in to the counselor.

She was a nice-enough counselor. Just didn't understand. So involved in her own views and taking Tony's side. She wouldn't be quiet long enough to hear Ginny's side. Just kept repeating the reasons. A whole list of reasons...financially impossible...Tony's obviously not ready—you see, he wants you to do this....You can't handle it emotionally. You'll drag the families in. There's no way it could possibly work....

Ginny listened silently to all the reasons 'til the very end. Then the courage came. "I don't believe all this that you're saying. I won't have an abortion. Abortion...is not...for me,"

191

she said in her softest but stubbornest voice, the one that Tony hated.

All she remembered after that was the running. Tony running down the hall, down the three flights of stairs from the clinic, running down the boulevard with her chasing him, tears blurring everything, calling to him, screaming to him, crying. And him running and yelling 'til he was out of sight. She'd stood there alone, sobbing, catching her breath, until he came back for her and took her home. Without a word.

She'd waited until she was six weeks along to tell her folks, hoping it would be too late for a safe abortion.

Then the real nightmare began. Her stepfather, shooting off words that made her skin crawl: slut, whore, your fault. And her mom, hurt and upset, trying to do the right thing. Only nobody knew what the right thing was. Then all of a sudden *everybody* knew: the right thing was abortion. Everybody except the mother-to-be.

More crying and hollering, more visits to the abortion counselors, and the baby growing in her and time passing. Then, somewhere, that billboard about Lifeline and a phone number. Sweet, comforting voice of a lady—listening. Listening to *her*, to *her* side, to *her* feelings. Telling her she was doing the right thing. Finally, an ally.

Ginny's thoughts were interrupted by the cautious knock on the bedroom door and Stephie's voice calling "Mommy" from the other side. The mommy glanced at the clock—7:30. Two hours she'd been lying there.

"Come in, honey," she called.

Stephie turned the knob and bounced into the room, surprised to see her mom still in bed.

"What's wrong, Mommy?"

"Nothing, Steph. Your mom's just being lazy today."

Ginny rubbed her fingers through the seven-year-old's silky blond hair, studying the child's long, pale face, a replica of her own with its grey-green eyes and high cheekbones and forehead. Suddenly she drew Stephie up in her arms, hugging and rocking her as she had done when the child was newborn.

"I love you, Steph."

Stephie looked surprised. The first-born of the Petri family wasn't used to being babied. Enjoying the surprise, she wrapped her arms around her mother's neck and returned some squeezes of her own.

"I love you, too, Mommy."

A wind had come up. Its shrill whistle through the cracked rubber seals on the side vents of the Great White Wheeler screamed at Tony in eerie mimicry of the silent screams inside his head. The sky was clouding over. Looked like rain coming. Raindrops keep fallin' on my head, he thought of the song title. Everything's fallin' on my head. They keep you walking scared. Keep you in the dark as much as possible. Don't they know that scared and angry are the same thing? When you can't cut it, you get scared. You're helpless—can't live on three bucks an hour, and can't even *do* the job when you're hurting so damn bad.

A Coors truck passed him, the first vehicle he'd noticed since he got on the highway. Coors, of all things. "Don't drink Coors beer because it's non-union," the every-other-week union news-letter used to preach. That was about the only piece of advice he'd ever got from that bunch of creeps. Big helpers. You get hurt on the job, you can go pound salt before they're gonna give you any help. Playing all these fool games with the money.

They could have their friggin' money. He could live in a tent. Yeah. *He* could. And Ginny. But not the kids. Frankie. It wasn't just scarlet fever. He hadn't wanted to think about the encephalitis that came with it. Not something you want kids to have. Doc says he's OK...well, he runs, he jumps, he screams and yells, he's fast and strong. But touchy. So sensitive these days. Who knows if he'll have trouble—need special school or something. All takes money. If you'd been a cop, this wouldn't have happened, Petri. A cop. Big macho dream. Maybe you used to lift two or three hundred pounds, but now you can't even push a market basket....

The mental reruns escalated Tony's fury. He wasn't noticing the miles disappearing behind him or the speedometer needle wavering somewhere around 80—the Red Zone for the Wheeler—or the warning sign that said "Stop Ahead."

Suddenly it was there. Lawton Road intersection. The only red glow of STOP since he'd entered the highway ramp from home. His leg arched to jam the brakes, his response slowed by months of idleness. He forced the brake to the floor, bracing

193

against the burst of pain moving up his back. The Wheeler squealed and weaved across the lanes of the still-deserted road, shuddered in its struggle to obey the command of its driver's foot, and came to a halt. A complete halt. A silent halt.

Tony sat a moment, shaken, disoriented by the abrupt intrusion into his hypnotic ride. The silence was complete.

He turned the key and waited. Nothing.

He jiggled the key and held it in the special way that usually worked on the truck he knew so well. Nothing.

He pumped the accelerator, teased the clutch. Still no sound.

Then came the smack of his palm against the dash. The stinging hand mocked him as if it had a life of its own. He glanced away, his eyes catching sight of the rifle barrel jolted out from under the passenger seat by the sudden stop.

From somewhere inside, he felt the scream start. A moan, born out of nausea, out of the constant dull pain of his sickness, out of the sickness with his pain. His last piece of personal power had died with his engine.

Two fists squeezed the steering wheel—squeezed the blood from the now ghost-white knuckles until his arms trembled out of control.

Inner-voice words, usually kept caged, spilled out into the privacy of the truck cab. "This too? Am I gonna screw this up too?" He heard the childlike wail coming out of his grown man's throat, challenging the awful impotency of the moment.

He had to move. To get out. To do something....

Ignoring the pain of moving after miles of sitting, ignoring the pain of walking around the truck and opening doors, fighting the pain of bending and lifting, Tony took the rifle from the floor of the cab, paced the length of the truck like a hunter stalking, and came to a stop, staring hard at the silent front end of the failed Wheeler.

One squeeze of his hand was all it took to begin the onslaught. Pounding, cutting, whining sounds punctuated the repeat punches of the gunstock against his belly as the weapon came to life, tearing at the truck. Windshield first—a face pierced with stab-wounds, its bits of glass flying like glittering spittle from a gaping mouth. The metal flesh of fenders, ripping like paper from a nonstop slice of bullets. Headlights hollowed as their innards burst like squeezed glass eyeballs. Pulling, pulling

194

on the trigger, hands frozen to the weapon, riddling the hood, destroying the truck's heart, lungs, brain.

The Wheeler's body fluids oozed, bleeding onto the highway, running in wet, dark trickles, becoming mini-rivers before the explosion of its gas-tank guts. The roar of the instant firewall shocked the truck-killer. He dropped the weapon and backed away from the orange cloud of flame that licked at the painted skin of the truck, whooshed upward in the wind, and completely swallowed its victim.

Tony watched with horror. Horror at himself.

From somewhere, a faint wail of sirens began to grow louder.

CHAPTER 19

"Somebody goes crazy, I want to know
why they went crazy, because
I've been there now."

"Tony?"
"Yes?"
"Hi, Tony. It's Diana Cotter. Just called to see
how you were doing."

He hadn't recognized her voice over the phone.

"Oh...hi, Mrs. Cotter. Did my mom call you?"

"No, I was just wondering how the back injury was doing
and all. I wondered if they ever came through on the settlement
check." Diana had been in contact with Tony periodically, following his life adventures since he'd left school to get married.
She knew about his accident on the job and had heard that the
trucking company was considering a cash settlement in addition to the rehabilitation program.

"It's been so long since I talked to you," she said.

"Yeah...well, I been goin' kinda nuts out here."

"I'll bet. It's not like you to just be sitting around. Did you
get the insurance all settled and the rehab job from the union?"

My God. She hasn't heard anything yet, Tony realized. "Naw,
they been really dragging their heels on this stuff. I keep calling
but I keep getting the runaround and the bills keep coming
and I keep on not being able to pay them. I can't seem to get
those fools at the insurance company to understand what that
feels like."

"Boy, no wonder you're going nuts."

"Yeah. I'm thinking seriously of going over and blowing them
all away." He said it flatly, testing her response to the idea
he'd already acted on and bungled.

She laughed. "You're kidding, aren't you, Tony?"

"I'm not sure. I bought a gun. A repeating rifle, as a matter of fact. Don't know if I'd ever have the guts to use it," he said, still holding back the facts, "but I bought it."

There was a long pause as the meaning sunk in.

"You're kidding me, Ton. You are kidding, aren't you? You really bought a gun? What's going on out there?"

He stopped the pretense, then, and slowly eased into the whole story, describing his deadly plan, aborted by a failed engine. He wanted her to know just how crazy he'd become, but he left out a few things. Like how scared he was since the police brought him home that day. Like how much he needed help.

She knew he needed help right away. Not a time for pride. But he wasn't asking. Too far down to ask? Now Diana felt frightened.

"Look, Ton, why don't you let me call the attorney for you? It'll be easier because I live in the city and it won't be long distance. Let me see what I can find out and if we can get this thing moving with the rehab and the settlement check."

She heard his "OK." So casual. Still 'Joe Cool' for the public.

"Look, I want you to come into my office—I want to see you. I'll get back to you as soon as I reach Mr. Jonas. But do us a favor, Tony," she pleaded before hanging up. "Get rid of the rifle. Don't even have it around. It's not a great thing to be staring at when you're so close to the bottom."

"Naw, don't worry. I'm OK now. You can just thank that old White Wheeler that it wasn't another piece of sick history."

Diana finally reached union attorney Harry Jonas that Wednesday afternoon and made him aware of the seriousness of his client's situation. Hard-to-reach Harry Jonas, once reached, was found to have a very sensitive ear. He delivered what he promised within three days. A $500 check arrived in the mail to tide the Petris over until the settlement was resolved, and a call came to Tony immediately about enrollment in a rehabilitation program that would provide training and help place him in a welding job.

"Come in, Tony. Great to see you. It's been a long time."

"Yeah. About eleven months, since my big craziness. I think that was the last time I was here."

"Is it almost a year? I can't believe it. What's been happening since our last phone conversation?" Diana motioned him to sit and poured some coffee.

"Still working at the welding place. Getting pretty used to it. They're tellin' me I've gotten more raises faster than anybody who's ever worked there. It's still not Easy Street, but I'm moving. 'Course, I'm freezing my lovely body to death riding the 120 miles a day, round trip, on the Harley. No way I could drive a car there. The gas would break me."

"A hundred and twenty a day?" Diana groaned. "You make that brutal trip on the Harley? I'd kill myself! How does your back stand that?"

"I have to go with what I can afford," he diverted the question.

She didn't press. "Well, thanks for coming down tonight. I'm sure you're not looking for more places to drive."

"It's OK. I'm staying in town for dinner with the folks tonight."

"Oh, good. Say hello for me. Do you still feel like filling me in on all that's been happening?"

"That's what I'm here for. There's been lots of changes." Diana could tell just by the voice. "I wanted you to know, because the last time…well, that was my real low, if you know what I mean."

She knew. "Well, where do you want to start?" Diana asked.

"I don't know. There's so much. So much that's happened. After Harry Jonas whipped them into shape and got me that advance and the rehab program, I had to trust the guy, 'cause what did I know about all this stuff? When the insurance company let those checks get behind, something just snapped in me. I learned, later on, from talking around, that that's a real common thing they do—kinda put the squeeze on people, so they don't get to like it too much. I wonder if they know how risky that trick is or how many guys get crazy from it.

"But I learned something real important from all that. I learned about self-pity and how it keeps going like this," his hand made a spiralling motion, "just down and down. And I found out that almost everybody who tries to help you does the wrong thing."

"How so?"

"They're always trying to cheer you up, right? And that's the worst thing you can do, as far as I'm concerned, for somebody that's way down. If you go down there with them and feel the pain and anger and the hate, or whatever it happens to be, it does a tremendous amount more good than sayin', 'Aw, it's OK.'

198

'Cause it's *not* OK. Everything is goin' wrong and some fool is tellin' you, 'It's going to be better.' Bullshit. You don't wanna hear that.

"Yeah, I learned firsthand about this depression stuff. I suppose I could've read a book on it, if I could read," he laughed, "but it's not the same. I learned firsthand how to go into instant depression, for bona fide reasons—I mean, I think I had pretty good reasons—and I learned what it feels like. And on the side, I learned how to handle somebody else that might be suffering the same thing. That was a pretty heavy lesson for someone my age, don't you think?"

"I'll say. It's heavy for someone any age. I don't know how you handled it, Tony. Did you break down—did you cry at all? I know that's a pretty personal question, and you don't have to answer, but I wondered how you let go of all that pain."

"It's funny—you asking that. No, I *never* cried. I wasn't smart enough to do that at the time. My controls were like the tungsten I work with at the shop—very hard and with a very high melting point. No, I didn't cry, but you know what I did do? I considered violence. Me. Tony Petri, the non-violent person who breaks things instead of people.

"Well, I found out people can put you in a position where one day you say that may be the only way out. Or at least, it seems to be. It's not sane, but you begin to think it is. They push you and hassle you. Physically, I was hurt and in pain, and then mentally they're hurting you. They take away all your money and they jerk you around and they don't talk to you on the phone. Hurting you, playing with your head."

"I think alot of them would change jobs if they knew how close they came to somebody that was ready to...I mean, don't you think everybody...at one time or another..." he struggled with the words, "...must have thought about blowing someone away? Or decided maybe life's not worth living any more? So for me to think of killing someone, or *all* of them in that office...I mean, I was capable of it! I had the weapon in my truck. I was ready. God, I was ready."

"So what stopped you?" Diana spoke extra-softly, respecting the painful confession.

"Well, first the Wheeler stopped me. When I stood there on that highway and saw what I'd done to that truck and realized I was thinking of doing it to people....When I told you—and

Ginny—what I was thinking, just *thinking*, I said to myself, 'Two other people know I said I was gonna kill somebody.' That's a heavy thing to say. Here I'd been thinking it, and I happened to actually say it. Maybe if you can't get it out, then you can do it. Well, I kept thinking to myself, 'Other people know I have these thoughts about rendering this horrendous violence. This is not COOL, Tony. It's not acceptable.

"Well, all of a sudden, there was this tremendous turmoil in me and I had to make a change right then. But I didn't know how. Well, once I got that call about the welding rehab program and those checks started coming, I started to feel a little hopeful, like maybe there's a way out of here, and that's when I talked to Harry Jonas and he said the company was offering a settlement. I still thought I wanted to sue, but Jonas said, 'Listen, Tony. I'd take their offer. It's pretty good. We could sue them but we very rarely get any more than what they're offering— sometimes we come out with less—and it'll take a long time, maybe a year or two.'

"Well, when you're ignorant of something, you trust somebody. You have to. I'm not a lawyer. I don't know the laws and I was inclined to believe, with what I was already experiencing, that he was right—it would have dragged on for a year or two, and I wanted to get it over. Jonas didn't think I had grounds either, 'cause they base it on how bad you're hurt, and pain is a weird thing. How do you prove pain if you can't see it? It wasn't something I could show in a picture, like a broken bone or something. So we took the settlement.

"And when the check came, it was the saddest moment of all because it was such a miserable end. Not one day was I ever as sick and depressed as when I saw that check in the mail. It was $3,600."

Diana was astonished. "That was all they gave you?"

"That was it. I remember, the girl in the bank said, 'You don't want to let go of this check, do you?' I said, 'No. I hate this check.' She looked at me like maybe she should hit the buzzer, and she said, 'Why?' And I said, 'This is fifteen months of my life. Isn't fifteen months of your life worth more than $3,600? Not to mention the suffering you go through. And I have to be careful how I even move, every day.' Poor girl. I laid it all on her. She thought I was whacko. Well, I was."

He rested a moment, shook his head, and went on, "Nope,

there was never a sadder day than when I saw that check—because I knew it was wasted time. I realized that only the very smart could've gained anything from this—could maybe sit down, read a book, study, maybe learn something while they were recuperating. Use the time for something meaningful."

"There's nothing wrong with your intelligence, Tony," Diana interrupted. "Maybe if someone was supporting you and you had no responsibilities then you could have used the recovery time to work on reading. But that wasn't your reality."

"No, it sure wasn't. My mind just wasn't there. I had too many pressures on me. For me, it was a waste, a total waste. To them in those offices though, I was just some outrageous number about that long!

"You know, I carried that settlement check around for two weeks. I had a terrible conflict in me 'cause I was so sick and so hurt that it was so little, even though I knew there was no amount of money that could pay it back."

"Who decided on that figure of $3,600? How do they determine it?"

"It comes out of a book. Wild, huh? They got this book with formulas on how much you're worth when you screw yourself up on the job. Well, you're looking at a guy who's worth $3,600! Nothing but the best, I always said."

His slight laugh told Diana the insult of the settlement had been dealt with and pretty much laid to rest now.

"I can't remember when it happened, but late one night I just decided I'm gonna change. I had to find a way to help people instead of hurting them. Now I got this welding job—well, all day I build things that are either parts of nuclear weapons or in some other way made for killing people and it bothers me a lot, but it makes the paycheck. There's two guys at work that need help so bad and the only way they can feel like men is to hurt somebody. And what's sad is, the one these sick guys are badgering is being made crazy himself."

"And now he'll go home and yell at the kids, eh?"

"Yep. And it goes on and on like a cancer. It's all over the place."

"I think you should have been a philosopher. How'd you get so smart without being able to read?" Diana asked the question she always asked herself about people like Tony who sucked up knowledge from everywhere and nowhere. She wished she could patent the process if anyone could define how it happened.

"I don't know," Tony answered. "It just seems to come to me. I think about a lot of stuff, stuff that I see, stuff that I hear. It all pieces together.

"We spend 98 billion zillion dollars a year institutionalizing people and prosecuting, and the schools spend absolutely nothing teaching them how to *be,* just to be happy with themselves, to be peaceful, to realize that if you hurt a person you've done a lot of damage, because now he's mad and he's gonna hurt somebody else, and you have to justify why.

"So many people are sheep. You notice that? They all yell about having better laws to put people away. If someone commits a crime, execute him—that's what most people want. They want bigger prisons, better laws, but nobody's going to the source.

"Somebody goes crazy, I want to know *why,* because I've been there now. I know what it's like.

"I don't want to know where they should be kept! I want to know who's responsible for not taking care of them. It's funny. They spend those zillions of dollars on housing people that have been pushed to the edge—the criminals, the crazies, whatever you want to call them. And they spend peanuts on trying to take care of them before they go crazy and can't be helped.

"People need a chance to prove themselves. In a lot of ways, I've spent a great deal of my life proving something. Like my eye-hand coordination. I have a hard time with that, 'cause my eyes lose track of where my hands are going, but here I am spending my life proving I can do it.

"At my welding job I have a torch about this small," he spread his index fingers apart about two inches, "and I have to hold it at all different kinds of angles and skim a little ball of tungsten at the end of it that's about one or two thousandths of an inch, and hold a wire and move it two or three thousandths of an inch, step-step-step-step—each drop has to be in a certain place, a certain way. You have to watch what the character of the weld is behind it and how it's melting in front of it, and keep the argon and helium flowing just right. Those welds are so specialized, they have to be so precise, since they're used on all this super-sophisticated electronic gear on airplanes and rockets, that I have to find an X-ray machine and X-ray each weld eleven different ways to make sure it's right on. They can't risk any half-assed welds on that stuff. I'm second in the chain of command of welders there, and the one guy above me has been welding thirty years.

"But it's a battle. I'm spending every day of my life fighting a battle against these things that are wrong with me. Each day, proving...that I can use...my hands...and my eyes...together." He spaced the words, slow and soft, marvelling at his self-discovery.

Suddenly self-conscious, he glanced at the clock and Diana knew it was getting late.

"Well, that's about it with the trials and tribulations of Tony Petri," he told her, indicating he'd pretty much said all he'd come to say. "What do you think of all the changes?"

Diana had so much she wanted to say to this young man, formerly of so few words, who had come so far and had so enriched her understandings. But she checked herself and reached out a hand to touch his shoulder as she told him how especially proud she felt of his growth, courage, and new directions.

She confessed she was disappointed in herself—that she hadn't completed the job she'd begun: to help him read with the ease he craved. She repeated her offer to be available whenever he had the time and energy to work once more—even if it didn't happen 'til he was thirty-five, she joked.

He looked at her for a moment and said, "Mrs. Cotter, you didn't completely teach me to read, but you taught me something I never knew before. You taught me that I *could* read. I guess the rest is up to me, isn't it?"

The gift of those words took away any Diana might have said. She returned the squeeze of his goodbye handshake and waved silently as he walked away. When he reached the door, Tony turned and said, "Oh, I forgot to tell you. You're gonna love this one. Stephie's teacher called last week and asked Ginny to come in. She said there was 'something wrong' with our daughter. We've heard that one before, eh?...Well...keep in touch," and he closed the door behind him.

EPILOGUE

READING, WRITING, AND RAGE shows beyond a doubt that Tony Petri had many problems—perceptual problems, possible neurological problems, visual problems, allergy problems, family problems. However, the extent of each of these, considered in isolation, does not justify the utter totality of his school failure. Tony possessed the capacity to become literate—he proved that at age sixteen. Furthermore, each of Tony's problems was, if not correctable, at least relievable.

But relief was never found. Why not? Because the intricate web of factors relating to his remediation created a whole *new* dynamic which, I suggest, caused him to fail. Tony Petri failed to learn because of rage—an abiding, sucked-in anger that began with a label of Wrongness and grew, cumulatively, with each new affront to his self-worth. Controlled anger led him, unconsciously, to sabotage remediation of his multiple problems. This secret emotion was the understandable by-product of the war between Tony's disabilities, his pride, and the abuse of that pride by his environment.

Tony was a strong-willed child forced into submission to people and a system he neither respected nor understood—to a system that neither respected nor understood him. He felt powerless in the hands of the more powerful. And he hated that feeling. Bright children can be especially uncomfortable with powerlessness. Unconsciously, Tony had to find some solution. But he dared not misbehave—mother, father, church, and God had taught him that.

We cannot precisely know at what point Tony chose his weapon—quiet refusal to perform—but the tendency for retreat was apparent in the first grade. By the time he realized that the weapon was damaging himself far more than his adversaries, the pattern was too well established and the secrecy so extreme he could see no way out.

Tony needed to make decisions about himself. He sought responsibility, creativity, and meaningful use of his time. At a precociously early age, he read his world as hypocritical, irrational, and insulting. He saw things as they were, fantasized how they ought to be, and tried through sheer will power to effect change. This drive for self-determination led to another internal conflict. His special kind of passive power created guilt. He was shamed by his thoughts—angry, hateful, retaliatory thoughts—and came to direct this hatred at a safe target: himself. He feared his capacity to destroy if he ever released what was held inside.

Tony grew to believe the enemy was himself. He was wrong. Tony's rage was created by ignorance, nurtured by insensitivity, and ripened by the failure of the school and professional systems to listen to what was really happening or to learn from each other how to administer help. Over and over in this story, one is struck by examples of gross communication failure—between parent and child, between teachers, between parents and teachers, between teachers and outside professionals, between teachers and testers. There was no hint of coordination of goals or, in fact, of any joint planning between elementary and secondary schools. Each level of Tony's schooling was run as a separate operation, unburdened by knowledge of what had come before or by preparation for what was yet to come. This breakdown in communication was most apparent, and most infuriating, during Tony's transition from junior to senior high schools.

Throughout Tony's school years, the professionals involved with him never saw themselves as part of the fabric of the problem. To most, home was the culprit. The evidence allows us to watch how professionals often operate in isolation, an isolation fed by disagreement among themselves, suspicion of other points of view, and elitism. Too often, they fail to ask for help from one another, to seek additional clarifying information, or to share recommendations with those in a position to implement them.

The evidence also shows that all the remediation attempts concerned methods and materials rather than Tony, the person. And herein lies the crux of the problem stated earlier: why did this child defy sincere remediation efforts? We can see from this autopsy of a school failure that Tony's and his parents' mistrust of the "helpers" interfered with every major helping effort.

Were the private, proud Petris innately untrusting people?

Would they have been guarded and secretive, refusing to confide, no matter what professional approach was used?

Of course not.

If the Petris lacked a capacity for trust, this book would not have been written. When the Petris felt genuinely liked and respected rather than blamed, they were able, even delighted, to confide. When the Petris felt that Tony's capabilities and strengths were recognized and accounted for, they readily granted full cooperation.

The Petris' mistrust stemmed from their perceptions that the various "helpers" considered Tony defective, incapable. Each testing or tutoring session began with an implied presumption of Wrongness or inadequacy. Experts felt compelled to justify remedies in terms of the specialty they were trained in. Yet the Wrongness label did not fit and never would. Tony's parents knew their child to be bright, coordinated, and eager to learn. They were proud and sensitive to the criticism of others. Unspoken labels and negative judgments led to the unconscious subversion of the treatment goals and created permanent walls against communication and trust.

Tony was a master of selective attention. He did well on the things he tried to do well on—the projects he selected as worthy of his concentration. That fact told us he was neurologically able to pay attention. Tony never corrected or compensated for his perceptual and directional confusions because he *chose* not to pay attention.

Why does a child so young refuse to attend? He tells us why, at sixteen, and shows us the method to which he can respond. At sixteen, he became a full participant, a partner in the process of his own remediation. Feeling respected and included in the goal-setting for the first time, he began to understand the code of the English language. His remediation addressed both academic and emotional needs. Once he was willing to listen, his native intelligence allowed him to understand, and his fully matured nervous system was able to integrate information it had formerly been unable to process. He responded to methods that gave him success and he used the confidence he gained to dare to learn things formerly associated with failure. Most important, he began to feel that he could learn—and developed the motivation to try.

In the research literature, one of the causal theories of juvenile delinquency is that anger, frustration, and aggressive behavior stem from feelings of powerlessness. Powerlessness is described as a "social emotion" created when social institutional needs become more important than human needs.

Diana's intervention in Tony's life helped him regain some measure of personal power. Diana served as his agent, interpreter of professional jargon, clarifier of needs, consultant in crisis. She listened nonjudgmentally and believed in his abilities. Perhaps she made the difference in his fate.

As I have lectured throughout the country about the lessons learned from Tony's story, I have most frequently been asked what has become of him. Today, Tony Petri is a successfully functioning adult, still a husband to his Ginny and a father of four--two sons and two daughters. Life has continued to challenge him on every front, and it would probably be hard for him to say which role has been the most demanding. The former teen father has matured, mellowed, and survived the seemingly endless trials of parenting four children (only one of whom has inherited the learning disabilities) and found time on the side to become a gourmet cook, specializing in Italian, Chinese, and Mexican cuisine (with **lots** of spice!). His marriage to Ginny has transcended the doomsday predictions about teen marriages as, together, they have faced major health problems (and a new kind of bureaucratic abuse in the health care system), frequent accidents and childhood crises that blur together in the constant stress of parenthood.

In the job world, Tony continues to work on his nation's most high-tech military aircraft, where he started out 7 years ago as a high-precision welder. He has now risen to a supervisory position in the mechanical assembly of this top-secret aerospace project, but he will not allow them to give him a supervisor's title (because, he confided only to me, that would mean a commitment to reports and written tasks he dare not allow his colleagues to see.) At times he has earned as much as $70,000 a year, working 50-to 60-hour work weeks at $22 an hour, leaving for work at 4 a.m. and returning home anytime between 4 p.m. and midnight. Known on the job as the man with the answers, Tony endures as a respected and quite permanent figure after countless other employees have come and gone, thus far weathering the ubiquitous corporate downsizing that has victimized so many in the nineties. He's even entered the computer world, working on a CAD (Computer-Aided Design) program, to log onto the mainframe, plot out his welding plans, and write the necessary text. Interestingly, he has no Spellchecker available and either has to know the words he'll use or copy them from print. In Tony's words, "I'm totally self-taught, and now I can do anything the engineers can do. In fact, I tell the engineers how to get from A to Z, but I don't know how to spell it. And they kid me, saying 'Apparently at your level of genius you just don't have time to learn to spell.'"

They don't know he **can't** spell.

They don't know he has learning disabilities. He never disclosed the fact. Given his keen ability to "read" people, he is convinced some of his superiors have the same problem--but, says he, **no one** dares disclose. "The sad part of being in a huge machine like this," Tony philosophizes, "is that you will be replaced--if not by one person, by two or three or whatever it takes." I have kept him appraised of the changes in laws, and his rights under the ADA (Adults with Disabilities Act, 1990) which mandates that any company with 25 or more employees must make "reasonable accommodations," i.e., ones that won't cause undue financial hardship to the company but will allow the employee to succeed (by use of assistive equipment like tape recorders, Spellcheckers, special computer software, and modified methods of training and communicating instructions, eg., spoken instead of printed instructions, or vise versa). But the long-violated trust from his past feeds Tony's caution to this day. He really believes they would never accommodate to his disabilities, no matter how good his skills on the job. Because of the top-secret nature of the project, there are vast, unique constraints. He is certain that no tape recorder could ever be allowed, and he would never risk possible job termination by requesting such an accommodation after all these years. But he confesses that the toll on him grows every year as the job requires him to do more and more reading, writing, and computer work. The written communiques he writes take longer and are harder for him than anyone else, because "words I could spell yesterday I can't spell today," a cry so frequently heard from dyslexics.

This is Tony's story.

There are an estimated eight million Tonys in our school, yet few have access to trained ombudsmen to guide them through the morass of helping services or to determine why remediation efforts are failing. As my educational therapy practice serves more and more adults, I observe daily the deep scars borne by the unserved--and the impact their learning disabilities have on **every** aspect of their lives.

The answer, to me, seems clear. We parents, teachers, administrators, and helping professionals must begin to Listen differently--to "hear" the **causes** of the silence, the sullen looks, the isolation, the disruptive behavior.

We must listen fully for the Rightness in each child and for clues to explain the Wrongness.

We must presume that no child wants to be a failure.

And we must make the child and his/her parents respected partners in the process of evaluation and remediation.

As we learned from all the Petris, the consequences of misunderstanding, needless blame, and induced powerlessness are way too high.

***

REFERENCES

Diagnostic Tests and Remedial Programs
Referred to in the Book

Frostig, M., and Horne, D., *The Frostig Program for the The Development of Visual Perception*. Chicago: Follett, 1964. References to "perceptual testing" pertains to this test.

Heckelman, R.G., "Using the Neurological Impress Remedial Reading Technique, *"Academic Therapy Quarterly*, 1(4): 235-239, 1966. The NIM was used with Tony when he was sixteen.

Jastak, J.F., and Jastak, S.R., *Wide Range Achievement Test*. Guidance Associates of Delaware, 1978. Referred to in the book as the "WRAT."

Spache, G., *Diagnostic Reading Scales*. Monterey, Calif.: CTB/McGraw-Hill, 1981. The list of Common Syllables referred to in the book was taken from this test.

Wechsler, D., *Wechsler Intelligence Scales for Children, Revised*. New York: The Psychological Corporation, 1974. Referred to as the "WISC," this was the intelligence test used on Tony in every instance of IQ testing.

A Definition of "Learning Disability"

1) In 1981, the National Joint Committee for Learning Disabilities (NJCLD), comprised of these national organizations--LDA, ASHA, CLD/CEC, DCCD/CEC, IRA, ODS, and NCLD in cooperation, recommended a definition of learning disabilities, due to the problems affecting theoretical and

service-delivery issues that arose from a 1967 definition by the National Advisory Committee on Handicapped Children (NACHC). The NACHC definition had been used in PL 94-142, The Right to Education of the Handicapped. The following is the NJCLD definition, including its 1988 revisions (underlined text):

"Learning disabilities is a generic term that refers to a heterogeneous group of disorders manifested by significant difficulties in the acquisition and use of listening, speaking, reading, writing, reasoning, (or) mathematical abilities, or social skills. These disorders are intrinsic to the individual and presumed to be due to central nervous system dysfunction. Even though a learning disability may occur concomitantly with other handicapping conditions (eg., sensory impairment, mental retardation, social and emotional disturbance, or with socioenvironmental influences (eg., cultural differences, insufficient/inappropriate instruction, psychogenic factors), and especially with attention-deficit disorders, all of which may cause learning problems, a learning disability is not the direct result of those conditions or influences."

2) In 1984, the Learning Disabilities Association (LDA), then called Association for Children and Adults with Learning Disabilities (ACLD), rejected the above definition and wrote the following:

"Specific Learning Disabilities is a chronic condition of presumed neurological origin which selectively interferes with the development, integration, and/or demonstration of verbal and/or non-verbal abilities.

Specific Learning Disabilities exists as a distinct handicapping condition in the presence of average to superior intelligence, adequate sensory and motor systems, and adequate learning opportunities. The condition varies in its manifestations and in degree of severity.

Throughout life, the condition can affect self-esteem, education, vocation, socialization, and/or daily living activities."

RESOURCES FOR ADDITIONAL INFORMATION

American Speech and Language Association (ASHA):
9030 Old Georgetown Rd., Bethesda, MD 20014
301-897-5700 or 800-638-8255 (action line)
> The national professional organization of speech/language therapists. Provides technical assistance to professionals seeking diagnostic resources. The Consumer Action Line serves the public with information on speech-, language-, and hearing-related questions.

Association of Educational Therapists (AET):
1804 W. Burbank Blvd., Burbank, CA 91506
818-843-1183
> National professional association designed to establish standards of practice and continuing education for practitioners in educational therapy. Welcome affiliate members in related professions. Publishes quarterly journal and referral directory.

Children with Attention Deficit Disorder (CHADD):
1859 N. Pine Island Rd., Suite 185, Plantation, FL 33322
305-384-6869
> A national resource and support group for parents of children with attention deficit disorders. Works for implementation of best educational practices for this population.

Council for Exceptional Children (CEC):
1920 Association Drive, Reston, VA 22091-1589
703-620-3660
> A national organization concerned with all types of exceptional children. Publishes journals and provides information to parents and professionals.

Directory of Facilities and Services for the Learning Disabled:
> Published annually by:
> Academic Therapy Publishers, 20 Commercial Blvd., Novato, CA 94947.

Higher Education and Adult Training for People with Handicaps (HEATH) Resource Center:
One Dupont Circle, Suite 800, Washington, DC 20036-1193
800-544-3284 or 202-939-9320

>National clearinghouse on postsecondary education for individuals with disabilities. Provides information on programs, services, laws, resource agencies, and publications to this population.

International Reading Association (IRA):
Dept. TE, Box 8139, Newark, DE 19714

>A worldwide organization for reading teachers and those concerned with reading, remediation and illiteracy. Sponsors conferences, legislative action, publications, newsletters.

Learning Disability Association of America (LDA):
4156 Liberty Rd., Pittsburgh, PA 15234
412-341-1515

>Federated organization of parents and professionals concerned with well-being and education of children with learning disabilities. Publishes informative newsletter updating subscribers on legislation, research, academic and social/emotional issues, relevant conferences and workshops, groups for parents, teens, and adult dyslexics.

National Center for Learning Disabilities (NCLD):
381 Park Ave. South, Suite 1401, New York, NY 10016
212-545-9665

>Founded to expand public awareness and fund grants for worthy programs in the field of learning disabilities. Publishes *Their World,* a resource and information magazine for parents and professionals.

The International Dyslexia Association (IDA) (Formerly Orton Dyslexia):
Chester Building, Suite 382
8600 LaSalle Road, Baltimore, MD 21286-2044
410-296-0232   Web site: http://www.interdys.org

>A national scientific, educational association. Membership open to parents, professionals, and others interested in dyslexia-related language programs, research, and publications. Write for list of publications, conferences, and local chapter addresses in each state.

HOW TO EVALUATE HELPING SERVICES
By Dorothy Ungerleider

The following are some questions you might ask yourself when seeking to evaluate helping services for your child or yourself:

1. What are the professionals' qualifications (training, degrees, philosophy, license/certification, etc.) for providing the services they claim? What evidence of those qualifications has been provided for you?

2. Is their remedial or therapeutic approach a traditionally established one or a radical and "out of the ordinary" one? If it is new and different, is there any research available to support the claims for effectiveness?

3. What were your feelings about them during and after the initial interview? Was it easy to relate and confide? Did you feel accepted and respected without feeling judged? Did you find yourself appreciating their concern for your problem and respecting their knowledge of how to deal with it?

4. What were your child's feelings about them after a session? Did there seem to be a "match" in terms of potential for trust and relating? (With youngsters who are particularly resistant to help, as is often true with young adolescents, compatibility may be harder to determine and and may require more than one or two sessions to assess.)

5. After the assessment, did they clearly explain the client's problem so that you understood it? Did it fit what you know about your child/yourself? Did you then gain enough understanding of the problem to be able to explain it to someone else?

6. What therapy goals were set forth for the client? Were you (and your child) a partner(s) in the goal-setting process? Is there a plan for goal revision at set time intervals as therapy progresses and needs adjusting?

7. For juvenile clients, how do they inform parents of treatment progress? How frequently and by what means will they be in contact--at each session, monthly, by phone, in writing, etc?

8. As the helping service progresses, are they doing what they claimed they could do?

9. Was there an estimated duration for the intervention? Approximately how long will this go on?

10. What criteria were set for ending the therapy or helping service? (The criteria should either be the successful achievement of goals for the client's increased independence of functioning--or, the failure to achieve those goals within a period of time relative to the severity of the problem.)

BIBLIOGRAPHY

The books listed here represent favorites of mine which will provide more information pertaining to issues raised in the book. The list of publications grows daily. This one is meant to be a starting point. Many of these references have their own bibliographies as well.

Books

Adler, M. & Van Doren, C., *How to Read a Book.* New York: Touchstone/Simon & Shuster, 1972.

Alley, G., & Deshler, D., *Teaching the Learning Disabled Adolescent: Strategies and methods.* Denver: Love Publishing Co., 1979.

Arnold, L.E., *Helping Parents Help their Children.* New York: Brunner/Mazel 1978.

Barkley, R., *Attention-Deficit Hyperactivity Disorder: A clinical workbook.* New York: Guilford Press, 1991.

Brutten, M., Richardson, S., & Mangel, C., *Something's Wrong with My Child: A parents' book about children with learning disabilities.* New York: Harcourt Brace Jovanovich, 1979.

Buscaglia, L., *The Disabled and Their Parents: A counseling challenge.* New York: Holt, Rinehare & Winston, 1983.

Chall, J., *Creating Successful Readers: A practical guide to testing and teaching at all levels.* Chicago: Riverside Publishing, 1994.

Clark, R.M., *Family Life and School Achievement: Why poor black children succeed or fail.* Chicago: University of Chicago Press, 1983

Cordoni, B., *Living with a Learning Disability.* Carbondale, IL: Southern Illinois University Press, 1987.

Craig, E., *P.S. You're Not Listening.* New York: New American Library, 1972.

Cruickshank, W., Morse, W., and Johns, J., *Learning Disabilities: The struggle from adolescence toward adulthood.* Syracuse, NY: Syracuse University Press, 1980.

De Hirsch, K., Interactions between educational therapist and child. *Bulletin of the Orton Society,* vol. 27:89, 1977.

Dunivant, N., *The Relationship Between Learning Disabilities and Juvenile Delinquency: Executive summary.* Williamsburg, VA: National Center for State Courts, 1982.

Field, K., Kaufman, E., & Saltzman, C., *Emotions and Learning Reconsidered: International perspectives.* New York: Gardner Press, 1993.

Fine, M., & Carlson, C., *The Handbook of Family-School Intervention: A systems perspective.* Boston: Allyn & Bacon, 1992.

Gardner, H., *Multiple Intelligences.* New York: Basic Books, 1993.

Gardner, R., *Psychotherapeutic Approaches to the Resistant Child* New York: Jason Aranson, 1975.

Gerber, A., *Language-related Learning Disabilities: Their nature and treatment.* Baltimore: Paul H. Brookes, 1993.

Gold, M., & Mann, D., *Expelled to a Friendlier Place: A study of effective alternative schools.* Ann Arbor: University of Michigan Press, 1984.

Goodlad, J., A Place Called School: Prospects for the future. New York: McGraw-Hill, 1984.

Gottesman, D., *The Powerful Parent: A child advocacy handbook.* Norwalk, CT: Appleton-Century-Crofts, 1982.

Hammill, D., *Assessing the Abilities and Instructional Needs of Students.* Austin, TX: Pro-Ed, 1987.

Healy, J., *Endangered Minds: Why children don't think and what we can do about it.* New York: Touchstone, 1990.

Huston, A., *Understanding Dyslexia: A practical approach for parents and teachers.* New York: Madison Books, 1992.

Jenkins, R., Heidermann, P., & Caputo, J., *No Single Cause: Juvenile delinquency and the search for effective treatment.* College Park, MD: American Correctional Association, 1985.

Johnson, D., & Mykelbust, H., *Learning Disabilities: Educational principals and practices.* Orlando, FL: Grune and Stratton, 1967.

Kinsbourne, M., & Caplan, P., *Children's Learning and Attention Problems.* Boston: Little/Brown, 1979.

Kozol, J., *Illiterate America.* New York: Anchor Press/Doubleday, 1985.

Kozol, J., *Savage Inequalities.* New York: Harper Perennial, 1991.

Levine, M., *Developmental Variations and Learning Disorders.* Cambridge, MA: Educators Publishing Service, 1987.

Levine, M., *Keeping a Head in School.* Cambridge, MA: Educators Publishing Service, 1990.

Levine, M., *Educational Care: A system for understanding and helping children with learning problems at home and in school.* Cambridge, MA: Educators Publishing Service, 1994.

Lewis, M., & Volkmar, F., *Clinical Aspects of Child and Adolescent Development,* 3rd. Ed., Philadelphia: Lea & Febiger, 1990.

Lyon, R., Gray, D., Kavanagh, & Krasnegor, N. *Better Understanding Learning Disabilities: New views from research and their implications for education and public policy.* Baltimore: Paul H. Brookes, 1993.

Mann, L., Goodman, L., & Wiederholt, J. *Teaching the Learning Disabled Adolescent.* Boston: Houghton-Mifflin, 1978.

May, R., *Power and Innocence: A search for the source of violence.* Toronto: George J. McLeod Limited, 1972.

Moss, R., & Dunlap, H. *Why Johnny Can't Concentrate.* New York: Bantam Books, 1990.

Murray, C., *The Link Between Learning Disabilities and Juvenile Delinquency.* Washington, DC: U.S. Department of Justice, National Institute for Juvenile Justice and Delinquency Prevention, 1976.

Osman, B., *Learning Disabilities: A family affair.* New York: Random House, 1979.

Osman, B., *No One to Play With: The social side of learning disabilities.* New York: Random House, 1982.

Redl, F., *When We Deal with Children.* New York: Free Press. 1966.

Sanders, B., *A is for Ox: Violence, electronic media, and silencing of the written word.* New York: Pantheon Books, 1994.

Sapir, S., *Children with Special Needs: Case Studies in the clinical teaching process.* New York: Brunner/Mazel, 1982.

Sapir, S., *The Clinical Teaching Model.* New York: Brunner/Mazel. 1985.

Silver, L.B., *The Misunderstood child.* McGraw Hill, 1984.

Simpson, E., *Reversals.* Boston: Houghton-Mifflin, 1979.

Smith, S., *No Easy Answer: The learning disabled child at home and at school.* Cambridge, MA: Winthrop, 1979.

Smith, S., *Succeeeding Against the Odds.* Los Angeles: Tarcher, 1992.

Stevens, S., *The Learning Disabled Child: Ways that parents can help.* Winston-Salem, NC: John F. Blair, 1980.

Thomas, A. & Chess, S., *Temperament and Development.* New York: Brunner/Mazel, 1977.

Turecki, S., *The Emotional Problems of Normal Children.* New York: Bantam Books, 1994.

Ungerleider, D., *Psychoeducational Perspectives.* Los Angeles: Association of Educational Therapists Publication, 1991.

Vail, P., *About Dyslexia: Unraveling the myth.* Rosemont, NJ: Modern Learning Press. 1990.

Vail, P., *Learning Styles: Food for thought and 130 practical tips for teachers K-4:* Rosemont, NJ: Modern Learning Press, 1992.

Weiss, H., and Weiss, M., *A Survival Manual: Case studies and suggestions for the L.D. teenager.* Great Barrinton, MA: Treehouse Association, 1976.

Westman, J., *Handbook of Learning Disabilities: A multisystem approach.* New York: Allyn & Bacon, 1990.

ABOUT THE AUTHOR

DOROTHY FINK UNGERLEIDER, is an educational therapist in private practice in Encino, California. As founding President, Advisory Board Chair and Fellow of the Association of Educational Therapists, a national organization, she pioneered the movement to standardize the profession of educational therapy. She is a columnist for the Association journal, *The Educational Therapist,* and author of *PSYCHOEDUCATIONAL PERSPECTIVES.* As the current President of MACE (Multidisciplinary Academy of Clinical Educators), a national invitational academy, she contributed to its document, *Strategies for Public School Reform.* She is also a Trustee on LEARN, (Los Angeles Educational Alliance for Restructuring Now), dedicated to the restructuring of the Los Angeles Unified School District. She served as a faculty lecturer for the National Council of Juvenile and Family Court Judges, providing workshops for juvenile court judges and probation officers, and has lectured to numerous professional and parent groups about the complex causes of learning disorders and their effects on behavior and personality. She spearheaded a pro bono Community Service Project for two Los Angeles agencies, the Juvenile Justice Connection Project and New Directions for Youth, bringing remedial and advocacy services to an underserved delinquent and high risk population.

Ms. Ungerleider received her training in special education of emotionally disturbed youth and learning/reading disorders from the University of Michigan and California State University Northridge. The mother of two grown children, she lives with her husband in Encino.

Made in the USA
San Bernardino, CA
01 September 2013